Doing Christian Ethics
from the Margins

Doing Christian Ethics from the Margins

Miguel A. De La Torre

ORBIS BOOKS
Maryknoll, New York 10545

Third Printing, July 2008

Founded in 1970, Orbis Books endeavors to publish works that enlighten the mind, nourish the spirit, and challenge the conscience. The publishing arm of the Maryknoll Fathers and Brothers, Orbis seeks to explore the global dimensions of the Christian faith and mission, to invite dialogue with diverse cultures and religious traditions, and to serve the cause of reconciliation and peace. The books published reflect the views of their authors and do not represent the official position of the Maryknoll Society. To learn more about Maryknoll and Orbis Books, please visit our website at www.maryknoll.org.

Published by Orbis Books, Maryknoll, New York 10545-0308.
Manufactured in the United States of America.

Library of Congress Cataloging-in-Publication Data

De La Torre, Miguel A.
     Doing Christian ethics from the margins / Miguel A. De La Torre.
       p. cm.
     Includes bibliographical references and index.
     ISBN 1-57075-551-5 (pbk.)
    1. Christian ethics—Textbook.   2. Marginality, Social—Moral and ethical aspects—Textbook.   I. Title.
     BJ1251.D38 2004
     241—dc22

2004008344

To my brother Ricky

Contents

PART III
CASE STUDIES OF NATIONAL RELATIONSHIPS

PART IV
CASE STUDIES OF BUSINESS RELATIONSHIPS

Preface

The (class)room is appropriately named, for it is indeed a room of class — a room where students learn the class they belong to and the power and privilege that comes with that class.[1] The fact that some students are able to pay sufficient money to attend particular rooms of class located on prestigious campuses indicates that they will have certain opportunities that are denied to those of lower economic classes, those who are more often than not students of color residing on the margins of society.

Our educational system is far from being objective or neutral, and students who attend classrooms, from community colleges to highly selective colleges, can either be conditioned to accept the present system of social structures or to seek liberation from it. All too often, the educational system serves to normalize these power structures as legitimate. The task of educators, specifically those who call themselves ethicists, is to cultivate students' ability to find their own voices by creating an environment in which individual and collective consciousness-raising can occur.

As an ethicist unapologetically grounded in a Latino/a social context, I create an environment within the classroom that attempts to perceive the will of the Divine from within the social location of marginalized people — that is, those who are not usually able to participate in the classroom where I teach. Such a process analyzes their reality, a reality tied to an ethical perspective that demands a socio-political response to oppression. In this way a relationship can develop between intellectuals aware of the structural crises faced by people of color and the disenfranchised in the United States.

---

[1] I am indebted to one of my mentors, John Raines, who constantly reminded me of this fact during my doctoral studies.

Nevertheless, the danger facing liberationist scholars is that they can become an intellectual elite disconnected from the everyday struggles of the marginalized and have little or no impact upon the churches in disenfranchised communities. Ethicists from the margins attempting to overcome this disconnect advocate connecting the work done by Christian ministers serving disenfranchised communities with the academic work done by faculty and students in our colleges and universities. These ministers and scholars attempt to learn from the disenfranchised while serving them as organic intellectuals (to borrow a term from Antonio Gramsci), that is, intellectuals grounded in the social reality of the marginalized, and acting in the consciousness-raising process of the faith community.

The pedagogy I employ in my classroom, and will attempt to unfold in this book, seeks to open Christian ethics to the rich diversity found among those who are usually excluded — those who are part of a multiracial and multicultural people. In my "room of class" I attempt to construct a collaborative ethics through studying and reflecting on the lives and circumstances of marginalized people. This is not to make students aware of some quaint or exotic perspective of those who are disenfranchised; rather, it is to help them realize that because the gospel message was first proclaimed in the marginalized spaces of Judea, those who reside in these disenfranchised spaces, then and now, hold the key to interpreting this message properly. In this way the salvation of the usually eurocentric dominant culture depends on hearing what is proclaimed by those from the margins.

This approach entails a response to injustice and oppression. By forcing my students to occupy an uncomfortable space, I feel I can provide them with a unique outlook, a view I believe enhances more traditional learning. I try to bring their lifetime of experiences and knowledge into conversation with people whose lives and experiences may be quite different from theirs, people who may often be thought of as having little to contribute to the educational process.

This pedagogy, however, is useless if it is restricted solely to the classroom. The liberating ethical praxis I advocate is pertinent to the larger community as well. For example, the community in which my school is located, called Holland, was settled by the

Dutch in the early 1800s. Located on Lake Michigan, Holland has wooden shoe factories, a windmill imported from the Netherlands, and an annual May festival called Tulip Time that attracts over 100,000 visitors to celebrate Holland's Dutch heritage.

But Holland is also a town where all are not Dutch. On the underside of Holland, we discover Hispanics who comprise approximately 22.2 percent of the overall population. (If those who are undocumented were counted, the numbers would hover at 30 percent.) In addition, 3.5 percent of the population is Asian and 2.3 percent black. In spite of these demographics, those who live on the margins of Holland are seldom seen walking or shopping on 8th Street, the main business center of the city, even if they live a few blocks away.

Holland is a town where many from the dominant culture may wish to live in a more just and equitable society, but they also find themselves trapped within social structures created long ago (and some more recently) to protect their privilege by masking racism and classism. Consequently, those who are oppressed by these structures, along with those who benefit, are in need of liberation, another word for salvation.

To bring about liberation as salvation, Christianity must become a way of life rather than just a doctrinal belief. If simple belief is all that is required for salvation, then complicity with structures that perpetuate oppression is inconsequential to the Christian life. Besides, do not the demons themselves believe Jesus Christ is Lord of all (Jas. 2:19)? The perspectives of Christian liberationist ethicists are crucial to help establish a more just society. Faculty and students alike can contribute to the struggle against oppression that has often become institutionalized. For this reason, my role as an ethicist must include participation in a faith community and the overall society. What I *do*—my praxis—is more crucial than any book I might write. Most Christian ethicists working in a liberation framework write, or teach, to give voice to the voiceless, to shout from the mountaintop that which is commonly heard among disenfranchised people, to put into words what the marginalized are feeling and doing. No doubt, such writing may anger or alienate those who view their power and privilege as a birthright; nonetheless, these things must be said to bring about repentance for those who participate in injustice through their privilege, and to bring about salvation for those who suffer from the injustice.

As can be imagined, this type of pedagogy does not come easily in a conservative religious and political environment like Holland, Michigan. It might be wiser to simply conform to the dominant culture and remain silent in the face of racism, classism, sexism, and heterosexism. There is a tremendous temptation to turn my back on the oppression that surrounds me. But it seems my scholarship has been influenced by Don Quixote and, like Don Quixote, I feel the need to charge the windmills of Holland. But in a world that normalizes oppression — our world today — maybe some Don Quixotes can bring hope as they set out on a path of a justice-based ethics to take on the foes of power and privilege.

Acknowledgments

Even Don Quixote had his Sancho. Likewise, this book is a reality because of the many who labored with me to bring it to fruition. It would be a travesty to take full credit for what appears on these pages. Many of the ideas and insights for this book took shape in a senior-level class I taught at Hope College by the same name, "Doing Christian Ethics from the Margins." Although the class was composed of approximately twenty students (Anglo students, save one) with most sharing in middle- and upper-class privilege, these students were committed to seeking justice. They seriously undertook the quite difficult task of reflecting upon ethical case studies by seeking the voices of those who are usually disenfranchised by the prevailing social structures. I give my deep-felt thanks to these students. Specifically, I wish to highlight three of them: Dustin Janes, Lauren Hinkle, and Phil Johnson, who worked with me for an additional semester as research assistants, spending countless hours gathering and organizing data.

Thanks to a McGregor Fund grant offered through Hope College, Phil Johnson was able to continue assisting me with this project through the summer months. I am also indebted to librarian Anthony Guardado at Hope College, who worked with us in locating hard-to-find sources. I also greatly appreciated the Religion Department at Hope College, whose faculty set up a colloquium to read early versions of this manuscript and provided valuable feedback. In additional, I am grateful to John Raines and Allan Verhey, who carefully read sections of the manuscript and provided much constructive criticism. Any success this book has is due to their wise counsel. I continue to be indebted to Jonathan Schakel for his faithfulness in proofreading my text, and to my editor Susan Perry, who was always ready to prod me toward excellence. As always, I owe eternal gratitude to my children, Vincent and Victoria, and my soul-mate Deborah, my moral compass who continues to be the source of my strength.

PART I

ETHICAL THEORY

CHAPTER 1

Doing Christian Ethics

Even the wicked are virtuous. The Ku Klux Klan, probably the oldest hate group in the United States, bases its beliefs and actions upon what it perceives to be Christian values and virtues. According to its official web site:

> The Knights' Party is a political organization and believes we rightfully place our foundation upon the word of Jesus Christ. This we feel is what made America great. . . . It is only by basing governmental policy and laws upon the Christian faith that our nation and people will retain our cherished liberties and freedom. Our nation must repent of its sins and return to the laws of God and the precepts which made America Great![1]

Likewise, the Church of the Creator, one of the newest and fastest-growing hate groups, operates according to its own code of ethics. But unlike the Klan, it is constructed as a non-Christian organization. According to its official web page:

> Christianity teaches love your enemies and hate your own kind, while we teach exactly the opposite, namely hate and destroy your enemies and love your own kind. Whereas Christianity's teachings are suicidal, our creed brings out the best creative and constructive forces inherent to the White Race. Whereas Christians are destroyers, we are builders. . . . Our

---

[1] See http://www.kukluxklan.org

3

Golden Rule briefly can be summarized as follows: That which is good for the White Race is the highest virtue; that which is bad for the White Race is the ultimate sin.[2]

In all fairness, hate groups such as these advocate motherhood, patriotism, and the welfare of children. They exhort their members to live by a code of ethics that celebrates and defends values and virtues that some of the world's great faith traditions also advocate. It would be somewhat reductionist simply to write off these groups as purely evil with no comprehension of good. In fact, as these two web sites indicate, they do have a set of ethics, a sense of proper behavior, and a self-imposed mandate to live an honorable life, hence proving St. Augustine of Hippo's dictum that "there is a kind of honor even among thieves."

The problem with the value systems of the KKK and the Church of the Creator is that others, among them people of color, disagree with their understanding of morality. The issue then is not so much *whether* humans should follow some set of ethical precepts, but rather, *which* ethical precepts. Moral relativism recognizes the variety of ethical beliefs existing between different racial and ethnic groups, economic classes, and gender preferences. But if ethics is simply relative, where no one group's ethics is necessarily superior or inferior to another group's, then adhering to the ethics spouted by the Klan, or the Church of the Creator, should be as valid as any ethics coming from the marginalized spaces of society, or any other spaces for that matter. It appears as though a preferential option needs to be made for some set of ethical precepts. The question is: Whose?

While the Klan or the Church of the Creator may appear as extreme examples, other ethical perspectives expounded by many Christians within the U.S. eurocentric culture also raise questions and concerns about the incongruence existing with what they conceive to be moral and day-to-day experiences of marginalized people. Regardless of the virtues expounded by the dominant culture, there still exist self-perpetuating mechanisms of oppression that continue to normalize and legitimize how subjugation manifests itself in the overall customs, language, traditions, values, and laws

---

2 See http://www.creator.org/faq

of the United States. Our political systems, our policing authorities, our judicial institutions, and our military forces conspire to maintain a status quo designed to secure and protect the power and wealth of the privileged few. In some cases, the ethics advanced by the dominant culture appears to rationalize these present power structures, hence protecting and masking the political and economic interests of those whom the structures privilege — in effect, an ethics driven by the self-interest of Euroamericans.

As long as the religious leaders and scholars of the dominant culture continue to construct ethical perspectives from within their cultural space of wealth and power, the marginalized will need an alternate format by which to deliberate and, more importantly, do ethics. Through critical social analysis, it is possible to uncover the connection existing between the prevailing ideologies (namely, the ethics of the dominant culture) that support the present power arrangement, with the political, economic, and cultural components of the mechanisms of oppression that protect their power and wealth. Anchoring ethics on the everyday experience of the marginalized challenges the validity, or lack thereof, of prevailing ideologies that inform eurocentric ethics.

For example, the fact that once upon a time in U.S. history the "peculiar" institution of slavery was biblically supported, religiously justified, spiritually legitimized, and ethically normalized raises serious questions concerning the objectivity of any particular code of ethics originating from that dominant white culture. At the very least, the marginalized are suspicious of the ethics of those who benefit from what society deems to be Christian or moral — then, as well as today. Although hindsight facilitates our understanding of how unchristian and unethical previous generations may have been, we are left wondering whether perspectives considered by some to be morally sound today might be defined as unchristian and unethical by future generations. Regardless, extreme groups like the Klan or the Church of the Creator are not, nor should they be, our focus. Instead, our concentration rests with ethics advocated by traditionally based Christian congregations found throughout this country.

I aim to describe how the disenfranchised struggle against societal mechanisms responsible for much of the misery they face, preventing them from living out the mission of Christ as recorded in

the Gospel of John: "that they may have life, and have it abundantly" (10:10).[3] Christian liberationist ethics becomes the process
by which the mechanisms that dehumanize life, as well as cause
death, are dismantled. All too often, ethics, as presented by the
dominant culture, explores Christian virtues without seriously considering the existence of the oppressed majority of people. The
hope of God, like the hope of the marginalized, is the re-creation
of proper relationships where all people can live full abundant lives,
able to become all that God has called them to be, free from the
societal forces (racism, classism, and sexism) that foster dehu-
manizing conditions. Within such relationships exist healing, whole-
ness, and liberation.

WHY CHRISTIAN?

One may ask why this book unapologetically centers ethical reflection upon the Christian perspective, relying mainly on Christian
sacred texts (specifically the Hebrew Bible and the New Testament) and Christian theological concepts (specifically the liberationist motif advocated by many marginalized groups). Should not
ethical perspectives incorporate a wide variety of responses, including those that are not necessarily Christian-based? Realizing the
absence of a homogeneous cultural and religious center upon which
to deduct moral reasoning, does it not make sense to reflect the
world's religious diversity when determining proper ethical
responses? Surely there is much to learn about ethical deliberation
from major world religions like Islam, Judaism, Hinduism, and

---

[3] The reader should be aware that all scriptural quotes are the trans-
lation by the author from the original Hebrew or Greek. Additionally, it
will be assumed that the stories and traditions appearing in the biblical
text have been accurately preserved by the early faith communities. Usually, biblical scholars discuss the authenticity of authorship, as well as the
accuracy of particular events, stories, or statements appearing in the text;
however, such an analytical endeavor is beyond the scope of this book.
Instead, my use of scripture attempts to read the text from the perspective of the faith community. Such a reading is conducted from the marginalized spaces of society, attempting to understand and apply the biblical
message to the reality of disenfranchisement.

Buddhism, as well as overlooked earth-based religions from Africa, Australia, and the pre-European Americas. As worthy as such an exploration of comparative religious traditions may be, it is beyond the scope of this book.

Ethics remains a reflection of the social location and theological beliefs (or disbeliefs) of a given people. We focus on the Christian perspective because this book is written by and for those who claim to be followers of Jesus Christ. Although ethics can be done devoid of Jesus Christ (as well as devoid of the influence of a supreme god-type deity), such ethics, although valid for those constructing it, is not necessarily Christian-based, even though agreement may be found in several areas of deliberation.

That being said, it is crucial to realize that the "Christianity" upon which the ethical perspectives of this book are based, is not necessarily Christianity as defined and understood by those privileged by the dominant culture. Rather, it is Christianity as forged from the underside of the dominant culture, by those who exist on the margins of society. For those who struggle within oppressive structures, the personhood of Jesus Christ as a source of strength becomes crucial. The life and sayings of Christ, as recognized by the faith community that searches the biblical text for guidance to life's ethical dilemmas, serve as the ultimate standard of morality. While eurocentric theology, and the ethics that flow from it, has a tendency to abstract the Christ event, those on the margins recognize that Christ remains at work in the United States today.

Theologian James Cone reminds us that it is from within the oppressed black community (and I would add any oppressed community) that Christ continues to bring about liberation from oppressive structures (1999a:5). For this reason, Jesus Christ, as understood by the disenfranchised faith community, becomes authoritative in how ethics develops within marginalized groups. For them, the incarnation — the Word taking flesh and dwelling among us — becomes the lens through which God's character is understood. Although Christ remains the ultimate revelation of God's character to humanity, the biblical text becomes the primary witness of this revelation and, as such, forms Christian identity while informing moral actions. The ultimate values advocated by the revelation of God through Christ as witnessed in the biblical text become the standards by which individuals and, more important, social structures are judged. Regardless of how many different ways the biblical text can be interpreted, certain recurring themes, specifically a call to justice and a call to love, can be recognized by all who call themselves Christians.

WHY ETHICS?

Neither the overall biblical text, nor the pronouncements of Jesus are silent or abstruse concerning the type of actions or praxis expected of those who claim to be disciples of Christ. The prophets of old would answer the ethical question of what God wants of God's people in a very straightforward matter. God was not interested in church services devoid of praxis toward the marginalized. As the prophet Isaiah reminds us, "Do not bring me [your God] your worthless offerings, the incense is an abomination to me. I cannot endure new moon and Sabbath, the call to meetings and the evil assembly" (1:13). Instead, the prophets proclaimed justice for society's most vulnerable members as true worship, a testimony of one's love for God and neighbor.

Jesus sounds an eschatological admonishment on what is expected from his followers. In the Gospel of Matthew, he warns, "Because lawlessness shall have been multiplied, and the love of many will grow cold, the one enduring to the end, this one will be saved" (24:12–13). In short, there can be no faith, in fact no salvation, without ethical praxis—not because such actions are the cause of salvation, but rather their manifestation. To participate in ethical praxis is to seek justice. For those on the margins of society, the ultimate goal of any ethical praxis is to establish a more just society. Yet justice has become a worn-out, hollow expression—an abstract and detached battle cry. Every political action initiated by the dominant culture, no matter how self-serving, is construed as just. The maintenance of an economic system that produces poverty is heralded as being based on the just principle of *suum cuique tribuere* (to each what is due). Sending military personnel into battle to protect "our" natural overseas resources is understood as securing our freedoms and way of life. The most unjust acts are portrayed as just by those with the power and privilege to impose their worldview on the rest of society. This is what sociologist Emile Durkheim meant when he insisted that the beliefs and sentiments held in common by the inhabitants of the dominant culture become the moral norms codified in laws, customs, and traditions. Consequently, the primary function of society becomes the reaffirmation, protection, and perpetuation of this "collective or common conscience" (1933:79–82). If this is true, then those on the margins of society must ask if it is possible to formulate a universal principle of justice apart from the definitions imposed by the collective conscience of the dominant culture.

Two of the most important components of ethics are the concepts of justice and love, both rooted within the biblical narrative. Although these are two separate concepts, for the liberationist they are forever connected. The importance of justice to ethical living is expounded by biblical scholar Gerhard Von Rad, who writes:

> There is absolutely no concept in the Old Testament with so central a significance for all the relationships of human life as that of "tsedaqah." It is the standard not only for man's relationship to God, but also for his relationship to his fellows, reaching right down to the most petty wrangling—indeed, it is even the standard for man's relationship to the animals and to his natural environment. (1962:370)

Justice, the English equivalent of *tsedaqah*, can never be reduced simply to some ideal to be achieved or a code of precepts to be followed. Rather, justice denotes how a real relationship between two parties (God and human, human and human, nature and human, and/or human and society) is conducted. The emphasis is not on some abstract concept of how society is to organize itself, but rather on loyalty within relationships, specifically those dealing with humans (Von Rad 1962:371). Right relationship with God is possible only if people act justly toward each other.

Such relationships are prevented from securing an abundant life, here understood as intellectual, physical, and material development, when one party, in order to secure greater wealth and power, does so at the expense of the Other. Injustice thus becomes a perverted relationship that ignores coordinating the proper good or end of individuals with that of their community. Such perverted relationships insist that its members should pursue their own self-interest, for only then will it be capable of contributing to the overall common good.[4] Such thinking asserts that everyone has a moral obligation to follow self-interest so as to establish justice.[5] Still, such an approach to relationships is fundamentally incongruent with how justice is defined in the biblical text, specifically Paul's admonition to put the needs of others before oneself (Eph. 5:21).

The danger of not incorporating the relational aspects of the term justice can lead to the rejection of God, even while one professes to belong to God and to live a pious life. Liberation theologian Gustavo Gutiérrez reminds us:

> To know Yahweh, which in biblical language is equivalent to saying to love Yahweh, is to establish just relationships among persons, it is to recognize the rights of the poor. The God of biblical revelation is known through interhuman justice. When justice does not exist, God is not known; God is absent. (1988:110–11)

If justice is what Christians are called to do, it is done in obedience to love. Love can never be understood or defined as an emotional experience (although such feelings could, and usually become a symptom of the love praxis). Neither is it a response due to pity nor a duty based on paternalism. Brazilian theologians Leonardo and Clodovis Boff remind us that "love is praxis, not theory" (1988:4). Love is an action verb that describes something that is done by one person to another, an action taken regardless of how one feels or, as the author of 1 John 3:18 stated, "Let us

---

[4] For example, Adam Smith makes such an argument within the economic sphere in his 1776 book *The Wealth of Nations*.

[5] Martin Buber best describes the consequences of such a perverted relationship. He writes that the I-You relationship is an intimate one consisting of caring, trust, and empowerment. In such relationships, participants discover their humanity and through mutual affirming discover the "eternal You." By contrast, the I-It relationship (which some have argued is prevalent due to racism, classism, and sexism) dehumanizes the Other. By identifying them as a commodity to be possessed, exploited, and disposed at the will of the "I," the "It" is oppressed while the "I" loses their essential humanity, creating a condition in need of liberation and salvation (1970:62, 84, 150, 160).

not love in words, nor in mere talk, but in deed and in truth." Love is the deed of justice or, as the Medellín documents eloquently stated, "Love is the soul of justice. The Christianity which works for social justice should always cultivate peace and love in one's heart" (CELAM 1968:71). For the Christian, this deed is done in spite of the Other deserving to be loved. Paul reminds us, "But God loved us by commanding Christ to die for us, even while we were still sinners" (Rom. 5:8). It is this same type of love that binds the believer to the abundant life of the Other. Hence, to love in this fashion is to question, analyze, challenge, and dismantle the social structures responsible for preventing people from reaching the fullest potential of the abundant life promised by Christ.

Love becomes the unifying theme of the biblical text, specifically when expressed as a relational love for God and for one's neighbor. The false dichotomy existing between faith (love the Lord your God) and ethics (love your neighbor as yourself) is collapsed by Jesus, who demands manifestations of both by those wishing to be called his disciples. The doing of love becomes the new commandment Christians are called to observe (Jn. 12:34–35). The Apostle Paul understood how paramount Christ's command was for all ethical actions committed by those calling themselves Jesus' disciples. Hence he wrote to the Corinthians: "If I speak in the tongues of humans, even of angels, but I do not have love, I become as a sounding brass or clanging cymbal. And if I have prophecies, and know all mysteries, and all knowledge, and if I have all faith so as to move mountains, but I do not have love, I am nothing" (1 Cor. 13:1–3).

The love that liberates can only be known and experienced from within relationships established upon acts of justice. Relationships with each other, and God, become a source for moral guidance, capable of debunking the social structures erected and subsequently normalized by the dominant culture. By first learning to love humans through just relationships, the ability to love God also becomes possible. For as 1 John 4:20 reminds us, how can we love God whom we cannot see, unless we first learn to love humans whom we do see? It is love toward the least among us, demonstrated through a relationship founded on justice that manifests love for God. Only by loving the disenfranchised by seeing Jesus among the poor and weak, can one learn to love Jesus who claims to be the marginalized. To love the marginalized is to love Jesus, making fellowship with God possible as one enters into just fellowship with the disenfranchised.

In conclusion, the basis for all ethical acts can be reduced to one verse from Galatians: "The whole Law is fulfilled in one word, Love your neighbor as yourself" (5:14). How do we love our neighbor? We can look to the biblical narrative, seeking concrete examples of love manifested as an act of God's work to create justice-based relationships. The very identity of those claiming to be Christian becomes defined by their relationship to their God and to their neighbor. To construct justice apart from a love relationship with others becomes a perversion designed to protect the privilege of the ones doing the construction. If, according to Luke 4:18, Jesus came to "proclaim liberation to the captives . . . [and] set those oppressed free," how then can the bondage of many be preferred simply because it protects the power and privilege of the few? For this reason, an option for the poor characterizes a sincere commitment to justice, not because the poor are inherently more holy than the elite, but simply because they lack the elite's power and privilege. Consequently, we must now ask, why then from the margins?

WHY FROM THE MARGINS?

If the dominant culture continues to be the sole interpreter of moral reality, then its perspectives will continue to be the norm by which the rest of society is morally judged. The danger is that, to some extent, the dominant culture's ethics has historically been and, some would argue, continues to be, a moral theorizing geared to protect the self-interest of those who are privileged. Consequently, which ethical perspectives are chosen or discarded becomes a decision that establishes power relationships. To choose one ethical precept over another justifies those who will eventually benefit from what is chosen. Once members of the dominant culture recognize the ethical precepts that support their lifestyle, claims of moral absolutism can be made. When members of the dominant culture legitimize the values that advance their power within the social structures as moral "truths," they fail to realize that at times the Christian ethics that they advocate in fact legitimize power, specifically, who has it, and how it is to be used. This form of eurocentric moral imperialism forces serious consideration of the question asked by Argentinian theologian José Míguez Bonino: "In this world of power, of economic relations and structures, a world that maintains its autonomy and will not yield to voluntaristic moral ideals imposed from the outside, a world in which power and freedom seem to pull in opposite directions — what can Christians say and do?" (1983:21). For those who do ethics from the margins, the issue of power becomes paramount in the development of any ethical discourse. Foremost for those who are marginalized is the ethical response to the use, misuse, and abuse of power rather than issues of character, values, virtues, or moral principles.

Because the Judeo-Christian faith is based on the God of Exodus who can hear the cries for freedom from the marginalized and enters history to lead them toward liberation, any ethics arising from that faith that wishes to remain faithful to that religious tradition must remain rooted in the praxis of liberation. Christian ethics should first struggle with the question of power and how to crucify power and the privilege that comes with it so that justice and love can instead reign. Yet, if those who are privileged by the present political, economic, and social structures refuse to acknowledge that being wealthy and white provides specific advantages over against the disenfranchised, then how can they participate with integrity in any discourse that addresses injustices? For Christian ethics to be relevant, the faith community's struggles with oppressive living conditions must be engaged, always with the goal of dismantling the mechanism responsible for creating the inhumanity faced within marginalized spaces.

Jesus can never belong to the oppressors of this world because he is one of the oppressed. The radicalness of the gospel message is that Jesus is in solidarity with the very least of humanity. The last shall be first, the center shall be the periphery. In Matthew 25:31–46, Christ returns to earth to judge between those destined for the reign of heaven and those who are not. The blessed and the cursed are separated by what they did or did not do to the least among us. Specifically, did they or did they not feed the hungry, welcome the alien, clothe the naked, and visit those infirm or incarcerated? Is the ethical lifestyle of individuals in solidarity with the marginalized demonstrated in liberative acts that led others toward an abundant life? So that there would be no confusion about God's preferential option, Jesus clearly states, "Truly I say to you, inasmuch as you did it to one of these, the least of my people, you did it to me."

The church of Jesus Christ is called to identify and stand in solidarity with the oppressed. The act of solidarity becomes the litmus test of biblical fidelity and the paradigm used to analyze and judge how social structures contribute to or efface the exploitation of the marginalized. To be apart from the marginalized community of faith is to exile oneself from the possibility of hearing and discerning the gospel message of salvation — a salvation from the ideologies that masks power and privilege and the social structures responsible for their maintenance.

Ideologies and social structures are shaped and formed by individuals who are in turn shaped and formed by these same ideologies and social structures. Like everyone else, Christians are born into a society where the dialectical relation between the person and the community informs their beliefs and their character — in short, their identity. For this reason, the socio-historical context of any people profoundly contributes to the construction of their ethical system. When Christians, in accordance with their faith, attempt to develop ethical responses to the conflicts of human life, they participate in a dialogue between Christianity and what their community defines as Christian.[6]

---

[6] H. R. Niebuhr was correct in observing that Christian ethics are fused and confused with what the civil social order determines is best for the common good. However, ethicist Darryl Trimiew calls H. R. Niebuhr to task for his underlying principle for Christian social action. According to Niebuhr, "Responsibility affirms: God is acting in all actions upon you. So respond to all actions upon you as to respond to his action" (1963:126). Niebuhr continues by claiming, "The will of God is what God does in all that nature and men do. . . . Will of God is present for Jesus in every event from the death of sparrows, the shining of sun and descent of rain, through the exercise of authority by ecclesiastical and political powers that abuse their authority, through treachery and desertion by disciples" (164–65). Trimiew finds Niebuhr's admonition troubling for marginalized communities because it encourages believers to interpret all actions, regard-

Unfortunately those who control the instruments of social power claim a monopoly on truth to the detriment of the disenfranchised. Black ethicist Katie Cannon succinctly captures the confusing of the dominant culture's self-interest with the interest of the public when she writes: "The welfare of the state is now fully identified with the interests of the wealthy class. Everything else is subordinate to the prosperity of the wealthiest business people and to the welfare of the commercial class as a whole. . . . Their control of taxation, judiciary, and the armed forces gives them free access to all political processes . . . the interest of the ruling class becomes de facto the interest of the public" (1995:150).

The common good becomes restricted to those who benefit from the privilege obtained within these same social structures. Yet seldom do those in power admit that they are disproportionately rewarded by society. Concealing this truth makes any ethics emanating from that same dominant culture incomplete and heretical. Appeals to Christianity or reason will fail to affect the existing power structures, for the dominant culture uses both to defend their interest. Thus, the disenfranchised can only bring liberative change through empowerment.[7]

The immoral hoarding of power and privilege by the dominant culture makes it difficult for those benefitting by the status quo to

---

less of how repressive such actions may be to the disenfranchised, as God's providence. Oppression becomes conformity to the will of God, who is chastising the marginalized for their sins. But how can any "responsible self," Trimiew wonders, claim that the death and misery faced by those marginalized at the expense of the privileged is God's providence? (1993:xi, 8).

[7] Reinhold Niebuhr makes a similar point. He writes:
Dominant classes are always slowest to yield power because it is the source of privilege. As long as they hold it, they may dispense and share privilege, enjoying the moral pleasure of giving what does not belong to them and the practical advantage of withholding enough to preserve their eminence and superiority in society. . . . It must be taken for granted therefore that the injustices in society, which arise from class privileges, will not be abolished purely by moral persuasion. That is a conviction at which the proletarian class, which suffers most from social injustice, has finally arrived after centuries of disappointed hopes. (1960:121, 141)

be able to propose, with any integrity, liberative ethical precepts. For this reason, James H. Cone, as well as many other theologians of color, concludes that there can exist no theology (and I would add ethics) based on the gospel message that does not arise from marginalized communities (1999a:5). Francisco Moreno Rejón, a Latin American ethicist, maintains that for ethics to be liberative, its origins must rise:

1. *From the underside of history* and the world: from among the losers of history, from within the invaded cultures, from dependent [peoples] without genuine autonomy and suffering the manifold limitations that all this implies. 2. *From the outskirts of society*, where the victims of all manner of oppression live, the ones who "don't count" — the ones whose faces reflect "the suffering features of Christ the Lord" (Puebla Final Document, no. 3). 3. *From among the masses of an oppressed, believing people:* it cannot be a matter of indifference to moral theology that the majority of Christians and humanity live in conditions of inhuman poverty. (1993:215)

Only from the margins of power and privilege can a fuller and more comprehensive understanding of the prevailing social structures be ascertained. Not because those on the margins are more astute, but rather because they know what it means to be a marginalized person attempting to survive within a social context designed to benefit the privileged few at their expense. Cone says it best when he writes, "Only those who do not know bondage existentially can speak of liberation 'objectively.' Only those who have not been in the 'valley of death' can sing the songs of Zion as if they are uninvolved" (1999b:22).

Is there any hope then for those who benefit from the present oppressive structures? Before answering this question, it must be realized that those who benefit from the current socio-political and economic structures are themselves oppressed. While not to the extent of intellectual, physical, and material deprivation felt in economically deprived areas, still, the oppressor lacks the full humanity offered by Christ. To oppress another is to oppress oneself. German philosopher Hegel's concept of "Lordship and Bondage," as found in his *The Phenomenology of Mind*, avers that the master (the oppressor) is also subjugated to the structures he creates to enslave the laborer (1967:238–40). Because oppressive structures also prevent the master from obtaining an abundant life (specifically in the spiritual sense), those supposedly privileged by said structures are also in need of the gospel message of salvation and liberation.

Participation in ethical praxis designed to establish justice bestows dignity on the marginalized "non-persons" by accentuating their worth as receptacles of the *imago Dei*, the very image of God, but it also restores the humanity of the privileged who falsely construct their identity through the negation of the Other. According to psychoanalyst Jacques Lacan, those from the dominant culture look into the mirror and recognize themselves as superior through the distancing process of negative self-definition: "I am what I am not." The subject "I" is defined by contrasting it with the Objects residing on the margins. In the formation of the "I" out of the difference from the "them," there exist established power relations that give meaning to those differences (1977:1–7). By projecting the "I" upon the marginalized, those of the dominant culture are able to define themselves as worthier of the benefits society has to offer, either because they are more industrious (the Protestant work ethic) or are simply wiser.

The ethical task before both those who are oppressed and those who are privileged by the present institutionalized structures is not to reverse roles or to share the role of privileged at the expense of some other group but, rather, to dismantle the very structures responsible for causing injustices along race, class, and gender lines, regardless of the attitudes bound to those structures. Only then can all within society, the marginalized as well as the privileged, can achieve their full humanity and become able to live the abundant life offered by Christ.

How then can those who are privileged by the present social structures find their own liberation from those structures, a liberation that can lead to their salvation? By nailing and crucifying one's power and privilege to the cross so as to become nothing. According to the Apostle Paul's letter to the Philippians, "[Jesus Christ], who subsisting in the form of God thought it not robbery to be equal with God, but emptied himself, taking the form of a slave, in the likeness of humans, and being found in the fashion of a human, he humbled himself, becoming obedient until death, even the death of the cross" (2:6–8). At the cross, Jesus becomes nothing so as to redeem the world.

Ethics begins with our own surrender, with our self-negation. Those who benefit from the power and privilege of social structures can encounter the Absolute only through their own self-negation by crucifying their power and privilege. The late sixteenth-century mystic Juan de la Cruz (John of the Cross) captures this concept of self-negation in his *Ascent of Mount Carmel:* "To reach satisfaction in all, desire its possession in nothing. To come to the knowledge of all, desire the knowledge of nothing. To come to possess all, desire the possession of nothing. To arrive at being all, desire to be nothing" (1987:45).

Jesus was fond of saying, "For whoever desires to save their life shall lose it, but whoever loses their life for my sake and the sake of the gospel, that one shall save it" (Mk. 8:35). True liberation takes place when the individual sees into her or his own nature and thus becomes Christ-like. This praxis liberates those trapped by their race, class, and gender privilege, so that they, in solidarity with the marginalized, can bring about a just society based on the gospel definition of justice.

Still, which marginalized group will those from the dominant culture stand in solidarity with? Does each group create its own ethical reflection, or do they work together to overturn oppressive structures which affect all marginalized people? Darryl Trimiew, a black ethicist, has asked similar questions. He warns that:

> The refusal of various liberation movements to concern themselves with the fates of others is the self-issued death warrant of these moral movements. This new universalism is daunting, as it will require the cooperation of strangers, even strangers who may be competing for the very same scarce resources. . . . Yet the tendency of liberationists to concern themselves with parochial interests cannot be underestimated. In this country alone, liberation ethicists show little interest in working together on projects of solidarity in order to overthrow common oppressions. (2004:Chap.8)

Unlike biblical interpretation, theology, or other religious disciplines, ethics should not be conducted from only one marginalized perspective. Although black theology, Latina/o hermeneutics, and/or Asian-American Christian history provide unique and distinctive perspectives to different religious disciplines, ethics from just one marginalized perspective may prove counter-productive. Nuances between the different races and ethnicities exist and must be articulated in the overall conversation. Still, if the ultimate goal of ethics is to create a Christian response that brings change to existing oppressive structures, then no one group contains the critical mass required to bring about the desired just society. In fact, keeping marginalized groups separated insures and protects the power and privilege of the dominant culture.

When a front-page article in the *New York Times* (January 22, 2003) proclaimed, "Hispanics Now Largest Minority, Census Shows," some Latino/as felt that they had finally come into their own, receiving long overdue recognition. Yet, an unspoken underlying message was being communicated to other marginalized groups, specifically African Americans: "Hispanics are now the top dog, so you are going to have to compete against them for resources." But as Justo González perceptively observed, justice can never be served by having marginalized groups compete with each other for the meager resources doled out. For example, within churches, seminaries, church agencies, and church colleges, a small portion of the budget, a few positions, and a couple of courses are reserved for minorities, who are encouraged to fight among themselves for their small slice of the pie (1990b:36). These Christian institutions can now point at programs run, in spite of such limited resources, to herald their political correctness, all the while continuing institutionalized oppressive structures that secure the dominant culture's privilege. In effect, marginalized groups are often prevented from working together to bring changes to these institutions.

This is not the first time the dominant culture has fostered division between marginalized groups to secure its power. In fact, this strategy is older than the nation. Thandeka, a professor of theology and culture, shows how Virginians in colonial America learned to better secure their power by forcing what could have been natural allies against their rule to compete against each other. The dominant culture succeeded in preventing allegiances from developing between two oppressed groups, slaves (blacks) and ex-indentured servants (poor whites), by endowing the latter with white privilege. Prior to 1670, little difference existed between poor white indentured servants, considered "the scruff and scum of England," and black slaves, considered possessions.[8]

As more slaves flooded the colonies, an economic shift developed from a white indentured servitude-based economy where the poor whites worked for a limited number of years, to a black slave-based economy where Africans, although costing twice as much as poor whites, worked, along with their progeny, for life. Fear of future rebellions and a changing economic base led the Virginia elite to pass legislation to create social divisions between blacks and poor whites in order to secure its privileged place in the emerging nation (Thandeka 1999:42–47). These laws effectively caused a division based on race between natural allies, a strategy that has continued to serve the privileged class well throughout this country's history.[9]

Then, as now, the dominant culture's privilege is maintained because different marginalized groups fight with limited resources for black justice, Latino/a justice, Amerindian justice, gender justice, Asian-American justice, and so on. Any intellectual resistance against injustice must include a concerted effort to eliminate the

---

[8] Both the indentured servant and the slave lived an underfed and underclothed existence in separate inadequate quarters, supervised by overseers who would whip them as a form of correction. Both groups would run away from the oppression, while others, specifically freemen (former indentured servants who were without property) formed alliances to rebel. The most intense challenge to the status quo came in the form of the "Bacon's Rebellion" of 1676, which ended with the burning to the ground of Jamestown. The last rebels to surrender were eighty slaves and twenty indentured servants.

[9] In 1670 the Virginia Assembly forbade Africans and Amerindians from owning Christians (hereby understood as white) and non-Christians from Africa were to be slaves for life; in 1680, any white Christian was permitted to whip any black or slave who dared lift a hand in opposition to a Christian; in 1682, conversion to Christianity would not alter life-long slavery for Africans; in 1705, white indentured servants could not be whipped naked, only blacks who could also be dismembered for being unruly; also in 1705, all property (horses, cattle, and hogs) was confiscated from slaves and sold by the church so that the proceeds could be distributed among poor whites (Morgan 1975:329–33).

abuses of all oppressed groups. Although it is obvious that differences, particularly in cultural expressions, exist among numerous marginalized groups within the United States, a shared common history of disenfranchisement and the common problems of such a history create an opportunity to work together to dismantle oppressive structures that affect all who live on the periphery of power and privilege.

Ethics must be conducted from the overall margins of society more so than from any one particular marginalized perspective to avoid what Cornel West fears would be equating liberation with the white American middle-class man (1982:112). Although equal access to the socioeconomic resources of our society is desirable, the marginalized must stand vigilant of the danger of simply surmounting the present existing structures that cause oppression. Ethics is, and must remain, the dismantling of social mechanisms that benefit one group at the expense of another, regardless if the group privileged is white, black, brown, yellow, red, or any combination thereof. Not until separate marginalized groups begin to accompany each other toward justice, understood here as the dismantling of oppressive structures, can the hold of the dominant culture upon resources be effectively challenged.

CHAPTER 2

The De-Liberation of Ethics

My mother is illiterate. She never had the opportunity to go to school and obtain an education. Growing up in Cuba, she spoke one language—Spanish. Upon arriving in this country, she had difficulty communicating in English. But what my mother lacked in formal education she overcompensated with in street smarts. Once in the United States, she knew she needed employment. Like so many other refugees, she did whatever had to be done to procure a job. Failure meant that the children would go hungry. "Do you know how to waitress tables?" she would be asked. "But of course, back in the old country I was the head waitress in one of the most famous and busiest restaurants in the city," she would respond, even though she had never carried a tray of dishes in her life. "But can you read English?" the potential employer would ask. "But of course, I have a high school diploma from the old country." In reality, she simply memorized some important phrases found on most menus. She did get the job, and I, her son, got fed.

If I had been an ethicist back then and approached my mother questioning her character, her virtues, or her values, she would have simply laughed at me for my naivete. If she demonstrated the virtue of honesty and confessed she had no work experience, no education, and could barely speak the language, she would never have been hired. Yet, the moral reasoning she employed enabled her to surmount societal structures fundamentally averse to her very existence. "Which is more ethical," I imagine her asking me, "doing what needs to be done to get the job, or letting the sins of others force us to live on the streets?" For her, living on the streets was not hyperbole or a hypothetical case study, but a reality she faced. She sought to meet the basic needs of her family, in other words to survive, while retaining her dignity. Because she was a woman and had been impoverished as a child (through sexism and classism), she had no opportunity to obtain a formal education. Because she was a Latina in the United States living within a social structure hostile to her presence, few employment opportunities were available (racism). She simply did not have the luxury to wait for the "art of the possible" to feed her family.

Although my mother never read the theological works of historically marginalized women, like Delores Williams's *Sisters in the Wilderness*, I have no doubt that Williams's alternative ethical paradigm would have resonated with my Latina mother's experience. Just as the heroes of the faith, Abraham and Sarah, exploited and abused Hagar their slave girl, so too was my mother exploited and abused by self-professing Christians who capitalized on her inability to resist structures designed to benefit them at her expense due to her marginalized status as a woman, specifically a poor Latina woman. Although God did not liberate Hagar from her oppression (no doubt a concern for those of us engaged in liberative ethics), God did empower her to survive and endure the institutionalized forces responsible for her marginalization. Williams balanced resistance to oppression (by whatever means possible—even escaping to the desert) and survival with a liberation that may be far into the future. A spring found in the desert, where none had existed before, enabled Hagar to survive, at least momentarily.

Likewise, God enabled my mother, who was without the language skills and the work experience, to "make a way out of no way" by waitressing. My mother may never be able to read Williams's book, but in the depth of her soul, she understands Williams's message, for she too is a sister in the wilderness. Although illiterate, she understands what black ethicist Katie Cannon claims is the essence of Howard Thurman's theological ethics: "that the religion of Jesus is a 'technique of survival for the oppressed.'" The hope of my mother is to rely on a God who always provides the means and resources to meet the harsh realities of life (Cannon 1988:21, 162). She has not written a thesis on this subject but in her often-stated aphorism: "*Dios aprieta pero no ahogar*" (God squeezes but does not choke), she has communicated to me the message of a survival ethics that relies on God.

How easy it is for the intellectual elite to dismiss my mother, along with the others who are disenfranchised, as unschooled and untrained in understanding the proper implementation of sound ethical principles. In their minds, her "opinions" are biased perceptions based on her circumstances, no matter how unfortunate her situation may be. Nevertheless, while she might lack the means to articulate her ethics properly to a learned audience, still, it is my mother, along with others who are marginalized, who is constantly in the back of my mind as I wrestle with the ethical paradigms constructed in the prestigious halls of academia. Their moral reasoning is not the product of neatly categorized concepts found in theological textbooks, but rather a product of the messiness of struggling to meet basic needs within a social structure that successfully facilitates the failure of the marginalized. What then does eurocentric ethical theory, formulated from the secure space of privilege where employment is taken as a given, have to say to my mother? And more important, what can my illiterate mother teach those at the center of society about their own "biased opinions" of ethics as it relates to the everyday?

THE DILEMMA

In the name of Jesus Christ crusades have been launched to exterminate the Muslim "infidels"; women seeking autonomy have been burned as witches; indigenous people who refused to bow their knees to God and king were decimated; the kidnaping, rape, and enslavement of Africans were justified; and today, the pauperization of two-thirds of the world's population is legitimized so that a small minority of the planet can consider itself blessed by God. Yet the ethical pronouncements articulated within traditional Christian institutions such as churches, seminaries, Christian colleges, or Bible institutes tend to reinforce the ideologies of the dominant culture—ideologies that have brought untold death and misery to humanity. If it is important for those in power to remain in power, then the moral precepts they create, the political states they fashion, and the religious orders they support must either explicitly or implicitly maintain the status quo.

Even when ethical pronouncements are made that are critical of the power or privilege amassed by few at the expense of many, little if any praxis is put forward to dismantle the mechanisms responsible for maintaining the status quo. Usually cosmetic reforms are offered, with no serious consideration of the structural forms of injustices or social sin. As long as oppressive social structures persist, actions by individuals, no matter how well intended, are incapable of liberating those existing on the margins of society. Liberation can occur only through radical structural change. Reform simply avoids questioning the basics of the dominant culture's lifestyle, a lifestyle many ethicists share.

White, male (and increasingly female) ethicists with the economic privilege that comes with endowed chairs or full professorships at prestigious academic institutions do not theorize in an empty vacuum. Like the rest of the privileged dominant culture, they live in a certain location — an environment or context — that influences, affects, and shapes their ethical deliberations, deliberations that tend to justify their social location while consciously or unconsciously disenfranchising those on the margins of society. If we are to deal with issues of ethics, grounded in the reality of today's world, then we are forced to deal with the structural forces that form the "habitus" of those who benefit from the present social structures. If Christian ethics, constructed at the center of society, is rooted in a cultural discernment of the Bible as understood from a position of power and privilege, then to do ethics from the margins becomes an attempt to transform how ethics itself is done. Some ethicists from the periphery or margins of the dominant culture believe that their voices, usually silent or ignored, are capable of radically changing the theology, the doctrine, the practices, the mission, and the teachings of Christian institutions, starting at the grassroots level. To participate in an ethical discourse from the margins is to engage the proactive practices that precede the liberation and salvation of the least among us.

DE-LIBERATING LIBERATION

Since the start of the twentieth century, ethicists of the dominant culture gradually moved away from discussing which praxis should be employed when facing an ethical dilemma and, instead, devoted more of their energies to issues that dealt with the nature of ethics, specifically questions concerning virtues and the good. The proclivity of the dominant culture to deliberate ethics by pursuing the abstract good usually concludes with ethics being de-liberated. Praxis leading toward a more just social order was a first casualty of abstract ethical thought. Even though such abstract deliberations may be sympathetic to the plight of the oppressed, they still fall short by failing to alleviate the root causes of disenfranchisement.

To some degree, eurocentric ethics has become a matter of explaining what is ethical. But for those doing ethics from the margins, the question is not to determine some abstract understanding of what is ethical, but, rather, in the face of de-humanizing oppressive structures, to determine how people of faith adapt their actions to serve the least among us. Thus, ethics becomes the process by which the marginalized enter a more human condition by overcoming oppressive or controlling societal mechanisms. For them the starting point is not some ethical truth based on church doctrine or rational deliberation; instead, the starting point is analyzing the situation faced by the disenfranchised of our world, our nation, and our workplace and then reflecting *with* them theoretically, theologically, and hermeneutically to draw pastoral conclusion for actions to be taken.

Still, when ethical perspectives are voiced from the margins of society, all too often they are easily dismissed, especially if their spokespersons have not developed their methodology along the lines of acceptable eurocentric thought, usually viewed as the only appropriate form to participate in academic discourse. For some euroamerican ethicists, the praxis of liberation is reduced to a "theological symbol"designed to garner support from Christians for a particular social movement. But liberation is not just a symbol, it should mean a radical break with the status quo designed to maintain oppressive structures. Nonetheless, several ethicists of the dominant culture respond by accusing those doing ethics from a liberationist perspective of "moving from theology to politics without passing through ethics." Such arguments dismiss the formation of ethics from the margins as a very limited understanding of ethics.[1]

---

[1] For example, see the works of James Gustafson, *Theology and Christian Ethics, Can Ethics Be Christian?* and *Ethics from a Theocentric Persepc-*

While proficiency with the eurocentric ethical canon is the admission ticket to academic discussions of ethics, those doing ethics at the margins of power and privilege concentrate on practical praxis — behavior and actions. It is not what is *said* that bears witness to the good news of the resurrection, but what is *done* to those still trapped in the forces of death. When abstract deliberations are applied to reality, the attempts, although admirable in their aspirations to create a more just society, most often fail to assist those who are marginalized. Such deliberations continue to reinforce the very social structures responsible for much of the oppression felt by the disenfranchised. In large part, this is due to the present social structures being viewed and accepted as necessary to maintain a well-ordered society.

In *The City of God*, Augustine explains that the ultimate good is eternal life, while the ultimate evil is eternal death. The ultimate moral response for those living in the earthly city is a life lived in faith, awaiting the heavenly city to come (19:4). Augustine goes so far as to suggest that if we remain loyal to the heavenly city through faith, all other aspects of living a moral life will ensue. Nonetheless, shaken by Rome's political vulnerability and eventual sack in 410 C.E. by the Goths, Augustine looked to the civil structure to provide peace and order.[2] While salvation could be achieved only through the church, the state, although usually corrupt, was a necessary evil that maintained law and order. "Every use of temporal things is related to the enjoyment of earthly peace in the earthly city, while in the heavenly city it is related to the enjoyment of everlasting peace" (19:14). Acknowledging injustices and advocating their redress, Augustine still insisted that correcting injustice could never occur to the endangerment of the social order and peace.

---

tive: Theology and Ethics. See also Dennis P. McCann and Charles R. Strain, *Polity and Praxis: A Program for American Practical Theology*, pp. 146–52.

    [2] Non-Christian writers such as Celsus and Porphyry blamed the deterioration of the Roman Empire on the rise of Christianity, which embraced such "weak" virtues as love. They claimed that Christianity was a seditious movement that undermined the traditional brute militarism that originally forged the empire. One of the reasons why Augustine wrote *The City of God* was to refute such accusations.

This social order is arranged according to a hierarchy where husbands rule over wives (sexism) and masters ruled over slaves (classism) so that peace could be maintained (19:14).

Martin Luther (1483–1546) was greatly influenced by Augustinian thought. Luther maintained that the gospel is to be placed in heaven and the law on earth, erecting a barrier between the two. Humans are to obey the laws on earth, even when those laws dehumanize people. When peasants fought for the abolition of serfdom, Luther reminded them that earthly kingdoms can exist only if there is inequality, where some are free and others subservient. Repudiating the oppressed peasants' demand for their full humanity, Luther wrote to them:

> You assert that no one is to be the serf of anyone else, because Christ has made us all free. . . . Did not Abraham and other patriarchs and prophets have slaves? . . . A slave can be a Christian, and have Christian freedom, in the same way that a prisoner or a sick man is a Christian, and yet be free. [Your claim] would make all men equal, and turn the spiritual kingdom of Christ into a worldly, external kingdom; and that is impossible. A worldly kingdom cannot exist without an inequality of persons, some being free, some imprisoned, some lords, some subjects. . . . (vol. 46:39)

Luther went so far as to advise those in authority to "smite, slay, and stab, secretly or openly" the rebelling peasants, who like "mad dogs" must be killed (vol. 46:50). According to Luther, political stability, even if maintained through the oppression of the marginalized, takes precedence over the humanity of the marginalized.

The influence of these patriarchs of Western Christianity continues to be felt today. Some ethicists of the dominant culture, such as James Gustafson, warn of the danger of "[upsetting] a necessary equilibrium in society" (1975:119–20). Liberative praxis is fine, as long as society's equilibrium is maintained.[3] Although those

---

[3] Ethicist John Rawls insisted that the pursuit of justice be constrained within the limits of ensuring a well-ordered society, for only through such a society can a sense of justice be acquired (1971:453–57). Yet, according to Reinhold Niebuhr, the quest for justice, by its very nature, will disrupt the peace of society. Niebuhr wrote:

from the dominant culture strive to maintain society's equilibrium — an equilibrium that secures their place within the overall social order — those who remain marginalized hope to disrupt that same equilibrium. They see clearly that their needs are subordinated to those of the "well-ordered" society (understood here as a society that continues to privilege one group). They also recognize that those who benefit from the status quo will never voluntarily forfeit their privilege.

While we may all agree on the need for a well-ordered society, the question under dispute is who determines *how* and *what form* of a well-ordered society is to be maintained. For example, in his 1961 book concerning the sit-ins being conducted by African-Americans protesting segregation at lunch counters, ethicist Paul Ramsey heaped praise upon these protestors and their calls for more equitable race legislation. Yet, he found the sit-ins to be contradictory to proper Christian social action because they disrupted a well-ordered society. For him, the sit-ins promoted "lawlessness" and violated the rights of others, specifically the orderly stewardship of private property (1961:xiv). While desiring to end the racist segregation of his time, he first insisted on the preservation of the existing well-ordered society.[4]

Raising the consciousness of the marginalized always endangers the secure space of those calling for "law and order" who envision

---

Since every society has an instinctive desire for harmony and avoidance of strife, this is a very potent instrument of maintaining the unjust *status quo*. . . . Those who would eliminate the injustice are therefore always placed at the moral disadvantage of imperiling its peace. The privileged groups will place them under that moral disadvantage even if the efforts toward justice are made in the most pacific terms. They will claim that it is dangerous to disturb a precarious equilibrium and will feign to fear anarchy as the consequence of the effort. (1960:129)

[4] According to Ramsey:
But in the Christian view, simple and not so simple injustice *alone* has never been a sufficient justification for revolutionary change. There is always also the question of order to be considered, and a need for restraints placed upon all and upon the injustice infecting even our claims for greater justice. The Christian stands, then, for the rule of law against every utopian liberalism, however highminded. (1961:48–49)

their privilege as being threatened. All too often, in the name of "law and order," structures oppressive to marginalized groups are legitimized. For those on the underside of society's equilibrium, upsetting the dominant culture's serenity is the primary goal. As Martin Luther King, Jr., reminds us, "We know through painful experience that freedom is never voluntarily given by the oppressor; it must be demanded by the oppressed" (1964:80). It can be expected that such demands will create disharmony within "well-ordered" societies.

Nevertheless, there have been great religious scholars (and occasionally still are) of the dominant culture who tolerate a social order, regardless of how unethical it may appear to be, where the marginalized are to respect and honor those who are at the center not just for the good of society, but because this is how God ordained the social structure. With suspicion those on the margins approach scholars like John Calvin (1509–1564), who insisted that those who are marginalized, specifically the poor, should respect and honor those who are economically their superiors because God in God's wisdom bestowed the "elect" with special material gifts. In the political realm, Calvin called citizens to submit to governments, regardless of how tyrannical their rulers may have been because it is up to the Lord to avenge such despots, while it is up to the citizens to simply "obey and suffer" (4:20:31). Furthermore Calvin stated that the "poor must yield to the rich; the common folk, to the nobles; the servants, to their masters; the unlearned, to the educated" (3:7:1–5). Clearly Calvin ignored how the amassing of power and privileged is connected with the marginalization of the poor, the common folk, the servants, and the unlearned. Thus for ethicist Sharon Welch, the danger of our present society is the assumption that those in the center of society, God's elect, possess "the prerequisites for moral judgement and that other groups [the poor, the common folk, the servants, and the unlearned] are devoid of those same prerequisites" (1990:126).

THE SOCIAL POWER OF ETHICS

Since the rise of modernity, specifically manifested in the eighteenth century as the Age of Enlightenment, ethicists have moved away from religious ethical systems founded on revelation, biblical hermeneutics, or church tradition. For the "modern" mind, there existed unambiguous universal truths about the very nature of reality, and reliable methodologies for arriving at the answers to all the dilemmas humanity faces. All that was required was their discovery. The process of discovering these truths made God, to some extent, irrelevant. God was, in effect, replaced with a scientific process of secularization that found the answers to ethical dilemmas in humanistic or naturalistic moral deliberations. The Enlightenment asserted that the individual was capable, via his or her own reasoning ability, of discovering absolute and universal moral laws. An instinctive moral compass found within human nature could guide the individual in determining to do good and in refraining from doing evil.[5] Other ethicists, employing a utilitarian approach, defined what is ethical by the principle that all actions can be numerically scaled, hence the action whose net benefits are greatest is the correct moral choice.[6] Yet, more often than not, such appeals to self-evident propositions become a justification for those in power to protect their self-interest.

As previously mentioned, ethical precepts do not develop in a social or cultural vacuum. Yet, ironically, the social context for the construction of ethics is usually ignored. What is termed moral is more often a product of the power residing within a person's social location than of a person's understanding of natural law or, for that matter, an "objective" reading of the scriptures or the product of enlightened moral reasoning or logic. Nonetheless, the reasoning or logic of the center is often inappropriate for the margins. As Malcolm X (1925–1965) reminds us,

What is logical to the oppressor isn't logical to the oppressed. And what is reason to the oppressor isn't reason to the oppressed. The black people [and I would add all who are from the margins] in this country are beginning to realize

---

5 Ethicists like John Rawls suggest that an intuitive sense of justice will guide humans in making correct moral decisions (1971:114–15).

6 Most ethicists today, however, would agree that if a society is unjust to a minority portion of it population, even though greater utilitarian benefits are enjoyed by the majority of the population, then that society as a whole is acting unjustly.

that what sounds reasonable to those who exploit us does-
n't sound reasonable to us. There just has to be a new system of reason and logic devised by us who are at the bottom.
(1968:133)

The reality from the margins of society is that those with power
impose their constructs of morality upon the rest of the culture.
Even though the privileged are quite adept at convincing themselves that their acts are altruistic, those who are disenfranchised
are seldom convinced of this. Virtues, no matter how desirable,
can be imposed to insure the subserviency of the marginalized.[7]

Ethics from the margins insists that racism, sexism, and classism
are the end products of the exercise of power. The power of the
dominant culture that creates Christian ethics can no longer be
explained simply as a group of institutions that ensures obedience,
or as a mode of subjugation, or as a form of domination exerted
by one group over another. Rather, power is used to *normalize*
what the dominant culture determines to be ethical; it does so by
harnessing the existing forces to which it has access (Foucault
1988:18). For this reason, power's hold upon people is based on
its ability to produce. Power creates pleasure, constructs knowledge, and generates discourse. In this sense, power can be understood as something positive, producing reality and creating the
subject's opinion of what is "truth" (Foucault 1984:60–61).
Whether consciously or unconsciously, Christians of the dominant

---

[7] Martin Luther King, Jr., made a similar point when discussing the
difference between just and unjust laws. In his letter from a Birmingham
jail he wrote:

> Sometimes a law is just on its face and unjust in its application.
> For instance, I have been arrested on a charge of parading with-
> out a permit. Now, there is nothing wrong in having an ordi-
> nance which requires a permit for a parade. But such an
> ordinance becomes unjust when it is used to maintain segre-
> gation and to deny citizens the First-Amendment privilege of
> peaceful assembly. (1964:83)

This is not to say that the law King refers to, or certain virtues, are unim-
portant; rather, it is to insist that whatever becomes law, or is defined as virtue,
is more often a product of power relationships than we are willing to admit.

culture, while truly wishing to remain faithful to their religious convictions, at times construct ethical perspectives to preserve their power, defining their self-serving ethical response as Christian. In their minds, their perspectives are viewed as "truth," answering the question concerning what Jesus himself would do.

These perspectives are then taught as truth to those who suffer at times from how these very same ethical perspectives are employed within society. The illegitimate power to subjugate the race, gender, or class of others is legitimized and normalized by the dominant culture. The French philosopher Michel Foucault explains how this process of normalization takes place through his analogy of an insane asylum. Individuals committed were freed from their chains if they promised to restore themselves; in other words, if they imposed upon themselves their own "domestication." Those deemed mentally insane were treated as children who needed to learn how to respect the authority of their superiors. The asylum became a religious domain without religion, where the mad were taught ethical uniformity. Although free, their chains could always be reinstated (1965:246–59).[8]

Like the patients in the asylum, the marginalized suffer from their own "madness" — their refusal to conform to the ethical standards of the "civilized" dominant culture. In the minds of those with power and privilege, marginalization is self-imposed, a refusal on the part of the disenfranchised to assimilate to what is perceived as the common good. When they behave, when they submit to the law and order of the dominant culture, they are "free." Those who reject the dominant view are eyed with suspicion. Their rejection of the superiority of the dominant culture, and the morality it advocates, proves that they have not yet been cured of their "madness."

---

[8] One cure employed for madness was tea parties. Because civilized people knew how to act during tea parties, patients, in order to prove they were no longer mad, had to behave with the proper decorum befitting civilized persons — learning in effect to become an anonymous "normal" person. Because the patients were always observed, they learned how to watch themselves. In short, they learned how to police their own actions. With time, the patient internalized the behavior that was acceptable through self-discipline (1965:246–59).

The danger of doing ethical reflection from the center of power and privilege is that any moral truth may be distorted or perverted when the perspectives of the marginalized are ignored. Yet, for these ignored voices to question the validity of how the dominant culture arrives at ethical precepts becomes an act of madness, or even sacrilege. As in Foucault's asylums, those who benefit from the present power structures get to legitimize their version of ethical truth for all, including the disenfranchised. The dominant culture operates within a framework constructed from the social location of privilege, and the resulting system of ethics functions to justify the norm. Even when such ethical deliberations assail poverty, the economic structures responsible for causing poverty — which are also responsible for assuring the privilege of the dominant culture — are seldom analyzed.

This process of normalizing the ethical views of the dominant culture can best be understood as a product of its "habitus," a product of the social location of its members. Habitus can be defined as a system of internalized dispositions that mediates between social structures and practical activities, shaped by the former and regulating the latter (Brubaker 1985:758). Those born into positions of privilege possess a socially constructed lifestyle that facilitates their ability to justify their privilege. This lifestyle, in a sense, unconsciously teaches them how to understand their economic and social success. Their identity is indebted to the community from which they come, which is primarily responsible for their so-called "personal" opinions. Their position within society, justified through customs, language, attitudes, dispositions, beliefs, traditions, values, and so on, existed prior to their birth and will continue to shape future generations after they are dead. As the "memory of the body," they bear the culture within them, assimilating from childhood the community's knowledge and experiences. From the moment of birth, these constructs were imposed on them, molding their childhood and guiding them through adulthood by decoding and adjusting to new situations. When their position within the privileged class is threatened, they protect their self-interest without realizing they are doing so. To protect their self-interest, they merely have to assert what they were born into in order to become what they are, an effort done with the lack of self-consciousness that marks their so-called "nature" (Bourdieu 1977:72–73, 78–87).

One's habitus so imprisons the mind that it becomes difficult to move beyond a particular social location without making a major shift in how reality is conceived and understood. Consequently, few members of the dominant culture question the construction of their conscience. Accordingly, those who approach ethics from positions of power and privilege must remain vigilant during their moral deliberations, lest they confuse what is ethical with what is their habitus. Their only hope is to move beyond their social location by forming relationships of solidarity with the marginalized. According to José Míguez Bonino, a Latin American theologian, ethical reflection done from the margins becomes a resource by which the overall society can be transformed, so that human possibility can be maximized at a minimum human cost (1983:107).

We are left questioning the role social factors play in influencing how ethical reflection is constructed and conducted. Those of the dominant culture often find it difficult to accept the thought that much of their moral understanding may in fact be a product of their privileged position rather than a gift handed down to them by a Supreme Being. The morality that protects the status quo is often mystified through religious symbols and taboos to insure that ethical precepts are regulated and enforced. By defining Christian ethics as commands proceeding from the Divine or as interpretations of scripture — rather than formulated by the center of privilege — any arguments that question privilege can be dismissed as a distortion of morality.

It is not that the marginalized lack the academic rigor to do ethical reflection or that they simply bypass ethical reflection altogether. Rather, their approach to their oppressive situation produces a different way of doing ethics. The schism existing between privileged academic centers and the ghettos or barrios that surround them is so wide that many Christian "principles" become abstract concepts that lack any application to the lives of the marginalized.

INCARNATION: EXPERIENCING IN THE FLESH

All that is known is filtered through the lens of our social location. What is perceived to be morally true is determined by experience. The danger of creating an ethical structure based on experience is that the experiences of those who write books, preach at influential churches, or teach at prestigious academic centers usually become the norm for making ethical determinations. By contrast, this book argues for an ethics rooted in the experiences of the marginalized, an experience that was, and continues to be, shared by God.

"In the beginning was the Word, and the Word was with God, and the Word was God. . . . And the Word became flesh and dwelled among us" (Jn. 1:1, 14). God does not stand aloof from human experiences, but rather enfleshes Godself in the concrete events of human history. Not only do we learn from the gospel how to be Christ-like, but God, through the Christ event, "learns" how to be human-like. God understands the plight of today's crucified people, who hang on crosses dedicated to the idols of race, class, and gender superiority. The crucifixion of Christ is God's solidarity with the countless multitudes who continue to be crucified today. Jesus' death on the cross should never be reduced to a sacrifice called for to pacify a God offended by human sin. Ignored for centuries by Christian theology is that Jesus, as fully human, was put to death, like so many today, by the civil and religious leaders who saw him as a threat to their power. There is nothing redemptive in the suffering of the just. The importance of the cross for the marginalized is that they have a God who understands their trials and tribulations because God in the flesh also suffered trials and tribulations. The good news is not so much that Jesus was crucified, but that Jesus rose from the dead, not to demonstrate God's power, but to provide hope to today's crucified that they too will be ultimately victorious over the oppression they face.

This God who became human continues to enflesh Godself in the everyday lives and experiences of today's crucified people. An important element in ethical reflection is what Hispanic theologians have called *lo cotidiano*, the Spanish word for "the everyday."[9] Ethics from the margins is contextual, where the everyday experience of the disenfranchised becomes the subject and source of ethical reflection.

---

[9] Latina theologian María Pilar Aquino, among others, avers the importance of the "everyday," *lo cotidiano*, in the doing of theology. For Aquino, the salvific experience of God in the here and now is experienced by the marginalized in their "daily struggles for humanization, for a better quality of life and for greater social justice" (1999:39). As such, I insist that *lo cotidiano* is the necessary source of all liberative ethical reflection.

To do ethics from the margins is to reflect on autobiographical elements to avoid creating a lifeless ethical understanding. "Story theology," a major theme within Asian-American theological reflection, attempts to challenge the West's hyper-emphasis on grounding all theological thought on the rational. Similarly, the "third eye," according to Japanese Zen master Daisetz Suzuki, is an Asian attempt to become open to that which is unheard due to one's own ignorance. To perceive reality with a "third eye" allows Christianity to turn to the abundant indigenous stories, legends, and folklore of the people, as well as the experiences of the marginalized. An autobiographically based ethic resonates among the disenfranchised who find that the inclusion of their stories provides a needed "heart" to the Western emphasis on the rational (Yang 2004:Chap.15).

Additionally, the methodological inclusion of one's story into an ethical dilemma powerfully connects reality with theory. Such an inclusion challenges the predominant assumption that all ethical deliberations must occur apart from and independent of the interpreter's social location or identity. Rather than verifying what is truth as explicated by those who are traditionally viewed as authorities (such as clergy or ethicists), or through sacred texts as historically interpreted by experts, the source of ethical deliberation begins with *lo cotidiano*, as experienced and understood by those existing on the margins. The perspective of those who are considered nonpersons because of their race, class, or gender becomes the starting point for any Christian ethical action. And this shatters the grip of those at the top of theological hierarchies on being the sole legitimate interpreters or arbiters of what is ethical.

CHRISTIAN ETHICS FROM THE CENTER

We live in a world where social, political, and economic offenses are common. Only a privileged few can use institutionalized racism, classism, and sexism to insulate themselves from the ravages of maltreatment. If doing ethics from the margins provides liberation for both the oppressed and the oppressor, then to insist on doing ethics only from the center of power and privilege frustrates the hopes of not just the disenfranchised but also of the privileged. Before we can begin to participate in a liberative ethics, we must explore how the ethics of the dominant culture can mask the oppression of those who are disenfranchised. How is ethics constructed so as to encourage the dominant culture to remain complicit with institutionalized racism, classism, and sexism?

A Wretch Like Me

Are humans innately good or innately evil? If human nature is good, is society then responsible for human corruption? If so, ethics is reduced to education in order to reveal the error that is responsible for present injustices, given the assumption that good people will not knowingly participate in evil actions.[10] If, however, human nature is evil, then legal sanctions are needed to force humans to live morally.[11] Regardless of how one answers questions concerning the inherent nature of humans, the fact remains that depravity does exist. The depravity found in humans is often caused by the sins of those who have power over other humans. Because all are created in the image of God, all are good and all have the potential to walk in righteousness, even those who are non-Christians. We are not evil vassals devoid of all good, as some would have us believe.[12]

When aligned with colonial and imperialist thinking, the sin that exists among humans can contribute to relegating people of

---

[10] Eighteenth-century French philosopher Jean-Jacques Rousseau, according to his Second Discourse, would then be correct in viewing the original human as living in a state of innocent harmony with nature. Even though today humans are wicked, originally they were naturally good in the state of nature. They were, in effect, a type of noble savage.

[11] Thomas Hobbes, the seventeenth-century English philosopher who formulated the doctrine of psychological egoism, would then be correct in his assertion that the state of nature is one "where every man is enemy to every man" so that human life in this state of nature is one that is "solitary, poor, nasty, brutish, and short" (1909:96–97).

[12] Karl Barth understood that the depravity of humanity forbade any goodness from residing within individuals, making it impossible for them to be ethical, that is, determining the Good. Only Christ can do this, and only by faith can the Christian rely on God's grace and participate in an authentic ethical dimension. Apart from grace, humans lack the capacity to distinguish good from evil. For those lacking Christ in their lives, anything proposed as the Good is simply a distortion. (1928:136–82)

color to the level of non-persons. As nonpersons, their land can be stolen, their bodies raped, their labor exploited, and their humanity disregarded. Some from the dominant culture repent and attempt to live a more humble life. For them there is an emphasis upon repentance for their depraved nature or acknowledgment, as the slave captain who penned the words to "Amazing Grace" wrote in self-deprecation, that grace exists "for such a wretch like me." For those who live a life of privilege due to advantages paid for by those who were made to believe in their non-personhood, such emotions of self-derogation may prove to be a healthy step toward a spiritual path of healing. The danger occurs when those with power impose upon the wretched of the earth the requirement that they be "saved" in similar fashion.

One size does not fit all. It was — and often continues to be — assumed that the salvation needed by those on the margins is the same yearned for by those from the dominant culture. An assumption is usually made that the sins of the dominant culture are also the sins of those on the margins of power. While those who formulated the theological concepts and ethical precepts — usually from locations of power and privilege — may have wrestled with the prideful sin of self-centeredness, the marginalized have instead suffered from a lack of self-identity. It is the images and thoughts of the dominant culture that are usually at the center. Thus, the marginalized often interpret reality through the eyes of their oppressors rather than through their own disenfranchised eyes. This is why many from the centers of society preach self-denial, submission, and unworthiness to the marginalized, when the disenfranchised should instead be hearing about pride in self, liberation, human dignity, and worth.

There is no need to preach humility to those who are already humble. Humbled by the sins of the dominant culture, they do not need to be exhorted to become still more lowly. Quite the contrary. Salvation for the marginalized is the transformation from non-person to personhood. The liberating message of the gospel they need to hear is that they are worthy, precious, and due dignity because they are created in the very image of God. Jesus understood that part of his salvific message was to humble the proud and lift up the lowly. As it is written in the Magnificat, "[God] pulled down the powerful from their thrones, and exalted the humble ones. He filled the hungry with good things, and the rich he sent away empty" (Lk. 1:52–53). It is the privileged who need to come to terms with their spiritual wretchedness. It is the wretched who need to come to terms with their infinite worth.

Grace, Not Works

Martin Luther, like Augustine before him, believed that good works would flow from any individual who was freed from the bondage of sin through the justifying love of God. For Augustine, grace did not free the moral agent from his or her obligations to perform good works; in fact, conversion generated a new creature in Christ now capable of doing good because his or her life was dominated by God's grace. Still, experiencing the forgiveness of Christ took precedence over any need to know the good. And although Luther fought against a misinterpretation of his doctrine of justification by faith that advocated a release from ethical obligations, nonetheless the Reformation formula *sola fide* (only faith) undermined the need to consider ethics crucial to the Christian identity. Contrary to what Augustine or Luther may have said or meant about the duty of Christians to do good works, the way some Christians from the dominant culture have put *sola fide* into practice has proven detrimental to the marginalized. It is wrong to reduce Christianity to an issue of grace where one can profess Christ as Lord without seriously implementing Christ's demands that justice affects and impacts the believer's life.

Sola fide as practiced by those who are privileged is harmful for those existing on the margins of privilege. Used in this manner, the doctrine of justification, which encompasses the forgiveness of sin, freedom from guilt, and reconciliation with God, fosters among the powerful and privileged a sense of impunity. It gives the impression that those who benefit from the present power structures can receive pardon for their sins from Christ without any need to convert from the practices and actions that contribute to oppressive social structures. Relationships are thus limited to the vertical, without seriously considering the neighbor who continues to be marginalized.

Sola fide can become the other extreme to the danger of solely relying on works for justification, as pointed out by Jesus Christ.

During Jesus' time, the Pharisees created a set of rules that excused them from fulfilling their obligations to their faith. Through a strict adherence to tithing, they ignored issues of justice. Jesus condemned them by stating, "Woe to you scribes and Pharisees, hypocrites! Because you tithe on the mint, the dill, and the cummin, yet you have left the weightier matters of the law, like justice, mercy, and faith" (Mt. 23:23). On another occasion, Jesus condemned the hypocrisies of the religious scholars who "dedicated" their property to God so as to avoid the just praxis of caring for their aging parents (Mk 7:11–13). Rather than being legalistic as were the Pharisees and religious teachers of the time of Jesus, some of today's ethicists and theologians from the dominant culture have gone to the other extreme. While blind obedience to the law undermines the establishment of a justice-based relationship with the marginalized, so too does a blind acceptance of grace contribute effectively to ignoring the needs and concerns of the disenfranchised.

Heaven-Bound

Ethical praxis that can lead to a more just society is at times ignored by emphasizing the hereafter rather than the here-and-now. If belief in Christ is all that is required for a blessed hereafter, those with the power to form theological discourse can present heaven to the wretched of the earth as a future place where they will be rewarded for their patient suffering. The present state of misery endured by the disenfranchised is justified as a consequence of original sin. Their doleful existence on earth will be compensated by heavenly mansions and ruby-crusted crowns of gold. Such escapist illusions only help to pacify the disenfranchised by encouraging them to shrug off their misery as God's will. But, as Charles Kammer reminds us, concepts like the reign of God are not spiritual escape hatches; instead they are evidence of the irruption of God's activity into history to transform personal, social, and political relationships (1988:44).

If the hereafter becomes a narcotic (similar to Marx's reference to opium), it negates what is of value in the here-and-now. Christian ethics, as formulated within the margins of society, rejects the notion that God somehow wills God's children to live under oppressive structures so that they can eventually live in everlasting riches. In fact, such a view of the afterlife, or eschatology, that justifies death is satanic. "The Reign of God is at hand," Jesus was fond of saying. God's reign is not in some far-off distant place disconnected from the trials and tribulations here on earth. No. God's reign is a present-day social, political, public, and personal reality evident among God's people. While not negating some form of final reward in the hereafter, the gospel message is primarily for the here-and-now. Salvation, understood as liberation in its fullness, has as much to do with the now as with a final resting place. And even though praxis (or what Luther called works) is insufficient for obtaining salvation, which remains a gift of God's grace, still praxis becomes an act of obedience, an outward expression of an inward conversion.

Juan Luis Segundo, a Latin American liberation theologian, insists that this genuine conversion makes true reconciliation with God and each other possible. Conversion requires a confession of the causes of estrangement (specifically those dealing with power and privilege) and an attempt to take action to eradicate these causes. If not, premature reconciliation will develop, masking unresolved structures of oppression. Although conversion is gospel language, Segundo uses it to indicate a change of attitude (1993:37, 51). If conversion does not establish justice-based relationships with God and fellow human beings, then salvation hasn't taken place. Any conversion devoid of actions for human liberation from structures of oppression is a façade that only normalizes present oppressions along gender, race, and class lines and masks forms of repression. Any salvation based on Jesus Christ should free the believer from the bondage, whether socially, culturally, or legally imposed, that reduces humans to disposable objects. In short, conversion, as a spiritual dimension, heals. If not, old enmities and unresolved hatreds from present systems continue in any supposedly reconciled future.

If conversion is understood as a rupture with and a turning away from sin (sin caused by individual actions *and* sin caused by social institutions), then salvation can occur only through the raising of consciousness to a level that can recognize the personal and communal sins preventing the start of a new life in Jesus. Conversion is a witness, a testimony to an unsaved world whose rejection of God, through the worship of the idol of self-interest, is manifested in oppressive relations according to race, class, and gender. Conversion to Christ does not correspond to some abstract concept of Jesus sitting on a throne in Heaven, nor is it an ethereal emotional experience. Rather, conversion to Christ serves the oppressed flesh and blood neighbor who, as "the least of my people," is in reality Jesus in the here-and-now. Salvation through Christ is at its essence a relationship with God and with each other, a justice-based relationship whose very nature transforms all aspects of humanity so that the abundant life can be lived by all to its fullest.

Unfortunately, in too many cases, the pursuit of salvation has been privatized. Peruvian theologian Gustavo Gutiérrez reminds us that:

> Faith cannot be lived on the private plane of the "interior life." Faith is the very negation of retreat into oneself, of folding back upon oneself. Faith comes alive in the dynamism of the good news that reveals us as children of the Father and sisters and brothers of one another, and creates a community, a church, the visible sign to others of liberation in Christ. (1984:67)

Too often personal salvation has become spiritual escapism rather than a justice-based transformation. Some conservative evangelicals are consumed with a passion to witness for life after death. While important, the real message the vast majority of those living in oppression hunger for is life *prior* to death. Such a message must be communicated through action, rather than just through words. Christian evangelism is thus understood as any action that leads toward the transformation of the individual, as well as the community, to the basic principles of justice lived and taught by Jesus Christ. The conversion resulting from such an evangelical venture does not lead toward a "once saved, always saved" understanding, but rather a lifelong process of working out the liberation made possible by Christ, or as the Apostle Paul would suggest, "[the working out of] your salvation in fear and trembling" (Phil. 2:12).

Sometimes attempts are made to Christianize the social order in order to remedy social ills, believing that society's "peccadillos" are caused by the decisions made by "non-Christians" within positions of power. Yet "saving" the powerful individual so that a

"Christian" will make decisions will not necessarily reform the social structure. As previously mentioned, most moral precepts reflect the cultural and philosophical milieu of a people, not of an individual. While the conversion of decision-makers within the social structures may be propitious, it often has little or no impact on how these social structures operate. Concentrating solely on personal morality or virtues without engaging the actual structures responsible for producing injustices will only lead to discouraging results. A change of heart of individuals usually is insufficient to produce a more just social order. The social structures themselves require transformation and conversion. Without such transformation, reform may occur, but more often than not, the marginalized will still find themselves disenfranchised due to race, class, and/or gender.

Salvation, in its truest sense, becomes liberation from sin — sins committed by the individual and, just as important, those committed to the individual through social institutions. Reducing salvation to personal choice, disconnected from the community, is foreign to the biblical text. Take the example of Moses in the Hebrew Bible or Paul in the New Testament. Both were willing to be cut off from God and face damnation for the sake of the community's liberation. Moses pleaded to God to blot him from the book of life if it would save God's people (Ex. 32:32), while Paul was willing to be condemned and cut off from Christ if it would help his Jewish compatriots find salvation (Rom. 9:2). Both Moses and Paul refused to exchange their quest to transform society as an expression of their love for their neighbor for some privatized faith that assured them of individual immortality. They serve as models of a self-sacrificing faith that places the needs of the community before personal reward. They understood the depths of the words of Jesus when he said, "A person can have no greater love than to lay down one's life for one's friends" (Jn. 15:13).

While belief in Christ is important, if not crucial, it remains insufficient. Jesus states, "If then, you offer your gift on the altar, and there remember that your companion has something against you, leave your gift there before the altar, and go. First be reconciled to your companion, and then come offer your gift" (Mt. 5:23–24). The implication is that God is more concerned with loving and reconciling with those who have a grievance than with the would-be worshiper's personal relationship with God or his or her attempt to gain moral perfection through obedience to religious law, tradition, or custom.

Although conversion is a gift from God, still the individual must choose to accept such a gift. How? Conversion for those of the dominant culture moves beyond simple belief. Rather, conversion moves toward a consciousness-raising experience that is linked to a specific praxis, a praxis that breaks with personal and social sin and leads the new believer to turn away from the old life of privilege and begin a new life in Christ manifested as solidarity with the same people Jesus sought to identify himself with, the outcasts. Consciousness-raising becomes the process by which persons become cognizant of their existential being, leading toward a self-reflective, critical awareness of how a person benefits or is oppressed by the prevailing social structures. For both the privileged and disenfranchised, conversion as a consciousness-raising praxis leads to the transformation of the person and society so that the convert can encounter the "neighbor" in the fulness of his or her humanity. Regardless of the neighbor's belief or confession in Christ, that neighbor still has worth before God.

Still, salvation can never be equated with a social system or agenda created by humans (such as socialism, capitalism, or neoliberalism); rather, liberation is a theological enterprise with a social ethical agenda of establishing justice so that all human beings can live in what Martin Luther King, Jr., called "the beloved community," where justice rolls down like living water. For Christian ethics to take hold, radical concrete changes are required in the public arena (as well as in the life of the believer) so as to bring salvation, understood as liberation, to both the marginalized and to those who benefit from that disenfranchisement. Such radical actions move the church from teaching ethics as a collection of moral precepts for private living to teaching ethics as political and social actions that reflect one's Christian testimony. The basic criterion for doing ethics from the margins becomes the salvation and liberation of all, both the privileged and the disenfranchised who are oppressed by political, social, and cultural structures that overtly or covertly foster racism, classism, and sexism. This evangelistic action for liberation is the ultimate love praxis.

A Personal Relationship

The pervasiveness of individualism, specifically the rugged individualism celebrated in the United States, relegates moral decisions to the private sphere, in a sense essentially relegating views on morality to the individual. This tends to weaken social bonds and hamper the development of a communal apparatus authorized to foster and implement ethical actions that can lead to a social order grounded on relationships. When morality is privatized, individual members of the dominant culture can shop for a set of values or virtues, like any other consumer good, that is appropriate to the particular individual at a given place and time. This is not to minimize the importance of the individual, but because the self should never be considered *apart* from the communal, ethics must be fashioned to acknowledge the relationships established by the interrelatedness of the individual and the community of faith, where actions committed by one profoundly affect the other.

Psychologist Carol Gilligan, well known for her work in gender studies, has proposed that psychology has ignored and misunderstood women's moral commitments because the discipline has historically focused on observing the lives of men. She maintains that men usually approach morality from an individualistic perspective that deliberates on issues of rights in a way that is interconnected with the celebration of personal autonomy. On the other hand, she observes, women approach moral dilemmas from the context of relationships grounded in the ability to care (1982:17). I would claim that the approach to moral reasoning of women, as described by Gilligan, is more similar to how ethics is conducted by both men and women in disenfranchised communities.

Lacking privilege and power, members of marginalized communities find themselves clinging to each other in order to survive oppressive structures. They are supported by these relationships of caring, which become crucial in understanding ethics from the margins. Ethical praxis from the margins arises from the relational links of communal morality and the injustices caused by social structures, whether manifested as traditions, customs, or laws. To divorce ethics from critical social analysis is to reduce ethics to an individualistic morality that is often of little use to those struggling to survive. Those doing ethics on the margins of society realize that unequal alignments of power within social structures (male over female, white over non-white, or wealthy over poor) are usually the root causes of injustice and the antithesis of the gospel message.

To counter this trend, Christian ethics as done from the margins becomes a *koinonia* ethics, a political calling for radical structural changes in how society is ordered. *Koinonia*, the New Testament Greek term used to describe the faith community, connotes relationships and fellowship, where all things are held in common. Not only are material possessions held in common (Acts 5), but also experiences. Paul writes, "If one member [of the *koinonia*] suffers, with it suffer all members, or if one member is glorified, with it, all members rejoice" (1 Cor. 12:26). *Koinonia* occurs when the faith community gathers to stand in solidarity, sharing the trials and joys of the human condition. Any ethic labeled Christian must reflect the response of *koinonia* to the dilemmas that prevent Christians from fulfilling Christ's mission that all experience "life abundantly."

Because ethics from the margins emphasizes praxis, it interacts with the political and social structures that normalize injustices. Consequently, ethics done from the margins influences the political realm. One cannot read the story of liberation found in Exodus, the call for justice found in Amos, the stories of Jesus, or of Paul's dealing with the imperial powers of Rome without coming to the conclusion that these are not simply religious documents, but also calls to political action. While Christian ethics from the margins is not a political ethics, it does influence change in the political sphere when it remains faithful to its Christian foundations. Consequently, the *koinonia* ethics[13] sought by those on the margins often conflicts with the individualistic ethics of the dominant culture; the former recognizes the unity Jesus expressed

---

13 Still, *koinonia* ethics is understood as being "of the political," rather than simply a *koinonia* political ethics. Following Clodovis Boff's lead, I use the preposition "of" to maintain a distance between the (political or social) object and its (theological or scientific) theory, "[keeping] what it unites at an appropriate distance" (1987:xxv).

between God and neighbor, while the latter emphasizes a personal relationship between Jesus and the individual.

To some extent, ethical responsibilities are often compartmentalized into two spheres: either as two cities as in Augustine, or two swords as in Martin Luther. These theological perspectives allow Christians to formulate two types of ethics, one for the private life (the heavenly city) and a different, if not contradictory, ethics for the public life (the earthly city). But there is no ethical dualism within the biblical narrative.

A major error made by ethicists of the dominant culture is to depend excessively upon the great reformers of the faith and to fail to recognize their limitations in bringing about justice in light of the oppression faced by the marginalized of their time. James Cone reminds us that great reformers such as Calvin and Wesley did little to make Christianity a religion of the marginalized. He writes, "Though no one can be responsible for everything that is done in their name, one may be suspicious of the easy affinity among Calvinism, capitalism, and slave trading. John Wesley also said little about slaveholding and did even less" (1999a:34).[14] Some philosophers, Kant, for example, insist that ethics belongs to the private and inner realm of human existence. Any public ethic that exists is simply the spillover of the individual conscience.[15]

Within this compartmentalized tradition, a dichotomy emerges between the Christian as individual and the Christian as public ser-

---

[14] In Calvin's case, this may partially be due to his following Luther's thinking in separating the private ethical sphere from the public. In the *Institutes* Calvin writes:

We may call the one the spiritual, the other the civil kingdom. Now, these two, as we have divided them, are always viewed apart from each other. When the one is considered, we should call off our minds, and not allow them to think of the other. For there exists in man a kind of two worlds, over which different kings and different laws can preside. (3:19:15)

[15] It is important to note that during the Reformation, the Anabaptists rejected the distinction between the Christian as individual and the Christian as public servant. This refusal to create a dichotomy between a private and public ethics led their spiritual descendants (the Amish, the Mennonites, and the Quakers) to become pacifists. Their refusal to justify war as a moral option for Christians can only be accomplished through their rejection of compartmentalization.

vant. For example, while a Christian might be inclined to follow God's commandment prohibiting killing and, in fact, may desire to offer the enemy the other cheek in obedience to Christ, still the Christian would have to remain responsible to the duty of the office placed upon his or her shoulder. For example, a soldier would have a duty to kill in order to preserve the overall social structure. Individual feelings must be put aside for the administration of this duty. The duty of obedience by the individual is so binding that the citizen should be willing to suffer death rather than rebel. Duty ensures that the government can continue to keep a check on the wickedness brought forth by humans. What reformers like Luther and Calvin ignored was that for the disenfranchised it is the government, working to preserve the rights of the privileged, that usually perpetuates wickedness. In such cases, the duty of the citizen may well be to reject the duality of responsibility established to maintain the status quo and actually rebel against it.[16]

Compartmentalizing Christian ethics into two cities or two swords, one spiritual and the other civil, places the former under the authority of the gospel message while it unbinds the latter from following the same set of precepts. The result is an ethical understanding, particularly prevalent within the United States, that is highly privatized with little commitment to transforming the social injustices caused by race, class, and gender oppression. To do ethics from the margins is to insist that while the two realms may be distinct, they are in fact related. The ethics advocated for the private life is the same as that advocated for the public life. The maintenance of a false dichotomy has facilitated the justification of some of the worst atrocities within Christian history, from the Crusades, to the Inquisition, to our very own "peculiar" institution of slavery.[17]

A dichotomy in eurocentric thought develops between the private and public life when moral purity is sought for the private life

---

[16] It should be noted that in the *Institutes*, Calvin, unlike Luther, did not see the magistrate as a substitute for divine rule and thus made allowance for the overthrow of tyranny if obedience to the ruler led one to disobey God (4:20:29–32). Karl Barth, on the other hand, exhorted Christians to obediently follow tyrants, for in so doing, they deprive the tyrant of power, for obedience is then freely given, not coerced.

[17] Even the neo-orthodox theologian Karl Barth blames Luther's form of compartmentalization for the rise of Nazism. According to Barth:

but not for the public life. This may stem from the conviction that the public life is incapable of obtaining the purity that only the private life can obtain. Justice, while desirable for earth, is reserved for heaven, so the only hope offered the oppressed is a spiritual liberation from their individual sins. Christians on the margins of power and privilege reject this interpretation of the dominant culture, which suggests that the intent of the biblical text is to liberate the soul, but not necessarily the body.

Influential ethicist Reinhold Niebuhr illustrated the fallacy of Martin Luther's severance between the experience of grace and the possibility for justice, which has the overall effect of reducing liberation to nothing more than liberation from God's everlasting wrath toward human sin (1943:192–93). However, Niebuhr continued the spiritual compartmentalization of Augustine, Luther, Calvin, and Kant by relegating love to the private sphere and social justice to the public realm. His commitment to Christian realism led him to conclude that the ideal of love as the basis for public action is simply impractical and unable to deal with the complexity of modern life. Nations, multinational corporations and other collective entities, unlike humans, are simply incapable of moral behavior.[18] In fact, he maintained that certain inequalities are necessary for society to function properly.[19]

> Martin Luther's error on the relations between law and gospel, between the temporal and the spiritual order and power . . . established, confirmed, and idealized the natural paganism of the German people of limiting and restraining it. (1941:7)

[18] Christian realism, rooted in the tradition of Niccolo Machiavelli, is usually associated with the neo-orthodox movement of the 1930s and '40s, which challenged the prevailing view that society was continuously evolving toward universal justice. The social optimism of the turn of the twentieth century held that the upward moving enlightenment of humanity was about to break through into an era of worldwide peace and prosperity. Even the ethical movement known as the Social Gospel, as articulated by Walter Rauschenbusch, saw the social ills of the time as soon being cured and eliminated through education and spirituality. Instead, a great worldwide depression and two world wars (the first optimistically called the "war to end all wars") culminated with death camps and the first use of the atomic bomb. Consequently, any remaining optimism from earlier in the century was dashed.

[19] According to Reinhold Niebuhr:

The impracticality Niebuhr feared is specifically the type of radical commitment to Christ that those from the margins demand from themselves and from those who benefit from the present social structures. Can a Christian who is committed to turning the other cheek go off to war and kill Muslims to ensure the flow of oil to the United States? Can Christians who are commanded to give their cloaks as well as their tunics to the person in need be entitled to bring a lawsuit against anyone? Can a Christian who is commanded to walk an extra mile for the one that asks be content simply to leave the "colored" urban centers after five in the afternoon for the secluded white suburbs where their children can receive a superior education and they can rest easy at night due to beefed-up security? Compartmentalizing love and justice into two separate spheres of human existence allows a person to claim to be a Christian (hence full of love) while supporting public policies that perpetuate mechanisms of death for marginalized persons.

But how then can a judge mete out punishment during a court procedure? If no ethical dichotomy exists between the public and private sphere, can a judge who is committed to unconditional love punish a wrongdoer? Can a soldier ever fight in a war? Such questions, while valid, miss how the status quo is detrimental to the most marginalized. Take the example of the judge. When we consider that 70 percent of those in prison are people of color from mainly economically deprived areas (Parenti, 1999:xii, 167), we can conclude 1) that people of color are engaged in crime as a negative consequence of their marginalization, where the lack of economic opportunities coupled with an inadequate education system contributes to wrong (legal and moral) decisions on their part; and/or 2) that the judicial and legal system is skewed to convict people of color at a greater rate than whites. While the question concerning how a judge should deliberate may appear to be an

---

No complex society will be able to dispense with certain inequalities of privilege. Some of them are necessary for the proper performance of certain social functions; and others (though this is not so certain) may be needed to prompt energy and diligence in the performance of important functions. . . . No society has ever achieved peace without incorporating injustice into its harmony. (1960:128–29)

issue of retributive justice,[20] in reality, at its very core, it is an issue of distributive justice.[21] Hence, the dominant culture, often refusing to deal with the causes responsible for crime and the procedures by which those accused of crimes are convicted, instead deliberates about how a judge can hand down punishment while remaining a faithful Christian.

While the dominant culture asks, "How does one remain ethical in a corrupt society like this?" those who are marginalized ask, "How does one make a corrupt society like this just?" Because different questions are being asked, different answers are being formulated. And while the question of how a Christian judge can reconcile love with meting out punishment may be crucial for the powerful and privileged, it remains irrelevant for the marginalized because it refuses to deal with the causes of injustice. Questioning how a judicial system metes out justice becomes an important discourse for the marginalized only after they have some sense that justice exists for them. The barrios and ghettos of this nation testify to the prevalence of systemic injustice in our society. Such injustice is maintained, in large part, by an ethical compartmentalization that allows those with power to continue benefitting from unjust social structures in the public sphere while claiming to be Christian in the private sphere.

Subjective vs. Objective

Any system of ethics reflects the activity of a given space. All of us bring our location to how we fashion our ethical perspectives. We also bring our subjective understanding of God based on our experience and our location. However, often systems of ethics tend to mirror more information about who we are than information about what God wants. And, in reality, ethics derives from theologies, which are themselves rooted in prior political commitments and thoughts. Even an "impartial" reading of a biblical text is understood by the reader within a particular socio-economic setting. All

---

[20] Retributive justice is concerned with determining a just punishment or penalty for those who commit illegal or immoral acts.

[21] Distributive justice concerns itself with the fair and equitable distribution of the benefits and burdens of society.

ideas are fastened to the social situation from which they arise and it would be naive to believe that we could develop objective ethical propositions in a vacuum. Still, some eurocentric Christian moral agents assume that they are able to arrive at an objective response to whatever dilemmas arise.[22] In the end, the question remains — whose understanding of Christianity?

Those doing ethics from privileged communities assume that "pure" reason or "proper" biblical hermeneutics are employed. These moral agents from the dominant culture assume that their conclusions are objective; similarly, these same agents assume that those coming from the periphery of society have to be subjective because they are influenced by their marginality. In reality, what moral agents from the dominant culture call "objective" is in fact highly subjective, as it is a product of the social location of the one engaged in moral reasoning. What the moral agent concludes is a universal morality is, in fact, a morality that resonates among those from the same background, those who possess so-called economic and racial "superiority." The ethical conclusions of marginalized groups are often considered viable depending on how close they come to the eurocentric ideal.

Nevertheless, the work of theologians such as James Cone helps define the meaning of ethical terms like "right" and "wrong" while showing why those of the dominant culture — or any culture for that matter — are incapable of fashioning an *objective* ethical code of behavior. Cone writes:

> All acts which impede the struggle of black self-determination — black power — are anti-Christian, the work of Satan. The revolutionary context forces black theology to shun all abstract principles dealing with what is the "right" and "wrong" course of action. There is only one principle which

---

22 Ethicists such as Emil Brunner conclude that non-Christian ethical systems are unable to provide the whole answer to any ethical problem. Indeed, he says, only a Protestant understanding of Christianity can (1947:41–43, 57). John Rawls, on the other hand, accepts the possibility of developing a neutral framework of basic rights, believing that society can objectively develop principles conforming to a concept of right (1971:130–36).

guides the thinking and action of black theology: an unqual-
ified commitment to the black community as that community seeks to define its existence in light of God's liberating
work in the world. . . . The logic of liberation is always incom-
prehensible to slave masters. (1999a:10)

What is true for the black community is not limited to the black
community. Cone's words ring true for all marginalized groups.
Here lies a major difference between systems of ethics advocated
by the dominant culture and systems of ethics constructed from
the margins of society.

By making a preferential option for the marginalized, ethicists
of the dominant culture are prevented from achieving the objectivity for which they strive. After all, their "objectivity" is only the
subjectivity of those who possess the power to make their view
normative. A harmonious narrative based on some value-neutral
analysis concerning the definition of justice simply does not exist.
Injustice, oppression, and abuse are part of the human condition.
Making a preferential option for the marginalized prevents the creation of neat ideologies that, theoretically, might help improve the
situation of the marginalized, yet fail to provide any holistic form
of liberation. No ethics, and no theology for that matter, can be
socially uncommitted. All ethics and all theologies are and will forever remain subjective — they are incapable of fully comprehending the infinity of the Divine.

Pie in the Sky

Unfortunately, the dominant culture often dismisses the hope of
the marginalized for a just social order as utopian. The idea of a
just society is as utopian as Isaiah's messianic dream where "the
wolf shall stay with the lamb, and the leopard shall lie with the kid"
(11:6). Yet, even though ethics from the margins stands in open
rebellion against the "opium" of otherworldliness, the "utopias"
of Isaiah and of the marginalized are still affirmed with an open-
eyed awareness of the present power structures, all the while moving toward a future reality. The hope of the marginalized is not a
utopian dream based on the fantasy world of imagination; rather,
it is usually a feet-on-the ground utopianism anchored in the real-

ism of the disenfranchised. Gustavo Gutiérrez insists that pessimism comes from reality because reality is tragic, while optimism comes from action because action can change reality (1984:80–81). Commenting on an ethic of solidarity, Gutiérrez claims:

> Today, more than ever, is the time to remember that God has given to all humanity what is necessary for its sustenance. The goods of this earth do not belong exclusively to certain persons or to certain social groups, whatever their knowledge or place in society may be. The goods belong to all. . . . We can call this a utopian perspective, but in a realistic sense of the word, which rejects an inhuman situation and pursues relationships of justice and cooperation between persons. (1998:121)

Hence, the desire for a utopia is not a flight from present reality to an illusionary world, rather it is a product of hope, the hope of perfecting our reality and preventing the status quo from absolutizing itself. The utopianism called for by those doing ethics on the margins of society is not some naive idealism where a future perfect social order is established. Utopianism, as understood here, is a rejection of the present social order grounded in structures designed to perpetrate racism, sexism, and classism. It is a utopianism that protests the way things presently are, and imagines, based on the reality of the oppressed, how society can be restructured to create a more just social order. The function of utopian thought is to guide praxis.

Latin American theologian José Míguez Bonino succinctly captures this so-called utopian vision. He writes: "The true question is not 'What degree of justice (liberation of the poor) is compatible with the maintenance of the existing order?' but 'what kind of order, which order is compatible with the exercise of justice (the right of the poor)?'" (1983:86). Míguez Bonino correctly points out the ineffectiveness of an ethics that refuses to challenge or change the status quo in the name of realism. The radical love ethic propounded by the gospel message of Christ is not served by compromising with the ambiguities of reality.

As Paulo Freire reminds us: "The radical, committed to human liberation, does not become the prisoner of a 'circle of certainty' within which reality is also imprisoned. On the contrary, the more radical the person is, the more fully he or she enters reality so that, knowing it better, he or she can better transform it" (1994:21). Because they fail to address the need to reform unjust social structures, realist or rationalist approaches are unresponsive to the social realities of the disenfranchised. What is needed is a feet-on-the-ground ethics, an ethics that is tied to the experiences of the marginalized in the midst of their reality in facing a particular dilemma or situation.

The system of ethics constructed from the margins is an ethics that proclaims a God who exists in the midst of the people's suffering and that seeks to be faithful to the praxis of the gospel message in spite of existing social structures that thwart the faith community's struggle for justice. In the following chapter, I will provide a fluid paradigm to elucidate how the disenfranchised, and those of the dominant cultures wishing to stand in solidarity with them, can operate as moral agents.

CHAPTER 3

The Liberation of Ethics

Choosing to do ethics from the margins is a proactive option made with, by, and for those who are disenfranchised. Christians make an option for the poor, for those on the margins, not so much because it is the "ethical" thing to do but because of the need on the part of believers to imitate God as fully revealed in the life of Jesus Christ. Two Latin American liberation theologians, Clodovis Boff and George Pixley, remind us:

> Before being a duty . . . the option for the poor is a reality of faith, or theological truth. . . . Before being something that concerns the church, the option for the poor is something that concerns God. God is the first to opt for the poor, and it is only as a consequence of this that the church too has to opt for the poor. (1989:109)

For Christians, no real dichotomy or separation can exist between ethics and social action if social action is understood as the praxis of ethics, the process by which privileged Christians are transformed into the image of Christ. Solidarity that comes from making an option for the poor is crucial not because Christ is *with* the marginalized but, rather, Christ *is* the marginalized. In the words of the Apostle Paul, "Remember the grace of our Lord Jesus Christ who for [our] sake, although rich became poor, so that [we] might become rich through the poverty of that One" (2 Cor. 8:9). Who Christ is is directly linked to what Christ does. Likewise, Christian ethics is directly linked to Christian praxis.

THE HERMENEUTICAL CIRCLE FOR ETHICS

God wills that all come into salvation — that is, liberation from sin. "Sin" includes individual sins as well as social sins, those that result from social structures. Ethics is the action by which liberation, or salvation, can be manifested. Any model or paradigm used to assist the faith community in developing ethical precepts must start with the experience of those most affected by the sin of oppression, those suffering most from the political and economic structures of society. Christian ethics should result in the transformation of such structures into a more just social order.

Liberation theologians have generally relied on a process called the "hermeneutical circle" as a guide for their reflection. Several ethicists from the margins have also adopted the hermeneutical circle as a paradigm by which to do ethics. Such a paradigm, motivated by a passion to establish justice-based relationships from which love can flow, begins with the lived experience of oppressive social situations and proceeds by working out a theory and then a course of action that will dismantle the mechanisms that cause oppression. It usually proceeds through different but closely related stages that are described below.[1] The purpose of the hermeneutical circle is to formulate a praxis — a system of Christian ethics — to change the reality faced by those living on the margins of society.

Step 1. Observing—An Analysis

To gaze upon an object is not an entirely innocent phenomenon involving the simple transmission of light waves. To "see" also encompasses a mode of thought that transforms the object being seen into a concept for intellectual assimilation and possession.

---

[1] The framework provided here is based on the model of 1) seeing, 2) judging, and 3) acting employed by liberation theologians in Latin American who have been influenced by the Catholic Church's encyclicals *Gaudium et Spes* (1965) and *Octogesima Adveniens* (1971). It is essential to keep in mind that this paradigm, like so many others, is a working model—not an absolute.

Think of the process of looking at a photograph of a loved one. Observing can be a very rich and emotional experience. We observe inanimate objects and persons and we also observe their interactions as they exist together to form a society.

Within a society people can be viewed both as subjects and objects. Those whom society defines as "subjects" normally have far more power, including the power to legitimize and normalize what they see. In "first world" countries, the dominant euroamerican culture, which tends to be white, defines reality for those on the periphery or margins (De La Torre and Aponte 2001:11–12). This is because seeing is political, a social construction that endows the person doing the observing with the power to provide meaning to an object. Probably the worst consequence to befall persons who are viewed as "objects" is that they then see themselves as inferior and lacking power. This is antithetical to the gospel message and an affront to the social dignity of all human beings. When persons viewed as objects accept their oppressors' worldview as their own, they often feel compelled to behave and act according to the way in which they have been constructed by others.

It would be naive to view power as centralized in the hands of the elite of the dominant culture. Power is everywhere as it forms in and passes through a multitude of institutions. It is most effective when it is exercised through coercion that appears natural and neutral—a coercion based simply on the ability to observe.

The starting point for doing ethics, then, becomes the observing, which is done in most first-world countries by members of a white, male eurocentric culture. Their understanding of morality and virtues have great importance for those who are disenfranchised. What can those who unjustly benefit from white, male privilege say about morality to those who suffer unjustly because of this privilege?

Distrust of and experience with the ethics constructed by the dominant culture lead those on the margins to observe and discern the reality faced by marginalized people for themselves. Using the eyes of the marginalized, or observing from below, becomes the first step in arriving at any ethical response; it informs about how God is understood, how scripture is read, and how society is constructed. As the causes for oppression are unmasked through this analysis, consciousness of what is happening is raised, and the object, which has now become the subject, gains a deeper understanding of reality.

During the process of observing, it is also essential to consider seriously the historical situation that gave rise to the present situation. If we define history as the memory of a people, how do those on the margins recall their history apart from the imagery imposed upon them by those with power? And most often the "official" history is devoid of the voices of the disenfranchised. In the words of Frantz Fanon, a radical political thinker and writer from Martinique, "The history which [the colonizer] writes is not the history of the country which he plunders but the history of his own nation in regard to all that she skims off, all that she violates and starves" (1963:51). The history of marginalized people in the United States is written primarily by those who have the power to determine the official story. It is, in short, the history of the dominant power. Nation-building normally requires an epic tale of triumphant wars, heroic figures, and awe-inspiring achievements that elevate the dominant culture while disenfranchising the history of the defeated, or their "other." Homi K. Bhabha, a post-colonial theorist teaching at the University of Chicago, has termed this the "syntax of forgetting" (1994:160–61). In the United States, the common narrative of nation-building not only disguises the complex political forces responsible for bringing forth that history, but, more important, it suppresses sexual differences, racial divisions, and class conflicts.

Any thorough understanding of an ethical dilemma must include the historical causes of the dilemma and a study of the ways in which the society maintains structures that caused the dilemma. Michel Foucault has pointed out that the domination of certain people by others creates values. Historical writings, in their turn, justify the values and social positions of those who write the history. This relationship of domination becomes fixed throughout history by means of procedures that confer and impose rights on one group and obligations on another. In this way, the dominant culture normalizes its power by engraving its memories on both people and institutions (1984:83–85).

The victors of U.S. history inscribe their genealogies upon the national epic, emphasizing military victories, technological advances, and political achievements. These deeds become the official history. Yet, the truth of the subject is not necessarily found in the history written by the subject. Psychoanalyst Jacques Lacan insists that truth is found in the "locus of the Other" (1977:286). Precisely for this reason, the dominant culture attempts constantly to obliterate the Other's locus. Or, as Frantz Fanon eloquently stated:

> Perhaps we have not sufficiently demonstrated that colonialism is not simply content to impose its rule upon the present and the future of a dominated country. Colonialism is not satisfied merely with holding a people in its grip and emptying the native's brain of all form and content. By a kind of perverted logic, it turns to the past of the oppressed people, and distorts, disfigures, and destroys it. (1963:210)

To seek the voices of those who do not inhabit history is to critique those with power and privilege for substituting their memory for forgotten history. On the other hand, ignoring the voices of those neglected by history can be used to justify yesterday's sexual, racial, and economic domination, while normalizing today's continuation of that oppression; it also prevents hope for tomorrow's liberation.

The approach to ethics from the margins seeks to understand what justice is by exploring and understanding how justice was historically denied. If the mechanisms that produce death, such as hunger, nakedness, and homelessness, can be recognized historically as part of the lives of the marginalized, then the reverse — praxis or actions leading to life, and this means abundant life — should inform any system of ethics. For this reason, ethics done on the margins is and must remain a contextual ethics that seeks to see the liberating work of God through the eyes of those made poor, those victimized, and those made to suffer because they belong to the "wrong" gender, race, or economic class. We exchange the history constructed by the academy, the affluent, and the power-holders for one created from history's underside, whose ongoing struggle is to overcome oppression. We not only search for the God of history but claim that God orients history to establish justice and takes sides with the faceless multitude suffering from oppression.

Step 2: Reflecting — Social Analysis

Social analysis is required before social structures can be transformed. Instead of turning to philosophical concepts or abstractions, an attempt is made, using the tools of sociology, anthropology, economics, and political theory, to ground ethics in analysis in order to best discern reality. By providing raw data, the social sciences provide a productive methodology to discern the structures of social phenomena and thus illuminate the reality faced by those marginalized by these structures.

It should be noted that Christian ethicists can legitimately borrow analytical methods from other academic disciplines. Whatever tools of human thought are available should be used to illuminate the social location of the marginalized and to identify oppressive structures. To engage in the self-liberating praxis of naming one's own reality and to point out how political mechanisms maintain institutionalized oppressive structures is to point out sin — sin being understood as the product of existing social, political, and economic systems designed to secure the power and privilege of one group through domination of others.

Analysis of social systems is an integral component of ethical deliberation because it provides a necessary critique of how the present social structures justify racist, sexist, and classist norms. Ethics can never adequately respond to oppressive structures if it fails to understand fully how these structures are created and preserved through economic, social, and political forces. Ignoring social analysis prevents ethics from providing an informed and intelligent practical response to oppression.

In the way that biblical interpretation is never totally objective, social analysis is incapable of being fully neutral. Both biblical interpretation and social analysis — or any similar thought process — encompass the biases of the group undertaking the reading or analysis. For this reason, more weight, termed "the epistemological privilege," is given to the marginalized. This privilege accorded the disenfranchised is based on their ability to know how to live and survive in both the center and periphery of society, unlike the dominant cultures, which generally fail to understand the marginalized experience. Consequently, the primary source for doing ethics is the lived, everyday experience of marginalized people.

As important as social analysis may be, it cannot become the totality of an ethicist's reflection. Ethical reflection must also be based on the life of Jesus and on Jesus' mission, as illustrated in his pronouncement in John 10:10: "I came that they may have life, and have it abundantly." Simply put, if the implementation of an ethical action prevents life from being lived abundantly by a segment of the population or, worse, if it brings death, then it is anti-gospel. When Christian ethics ignores how minority groups are denied access to opportunities, or reinforces the power and privilege amassed by one segment of the population, or when ethics is relegated to abstract discussions that seldom question how our social structures are constructed, then such ethics ceases to be Christian. Only ethical reflections that empower all elements of humanity, offering abundant life in the here and now instead of the hereafter, can be determined to be Christian. Jesus Christ and his life-giving mission become the lens through which Christian ethical reflection is conducted. Such reflection leads to the praxis of liberation, a process of using reflection to develop actions that bring about the transformation — understood as both liberation and salvation—of all individuals and social structures.

Step 3: Praying—A Theological and Biblical Analysis

If we move directly from observing and reflecting to actions for liberation, ethics from the margins can be accused of being some sort of radical reaction to a given situation. For this reason, praying becomes a crucial step in the ethical paradigm as it ties theory based on observation with the faith community most affected by the ethical dilemma. As Francisco Moreno Rejón, a moral theologian working in Latin America, reminds us:

> A salient note in liberation theology and ethics is rooted in their effort to reconcile the requirements of a theoretical, academic order with a pastoral projection. Thus, we are dealing with a moral theology that, far from repeating timeless, ahistorical principles, presents itself as a reflection vigorously involved with the people's daily experience. (1993:217)

As used here, prayer is not limited to an individual closed in a room to have a private conversation with God in hopes of gain-ing wisdom and guidance. While personal prayer is important and not to be neglected, prayer is also understood to be communal, bringing together the different members of the spiritual body to pray together. Prayer can be a communal process by which a disenfranchised faith community accompanies its members and stands in solidarity during its trials and tribulations. Ethics is also a communal activity. As such, it is within the faith community (often called by the Greek word *koinonia*), particularly those established on the margins of power and privileged by the Christ event that happened in their midst, that God's ongoing activity within humanity finds its locus. God continues to move in history within the faith community. Ethics, then, can never be reduced to a personal choice or an individual morality; it must instead remain a communal action guided by the relationships established in *koinonia*.

Koinonia is based more on the relationships within the faith community than with precepts or principles. Solidarity and constant communication with the people of faith situated in marginalized communities afford a perspective that is lost on ethicists who confine their deliberations to theories found in academic books. Because morality is communal, ethics from the margins means listening critically to the stories of the marginalized and committing to work in solidarity with them in their struggle for full liberation, both spiritually and physically. Failure to incorporate the voices of the voiceless makes ethics useless for the vast majority of the world's humanity who struggle each day for the basic necessities of life: food, clothing, and shelter.

Praying also includes a critical application of the biblical text to the ethical situation faced by the marginalized. For Christians, the concept of justice is rooted in the life and acts of Jesus Christ as articulated in the biblical text. The biblical text should influence how moral decisions are arrived at and implemented. The Bible is read as a book of life, one that should shape all of existence, providing keys to an abundant life now and an eternal life later. As such, the Bible becomes a source of inspiration by which both individuals and communities can undergo radical changes, otherwise known as conversion, from a life dominated by sin to a life in solidarity with Christ and with "the least among us," those whom Christ chose to be in solidarity with.

For black biblical scholar Brian Blount, fusing the biblical narrative with the life situation of the marginalized produces a biblical witness uniquely capable of addressing their tragic circumstances. "In other words, they contextually construct *their* biblical story" (2001:24). Doing ethics through prayer and biblical reflection becomes a process of interconnecting the reality faced on the margins of society with the scriptures, fully aware of the contradictions existing between the biblical mandate for the fullness of the abundant life in Christ and how those from the center of society interpret sacred texts. All too often, the dominant culture views the Bible as God's "Owner's Manual," a book of moral precepts from which a "thou shalt not" list can be derived. Codifying the biblical text as a scriptural law book to be obeyed was an error made by the Pharisees of Jesus' time as well as an error that can be made today. Following specific precepts tends to excuse a person from living a life faithful to the call of Christ. Jesus did not provide a legalistic moral code for his disciples to follow. Even if he had, the world in which we live, with all of its global complexities and technological advances, is vastly different from the social context in which Jesus found himself. Jesus had no need to speak of issues concerning affirmative action or the ethical dimensions of driving an SUV.

For the Bible to be taken seriously as a source of ethical guidance, we must examine the relationships that Jesus established. By examining the actions taken by Jesus toward others, a pattern emerges that can inform present-day praxes. Jesus articulated moral values that he contextualized within his social location, that of a Jew living in a basically agrarian economy in first-century Palestine, a land that formed part of the Roman Empire.

For liberation theologian Jon Sobrino, who lives and teaches in El Salvador, applying the values proclaimed by Jesus to present situations is informed by the recognition that Jesus' message of justice and love was brought to all people through his identification and solidarity with one particular group, the marginalized. In Palestine, as today, the marginalized lived in conflict with the privileged and powerful. In addition, Jesus battled against sin manifested as specific social injustices, a conflict that found its conclusion in the execution of Jesus. The Bible's authoritative role in the formation of Christian ethics is established if and when the principles lived and spoken by Jesus are contextualized for the present day. In this way, ethics can move away from abstract notions toward concrete praxes, that, when arising from marginalized communities, become universally valid (1978:124–25, 138).

Nevertheless, there is not always a clear biblical mandate as to what action is moral. At times the biblical text even contradicts itself. For example, although the sixth commandment clearly states, "Thou shalt not commit adultery" (Ex. 20:14), the Leviticus code suggests that men can have multiple sex partners, even to the point of maintaining a harem (Lev. 18:18). Other laws simply cease to be applicable, as in the case of dietary regulations throughout the Book of Leviticus. Still other pronouncements offend modern Christian sensitivities, specifically sections that reduce women and slaves to objects, as in the case of the tenth commandment, which prohibits the coveting of another man's possessions, specifically his ox, donkey, house, *wife and slave.*

Even though those on the margins look toward the scriptures for the basis of ethical reflection, it is important to remember that a certain amount of self-criticism should also be employed. How do one's race, class, and gender influence how the text is interpreted? Even though the Bible remains, apart from Christ, the highest authority for most Christians, turning to the biblical text for guidance requires a critical analysis of the social context that gave rise to the text, a social context whose own milieu (such as patriarchy, for example) affected how the text was written. A social order that advanced patriarchal structures would likely not criticize the creation of harems or the sanction of bigamy. This kind of examination of a biblical text is termed the "hermeneutic of suspicion." A second type of danger exists when those in power use a biblical text to advance or justify their own ideologies; this is known as "prooftexting." For these reasons, the Bible is not read literally to determine how one group interprets a certain passage, but to learn God's character and how that character manifests itself throughout history.

Step 4: Acting—Implementing Praxis

Even the most liberal-minded member of the dominant culture must recognize that in spite of laudatory statements concerning the plight of those of other races, genders, and classes, the privilege of the dominant culture remains protected through social structures that normalize and legitimize the status quo, even if it is oppressive. Theorizing about justice, regardless of a person's best intentions, changes nothing. Matthew 7:12, also known as the Golden Rule, clearly states, "All things, whatsoever you desire that others should do to you, so also you should do to them." Simply stated, ethics from the margins is about *doing* rather than theorizing. While theory is not totally dispensed with, ethicists on the margins commit to grounding their praxis in the experience of the disenfranchised; ethical theory, then, is a reflection of that action, and theory is subordinated to the praxis.

While all may agree with the concept that poverty should be eliminated, specific acts need to be taken to move this "utopian" concept toward a reality. All too often, concepts remain simply concepts and never become praxis. Because the basic needs of the marginalized are most often impeded by social structures established by the dominant culture, most praxis will concentrate on transforming the social institutions from being disabling to being enabling. This action can attempt to meet such basic human needs as feeding the hungry, clothing the naked, and visiting the imprisoned; or, on the other hand, such action can attempt to change the actual social structures responsible for causing hunger, nakedness, imprisonment. In the end, both forms of action are needed; however, while those of the dominant culture are often willing to participate in the former through undertaking "charity work," seldom does the desire exist to participate in the latter because it threatens their privileged space.

As a result, eurocentric ethics, usually beginning with a "truth" discovered based on some teachings, revelation, sacred text, or rational analysis, lacks the ability to transform the overall power structures. When conducted from the margins, ethics attempts to work out truth and theory through reflection and action in solidarity with the oppressed. In this sense, praxis is not guided by theory. Ethics done from the margins is not deductive, that is, beginning with some universal truth and determining the appropriate response based on that truth. Those on the margins tend to be suspicious of such universal claims that have been used in the past to justify their oppression. The function of theory is an intellectual way of comprehending the reality experienced by the marginalized. It is not, nor should it be, construed as a truth by which a course of action is deduced.

Praxis becomes the Christian's pastoral response toward the structures responsible for racism, classism, and sexism. Although pastoral, the Christian response can also be highly political because, by its very nature, it challenges the overall political structure designed to benefit one group over others. Ethics can thus be understood as orthopraxis, which is the "doing" within a reality informed by theory and doctrine. Orthopraxis is opposed to orthodoxy, which means the arriving at the correct theory or doctrine. This doing of ethics attempts to bring the social order into harmony with the just society advocated by Christ's example, a community devoid of race, class, and gender oppression.

Still, given the multiplicity of possibilities, how do Christians decide what praxis should be used for the liberation of God's people? José Míguez Bonino provides us with an ethical thesis to inform the decision-making process. He writes, "In carrying out needed structural changes we encounter an inevitable tension between the human cost of their realization and the human cost of their postponement. The basic ethical criterion is the maximizing of universal human possibilities and the minimizing of human costs" (1983:107).

Bonino's thesis, when coupled with the above mentioned four steps of the hermeneutical circle for ethics, provides sufficient information for a moral agent to decide on an ethical process. Will it be the correct action? This is unknown until the final step, which reassesses the action taken. For now, the moral agent must take a "leap of faith" that his or her action is congruent with the liberative message of the gospel.

Step 5: Reassessing—New Ethical Perspectives

The praxis of liberation, at its core, can be understood as the process by which consciousness is raised. But praxis, in and of itself, is insufficient. At most, it informs ethicists about the validity of their interpretations of the oppression faced by a faith community. Further reflection is needed. Has the implementation of praxis brought a greater share of abundant life to the disenfranchised? If so, what additional praxis is required? If not, what should be done to replace the previous praxis with new and more effective action? The implementation of any additional praxis or a totally new praxis will depend on a reassessment of the situation.

Besides analyzing the effectiveness of the course of actions being taken, the process of reassessing also creates systems of ethics. As we have seen, euorocentric ethics is deductive, beginning with a "truth" and moving toward the application of that "truth," subordinating ethics to dogma. Doing ethics from the margins reverses this model. After praxis, as part of the reassessment, the individual returns to the biblical text with an ability to more clearly understand its mandates. Through actions, the moral agent experiences the fullness of the dilemma, allowing him or her to ascertain better the proper moral response. As this response is formed, it is again tested by the hermeneutical circle. And the process continues through additional reassessment and further corrections, if necessary. In the end, it is praxis that forms doctrine, informs the interpretation of scripture, and shapes the system of ethics.

The Hermeneutical Circle for Ethics

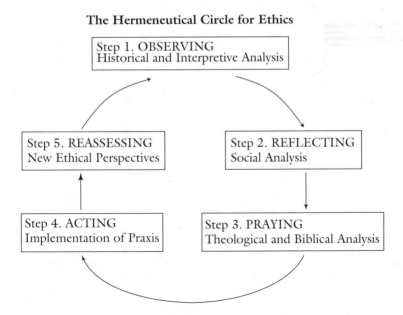

Step 1. OBSERVING
Historical and Interpretive Analysis

Step 5. REASSESSING
New Ethical Perspectives

Step 2. REFLECTING
Social Analysis

Step 4. ACTING
Implementation of Praxis

Step 3. PRAYING
Theological and Biblical Analysis

PART II

CASE STUDIES
OF GLOBAL RELATIONSHIPS

CHAPTER 4

Introducing Global Relationships

Every person remembers the horror of 9/11. More disturbing than the memory of the Twin Towers collapsing is the fact that close to three thousand individuals created in the image of God perished. Some died because they were at work on time and others were heroes who rushed into collapsing buildings in an attempt to save lives. In their honor, *The New York Times* published short biographies of those who perished that fateful day.

While we all know about the three thousand who died during the terrorist attacks, how many people are aware that according to the United Nations Development Programme (UNDP) ten times that number, thirty thousand children, died of hunger and preventable diseases that same day, or that thirty thousand children have died of hunger and preventable diseases every single day since (Fukuda-Parr 2003:8)?[1] While these children perish, impoverished countries are spending three to five times as much to pay off foreign debt as they spend on basic services to alleviate the silent genocide of children. While many of those targeted by terrorists die

---

[1] According to the 2002 United Nations Summit on Sustainable Development 1.1 billion people lack clean drinking water and 2.4 billion need access to sanitation. See Rachel L. Swarns, "Lack of Basics Threatens World's Poor," *The New York Times*, August 29, 2002. In addition, the United Nations estimates that about 300,000 children are involved as soldiers fighting in wars. Sadly, the United States, along with Somalia, are the only two nations in the world that have yet to ratify the United Nation's 1989 landmark treaty on children's rights. See Somini Sengupta, "U.N. Prepares for a Debate on Dire Needs of Children," *The New York Times*, May 8, 2002.

quickly, these children die slowly over time. Their pictures rarely appear in newspapers and their deaths may not even be noted in any special way. Nonetheless, they too are created in God's image. They have worth and dignity. If we can agree that their deaths are an affront to God, then their deaths should also be an affront to our humanity.

The targeting of the World Trade Center in New York and the Pentagon in Washington, D.C., was no coincidence. These structures served as symbolic headquarters of the world empire established by the United States and the consequences of that empire. In a world where over thirty thousand children die each day of hunger and preventable diseases, people in the United States spend millions of dollars annually trying to lose weight. The poorest 60 percent of the world's population owns only 6 percent of the world's wealth while the richest 20 percent owns 85 percent of the world's income, produces 66 percent of the world's greenhouse gases, and consumes 70 percent of the world's energy, 75 percent of the world's metals, and 85 percent of the world's wood (Sider 1997:2, 10, 29, 233).

The global policies that make this possible are also responsible for much of the world's poverty, hunger, destitution, and death. The gluttonous consumption of many first-world countries is not only morally indefensible, but also the root cause of much of the present instability in the world. This instability is a breeding ground for violence, fertilizing the mindset that birthed the 9/11 tragedy. Massive poverty is, without a doubt, the greatest threat to world peace and security. According to the general secretary of the United Nations, Kofi Annan, "No one in this world can feel comfortable or safe while so many are suffering and deprived."[2]

We have passed the era when the marines were used to secure the interests of U.S. corporations (such as the United Fruit Company) throughout Latin America. Today the greatest military force ever known to humanity, simply by its presence, creates a global hegemony that secures the expansion of the global market. If we can come to understand the depth of the misery of the world's

---

[2] Tim Weiner, "More Entreaties in Monterrey for More Aid to the Poor," *The New York Times*, March 22, 2002.

marginalized as a by-product of U.S. affluence created in part by its global economic policies of exclusion, we might begin to appreciate why "they" hate "us" and why our symbols of power become terrorist targets.

THE ECONOMIC MIGHT OF THE UNITED STATES

The cultural influences of the Greek empire, the imperial might of the Roman empire, the religious supremacy of the Holy Roman Empire, and the global reach of the British Empire all pale in comparison with the cultural dominance, the military might, the capitalist zeal, and the global influence of the U.S. empire. The term "empire" can no longer be narrowly defined as the physical possession of foreign lands that must pay tribute. Empire is understood today as a globalized economy that provides economic benefits to multinational corporations whose influences are secured through the military might of one superpower.

Indeed, the sun never sets today on the dominating influence of the United States. At no other time in human history has one nation enjoyed such supremacy of power. While empires of old relied on brute force, the U.S. empire relies mainly on economic force. Through its economic might, the United States dictates terms of trade with other nations, guaranteeing that benefits flow to the United States and the elite of countries that agree to the trade agreements. Take corn, for example, a staple of life in many parts of the world.

While Mexican farmers cultivate corn the way they have for centuries by using plows pulled by burros on small plots of land and relying on rain for irrigation, their U.S. counterparts operate heavily mechanized mega-farms that rely on satellite images to mete out water and fertilizer. Because corn grown in the U.S. is heavily subsidized, it is cheaper for Mexicans to buy what is exported from the U.S. than their home-grown crops. According to the Institute for Agriculture and Trade Policy, U.S. corn sells for 25 percent less than what local Mexican growers earn, meaning that those growers lose money with every acre they plant. Today, subsidized U.S. corn accounts for almost half of the world's stock, setting a world price so low that it eliminates all indigenous competition. It effectively robs three-quarters of the world's poor who live in rural areas (the poor are mostly farmers) and depend on exporting their crops for their livelihood.

Originally, the NAFTA agreement set a fifteen-year period for gradually raising the amount of U.S. corn that could enter Mexico without tariffs; however, Mexico willingly lifted the quotas in fewer than three years to assist its chicken and pork industries. According to Mexican NAFTA negotiators, the suspension of quotas directly benefitted fellow negotiator Eduardo Bours, whose family owns Mexico's largest chicken producer. Although the lifting of quotas rewarded his family business, Mexico lost some $2 billion in tariffs while half a million corn farmers abandoned their lands and moved to the cities in hope of finding a new livelihood. And the flow of cheaper U.S. corn did not translate into cheaper food prices for Mexicans. Quite the contrary. Price controls were lifted on tortillas and tortilla flour, causing their prices to triple. Not surprisingly, while the World Bank continues to sing the praises of NAFTA, a study conducted by the Carnegie Endowment for International Peace has concluded that a decade of NAFTA has failed to generate substantial job growth in Mexico and has brought hardship to hundreds of thousands of subsistence farmers. Real wages in Mexico are lower in 2004 (adjusted for inflation) than they were when NAFTA was adopted in 1994. Additional income inequality is greater and immigration to the United States continues to soar.[3]

In the early part of 2002, the United States Congress passed a bill signed by President George W. Bush authorizing $100 billion in farm subsidies over an eight-year period. By 2003, the world's wealthiest nations were giving their farmers more than $300 billion in subsidies. These subsidies privilege industrial-size farms that produce more acres of crops than are needed for domestic consumption and sell the surplus overseas at prices lower than indigenous farmers require. Even James D. Wolfensohn, president of the World Bank, accuses wealthy nations of "squandering" $1 billion

---

[3] See Tina Rosenberg, "The Free-Trade Fix," *The New York Times Magazine*, August 18, 2002, and "Why Mexico's Small Corn Farmers Go Hungry," *The New York Times*, March 3, 2003; see also Celia Dugger, "Report Finds Few Benefits for Mexico in NAFTA," *The New York Times*, November 19, 2003.

a day on farm subsidies that have devastating effects on impover-ished countries. Ian Goldin, the World Bank's vice-president stated it clearly: "Reducing these subsidies and removing agricultural trade barriers is one of the most important things rich countries can do for millions of people to escape poverty all over the world."[4] Every rural peasant forced to leave the land means another pro-ducer who is forced to migrate to the city, becoming, along with a family, one more consumer. This migration greatly contributes to the perpetual need for future food aid (George 1987:8).

THE RISE OF NEOLIBERALISM

The rise of the U.S. empire was neither an accident nor the result of luck. At the close of World War II, the Bretton Woods Confer-ence (1944) attempted to create an economic order that would rebuild Europe so as to prevent any further world wars. Free trade was perceived as the means by which to bring stability to the global order. Although the original intentions may have been noble, in the end, the new economic order promoted the development of first-world banks and institutions (the World Bank and the Inter-national Monetary Fund [IMF] were both created at Bretton Woods), and transnational corporations. The United States and its Western European allies developed their economic wealth at the expense of the peripheral nations, which provided raw materials and cheap labor. Underdevelopment of the periphery became a by-product of development of the center. What was once accepted as colonialism, where world powers directly occupied the lands of others to extract their national resources and human labor, was replaced with a more modern form of global exploitation, often

---

4 Edmund L. Andrews, "Rich Nations Criticized for Barriers to Trade," *The New York Times*, September 30, 2002; and Elizabeth Becker, "West-ern Farmers Fear Third-World Challenge to Subsidies," *The New York Times*, September 9, 2003. Wolfensohn also states that tariffs (at times exceeding 100 percent) placed by developed nations on agricultural prod-ucts imported from two-third nations make a "sham" out of any attempt at market accessibility. See his speech: "The Challenge of Globalization: The Role of the World Bank," April 2, 2001, World Bank's official web site: www.worldbank.org/html/extdr/extme/jdwsp040201a-en.htm.

termed neoliberalism. Underdevelopment will continue to persist so long as neoliberalism continues to privilege the nations that have placed themselves at the world's center. This is why any Christian ethical response to global injustices must start with a comprehension of neoliberalism.

Neoliberalism is a relatively new economic term. It was coined in the late 1990s to describe the social and moral implications of the free-trade policies of global capitalism (liberalism) since the collapse of the Eastern Bloc (neo-, meaning new or recent). Critics maintain that neoliberalism is responsible for the increasing disparity in global wealth and that it has created a parasitic relationship where the poor of the world sacrifice their humanity to serve the needs, wants, and desires of a privileged few. It provides the few with the right to determine what will be produced, who (nation-state or group of individuals) will produce it, under what conditions will production take place, what will be paid for the finished product, what will the profits amount to, and who will benefit from the profits. In spite of foreign aid programs designed by rich nations to assist so-called underdeveloped nations, more of the world's wealth, in the form of raw materials, natural resources, and cheap labor, is extracted through unfair trade agreements than is returned under the guise of humanitarianism or charity. The first world continues to appropriate the resources of weaker nations through the open market, causing internal scarcities in basic living needs required to maintain any type of humane living standard.

Insuring stable political systems, regardless of how repressive they may be, is a prerequisite for the economic marketplace to function. Political stability, which is needed to insure the steady and profitable flow of goods, supersedes the need for freedom and liberty. Thus, a history exists of U.S. pressure to topple democratically elected governments and install tyrants who secured stability (as has happened with the governments of Abenz in Guatemala, Allende in Chile, and Mossadegh in Iran). Ironically, supporters of the continuing expansion of neoliberalism often confuse this economic structure with democratic virtues like liberty. Hence, raising questions about ethics of the present economic structure can be construed as an attack on democracy itself (George 1999).

To some degree, neoliberalism can be understood as a movement within the World Bank akin to that of religion. According to economic development experts Susan George and Fabrizio Sabelli, the World Bank is "[a] supernational, non-democratic institution [that] functions very much like the Church, in fact the medieval Church. It has a doctrine, a rigidly structured hierarchy preaching and imposing this doctrine [of neoliberalism] and a quasi-religious mode of self-justification" (1994:5).

For theologians Clodovis Boff and George Pixley, "The theological status of [neoliberalism] today is precisely that of a vast idolatrous cult of the great god Capital, creator and father of so many lesser gods: money, the free market, and so on" (1989:144). Like most religious beliefs, the economic pronouncements expounded by the World Bank or IMF can be neither validated nor invalidated, but are usually accepted on faith. Ironically, the ethics employed by these institutions are not based on concepts of morality, but on interpreted principles of economics and the power amassed by the institution. This point is best illustrated by a statement of Brian Griffiths, vice-chairman of Goldman Sachs International and member of the British House of Lords: "What should be the Christian response to poverty? First, to support global capitalism by encouraging the governments of developing countries to privatize state-owned industries, open up their economies to trade and investment and allow competitive markets to grow" (2003:171).

For neoliberalism, market forces are more important than ethics, even when the market causes widespread hunger and poverty. Economist Milton Friedman once said, "Indeed, a major aim of the liberal [market] is to leave the ethical problem for individuals to wrestle with. The 'really' important ethical problems are those that face an individual in a free society—what he should do with his freedom" (1962:12).

Any focus on *individual* and *personal issues* of faith and redemption poses problems for Christian ethicists, especially those working on the margins. Daniel Bell best captures this new neoliberal attitude toward ethics in the words, "Capitalism has put a new twist on Augustine's famous dictum, 'Love and do as you please.' Now it is, 'Produce for the market and do as you please'" (2001:18). The pursuit of gain for the few most often creates scarcity for the many. Liberation theologians such as Peruvian Gustavo Gutiérrez insist that "In the Bible, material poverty is a sub-human situation, the fruit of injustice and sin" (1984:54). Here then is the crux of the conflict between neoliberalism and the gospel message of liberation: neoliberalism lacks a global ethical perspective because it reduces ethics to the sphere of individualism.

The dichotomy between communal and personal ethics—or between market forces and human development—allows Christians to accept the market as a "good." The market, then, determines the fate of humanity and humans exist for the market. Maximization of wealth becomes a virtue in and of itself, as well as a reason for being, and competition separates the sheep from the goats. Economic "losers" result from a lack of personal ethics to manage their own lives properly. Failure in being employable indicates a collapse of moral duty to maximize one's potential in the labor marketplace.

Transnational corporations also compete by eliminating competitors through mergers and acquisitions, which usually result in job losses. As technological advances reduce the need for manual labor, humans become dispensable, nonessential units that are rendered superfluous. Although raw material remains in high demand, the populations of the two-thirds world are no longer needed (Hinkelammert 1995:29–30).[5]

Neoliberalism tends to encompass and dictate every aspect of human existence. Nothing can exist outside the market. Even nations are reduced to "companies" with which the transnationals form alliances. Every thing and body is reduced to a consumer good. If a nation is unable to compete in the global marketplace, then a process of financial prioritizing, known as "structural adjustments" or "austerity programs" takes place so that the nation can

---

[5] The term *tiers monde* was coined by Alfred Sauvy in 1952 by analogy with the "third estate," a reference to the commoners of France prior to the French Revolution. The third estate stood in contrast to nobles and priests of the first and second estates respectively. The term implies the exploitation of the third world, similar to the way the third estate was exploited. Although a better term to describe the relationship between the first- and third-world nations might be "dominated" and "non-dominated" nations, or sometimes "developed" and "undeveloped," I choose to refer to these countries as the two-thirds world, a term used by others who come from these areas. Two-thirds refers to approximately two-thirds of the land masses, resources, and humanity contained within these countries.

become a stronger player, usually at the expense of their populations, whose living conditions worsen.

THE STRUCTURES OF NEOLIBERALISM

The World Bank and the IMF are key institutions of neoliberalism. They impose "conditions" and "structural adjustments" (normally severe cuts in health, education, and social services) on member states starving for credit. A key component of "structural adjustments" is turning national enterprises over to private investors. The privatization of national economies shifts the emphasis from achieving social goals to profit-making. Workers most often face massive wage cuts and layoffs as private owners seek to improve their bottom-line by cutting labor costs. The result of privatization in many underdeveloped countries entails a disappearance of social benefits and a direct reduction of the standard of living for workers.

It is now the market that dictates how a society is to be ruled. Global financial institutions set political policies that impact millions of lives. The power of the World Bank and IMF to impose structural adjustments facilitates their ability to force nations to participate in the world economic order even if the terms of participation are unfavorable, especially to those who are disenfranchised (Hinkelammert 2001:29). These structural adjustments invariably include devaluing the currency, correlating price structures to global markets, terminating import restrictions and exchange controls, imposing user fees on services (such as water, health care, and education), and reducing national sovereignty. The result is usually that the world's marginalized witness the weakening if not the outright dismantling of their economic safety net (protection for women and children in the workplace, social security benefits, labor unions), coupled with increased unemployment and pending ecological collapse. In a twisted form of logic, the increase of unemployment, which leads to increasing poverty and misery among the world's poor, is hailed as a plus. For the World Bank, unemployment means that "bloated" enterprises become lean units capable of competing in the open world market.

In the end, the state can become the servant of the capitalist structures responsible for maintaining "law and order" by squelching any resistance to the status quo. Human freedom and liberty are redefined to mean freedom for the flow of capital and goods, access to a ready and flexible labor pool, and the dissolution of state's rights to determine a separate and contrary destiny.

Those who question neoliberalism are not necessarily opposed to globalization, which has become a reality of modern life. Rather, they are against how globalization has come to be defined. The new political, social, and economic order that neoliberalism represents negatively impacts all humanity, especially the marginalized. Nevertheless, the good news is that God traditionally sides against the empires of history. In closing, consider the words of former Brazilian Archbishop Hélder Câmera: "When I feed the hungry, they call me a saint, when I ask *why* they are hungry, they call me a Communist." Any ethical praxis geared to dismantling global injustices must begin here — by asking why people are hungry. We cannot begin to deal with the liberation of the world's marginalized unless we first deal with the root cause of all their misery and suffering—economic injustice. The next three chapters will briefly explore three consequences of neoliberalism: global poverty, war, and the environment.

USING CASE STUDIES IN ETHICS
FROM THE MARGINS

Traditionally, the usual approach to teaching ethics is to emphasize theory: the student learns an ethical theory and then applies it to a hypothetical case study. The purpose of the case study is to determine objectively which ethical response is proper, based on a multitude of possibilities. The focus is not on the dilemma outlined in the case study but, rather, the methodology employed to arrive at the ethical response. Such a case study might involve a man trapped in a burning car with no way of getting out. An observer has a gun. Should the observer kill the man, sparing him the anguish of slowing burning to death?

Such case studies form a false dichotomy between ethical theory and practice. The purpose is not to determine what moral action should be taken when approaching burning cars but, rather, to answer the abstract question: is there ever a situation in which killing is justified? Regardless of how clever or creative such case studies may appear to be, they are useless to those residing on the margins of society because they fail to foster a concrete act to bring about change. While the question concerning a trapped person in a burning car may prove intriguing, the fact remains that most people will never come across such a situation. Such case studies reinforce a spectator-type ethics where debating theory, rather than transforming society, becomes the goal.

For those doing Christian ethics from the margins, relevant case studies must be contextualized in *lo cotidiano*, the everyday experience of marginalized people, the subject and source for all ethical reflection. Unfortunately, many ethicists of the dominant culture maintain that considering the interpreter's identity or social location interferes with the job of ascertaining a so-called "objective" rendering. The approach employed in this book, and particularly in the following case studies, challenges the assumption that ethical deliberation can be understood apart from what the interpreter brings to the analysis. The case studies and analysis in this book are unapologetically anchored in the experience of society's disenfranchised communities. The theologian Karl Barth once said that theology should be done with the Bible in one hand and the newspaper in the other. In reality, it is ethics that needs to be done with an open newspaper. By grounding case studies in the everyday reality the margins are brought to the center.

The remaining chapters will deal with ethical dilemmas from the perspective of the disenfranchised. The subsequent chapters will apply the hermeneutical circle for ethics described in Chapter 3 to a particular social issue in the world, such as globalization or poverty, through the eyes of the marginalized. The reader is invited to analyze and reflect on the situation in order to determine what praxis may be appropriate. After the third step of praying (theological and biblical analysis), the chapter will present several short case studies. The fourth (taking action) and the fifth steps (reassessment) are missing so that the reader can ponder the case studies through the worldview of the marginalized.

CHAPTER 5

Global Poverty

STEP 1. OBSERVING

Since the collapse of the Soviet Union, the United States has emerged as the undisputed world power, both economically and militarily. The might of the U.S. military facilitates the ever-expanding influence of transnational corporations whose single goal is to satisfy their stockholders by increased profits. One way to keep profit margins high is to pay low wages. Wages paid to workers, especially workers who are part of the world's poor, are not determined by textbook economics or the laborer's need to survive, but by the needs of the transnational corporation to increase profits. Yet, as many theologians, such as Enrique Dussel of Mexico, have pointed out, God's reign in community is an affirmation that people are created to live in a positive relation with the Divine and with each other. This cannot happen when individuals are reduced to their economic value, when they become objects or resources to be exploited (1988:17).

This happens today throughout the world. The disenfranchised become a commodity, an object, within an integrated global market; their sole purpose is to provide the world's powers with a reservoir of cheap labor. As theologian John Cobb observes, "Now that Marxism has been discredited, however, the capitalist countries no longer find it necessary to check the concentration of wealth in fewer hands. By moving from national economies to a single global economy, they can pit the workers of one country against the workers of all others" (1998:36).

The ever-present corporate goal of increasing profits creates a race among transnational corporations to the bottom as they seek the lowest possible wage to be paid. A quick look at one company illustrates this point. A Maytag refrigerator plant employing 1,600 workers was located in the prairie town of Galesburg, Illinois, home to 34,000 residents. On October 2002, Maytag announced the moving of its profitable Galesburg plant to Reynosa, Mexico, by 2004. Why close a profitable plant? Because Maytag paid an average of $15.14 an hour to its Galesburg employees. By moving the plant to Reynosa, Mexico, Maytag can now expect to pay an average of $2.00 an hour. Even though the city of Galesburg raised $3 million to assist Maytag, and the Illinois State House made concessions of $7.5 million in grants and loans, it was still more cost effective to shut down the plant and move it out of the country.

On the day the plant closure was announced, Maytag's stocks jumped 6 percent as Wall Street analysts applauded. The impact of the plant's relocation upon the community became irrelevant, as the good of the market superceded the good of the community. Besides the direct loss of sixteen hundred jobs at the plant, an additional two thousand jobs that depend on the plant (in distribution and auxiliary industries) are expected to be phased out. Moving the plant has begun to take its toll on the town of Galesburg, as home prices begin to slip and an oversaturated pool of unemployed workers depresses wages.[1] The problems Galesburg faces are being repeated in towns and cities throughout the United States. From 1965 through 1990, over eighteen hundred manufacturing plants employing more than half a million workers have been built in Mexico after closing their plants in the U.S. (Barlett and Steele 1992: 31). In 2001 and 2002 alone, the United States lost over two million factory jobs, bringing manufacturing employment to its lowest level in forty years.[2]

The economic consequences to the U.S. economy go further than the loss of jobs. Higher-paying manufacturing jobs have been disappearing at a rate unmatched since the Great Depression of the 1930s. Peaking in the late 1960s at almost 19.6 million manufacturing jobs, their disappearance has occurred at an average

---

[1] Steven Greenhouse, "City Feels Early Effects of Plant Closing in 2004," *The New York Times*, December 26, 2002.

[2] Source: U.S. Department of Labor Bureau of Labor Statistics, www.bls.gov/iag/iag.manufacturing.htm.

yearly rate of 1.3 percent (Barlett and Steele 1992:18–19). These jobs, according to the U.S. Department of Labor and the Bureau of Labor Statistics, have been replaced mainly by governmental jobs (increasing the size of the bureaucracy) and service jobs (including retail), a category that has skyrocketed since 1970 to 21.3 million government jobs in 2001 (16 percent of all jobs) and 64.5 million service and retail jobs in 2002 (59 percent of all jobs). When we consider that an average manufacturing job in 2002 earns $15.24 an hour for a 40.9 hour work-week, while an average retail salary is $10.04 an hour for a 29 hour work-week (a difference of $334.61 a week), we can appreciate the extent to which transnational corporations and neoliberalism, in their quest for the cheapest labor, are dismantling the U.S. middle class. (See Table 1, p. 99.)

The loss of jobs is not limited to blue-collar positions. One research firm, Forrester Research, estimates that over the first fifteen years of the new millennium, U.S. corporations, in an attempt to save 50 to 75 percent of wage costs, will move overseas (or "offshore") an estimated 3.3 million white-collar service jobs (representing 2 percent of all American jobs) and $136 billion in wages.[3] In 2003, IBM recently announced a shift of three million service jobs, including software design jobs, to other countries, mainly India. Why pay $60,000 a year for a skilled Java programmer in the United States when you can get one in India for $5,000 a year? IBM is not alone. Oracle, specializing in business software, plans to increase the number of jobs in India to 6,000 from 3,200. Microsoft plans to double its India software development operation to 500, and Accenture, a leading consulting firm, has increased its off-shore jobs to 4,000 in India, as well as others in China, Russia, and the Philippines.[4] The total savings to a U.S. company that shifts its job overseas can be as high as 50 percent, even when allowances are made for the extra cost of transportation, communication, and other expenses not needed if the work is done in the United States.[5]

---

[3] Ibid.; see also Diane E. Lewis, "Shift of Tech Jobs Abroad Speeding Up, Report Says," *Boston Globe*, December 25, 2002.

[4] Steven Greenhouse, "I.B.M. Explores Shift of Some Jobs Overseas," *The New York Times*, July 22, 2003.

[5] Louis Uchitelle, "A Missing Statistic: U.S. Jobs That Have Moved Overseas," *The New York Times*, October 5, 2003.

Of the 3.3 million service-sector jobs Forrester Research estimates will be conducted overseas by 2015, 70 percent of these positions will migrate to India, which has a large pool of English-speaking inhabitants, two million of whom have a college education. Ironically, even the U.S. government participates in the exportation of its bureaucratic labor force. Today's operators in Bombay handle calls from welfare and food-stamp recipients residing in nineteen American states. Not only do they assist U.S. citizens who have questions about their welfare benefits, they also prepare U.S. tax returns, evaluate health insurance claims, handle airline reservations, transcribe doctors' medical notes, analyze financial data, and read CAT scans. These skilled workers may earn about $200 a month, less than received by the welfare recipients they are helping.[6]

Besides participating in the quest for the lowest possible wage, the U.S. government encourages U.S. industry to outsource jobs to countries like India based on the theory that it benefits the market. During a March 30, 2004, interview with *The Cincinnati Enquirer* John W. Snow, the Treasury secretary, explained the government's position. The practice of moving American jobs to low-cost countries "is part of trade. . . . There can't be any doubt about the fact that trade makes the economy stronger." His comments are reminiscent of the remarks made by N. Gregory Mankiw a month earlier. Mankiw, the chairman of the White House Council of Economic Advisers, defended outsourcing as merely another form of international trade that ultimately would be a "plus" for the United States. William Poole, the president of the Federal Reserve Bank of St. Louis agrees. He sees outsourcing as benefiting the United States by reducing prices domestically while expanding export markets.[7]

However, it would be erroneous to believe that countries like India or Mexico have achieved a financial windfall from the importation of manufacturing jobs. For example, Mexicans have sunk

---

6 Jennifer Bjorhus, "U.S. Economic Slowdown Sends Technology Jobs Overseas," *San Jose Mercury News*, October 21, 2002; and Amy Waldman, "More 'Can I Help You? Jobs Migrate From U.S. to India," *The New York Times*, May 11, 2003.

7 Edmund L. Andrews, "Treasury Chief Defends Outsourcing of U.S. Work," *The New York Times*, March 31, 2004.

deeper into poverty, in spite of the opening of *maquiladoras* (assembly plants) along the border. Many Mexican peasants, many of whom used to live off the corn they grew, have surrendered to the fact that they can no longer compete with agricultural goods imported from the United States. Because the land could no longer support them, they abandoned their homesteads and moved to *colonias* (poor, sprawling slums of shacks patched together from pieces of metal, wood, and plastic) surrounding the *maquiladoras*.

And the towns straddling the border offered few other opportunities. Mexican wage earners have lost 20 percent of their purchasing power since NAFTA spurred the growth of *maquiladoras*, even though wages and benefits for *maquiladora* employees rose by 86 percent from 1997 to 2002 to an average of $6,490 a year. The increase in wages is deceptive when we consider that the national minimum wage fell by nearly 50 percent over the last decade. In 1975 Mexican production workers earned 23 percent of U.S. wages. Since the relocation of U.S. jobs to Mexico, that number has continued to drop, one reason why more dissatisfied workers attempt the hazardous border crossing to the North.[8]

The move from the United States to Mexico is only the first step. As the worsening conditions of Mexican workers brought up questions about plant safety, living wages, and the environment, factories began to look elsewhere. Although first attracted to Mexico by low wages, low taxes, and little if no environmental regula-

---

[8] The difference in the standards of living between the United States and Mexico, which was about three to one in the 1950s, is eight to one since the new millennium. The Mexican government estimates that forty million of its citizens live in poverty, with an additional twenty-five million living in extreme poverty, most of whom reside in the rural areas. Mexico's independent union federation, the National Union of Workers (UNT) places unemployment at over nine million people, a quarter of the workforce. Half of those who have jobs are employed by companies, who despite the law, pay less than the minimum wage, and offer no health insurance or retirement benefits. While the economic situation differs from country to country, the situation faced by Mexican workers indicates what is occurring globally. In many cases, it is even worse. See David Bacon, "World Labor Needs Independence and Solidarity," *Monthly Review* 52:3 (July/Aug. 2000): 84–102.

tions, some of these multinational corporations are again seeking to relocate. In the race for the lowest wages and labor standards, China is emerging as the new leader. Jobs in Mexico that pay $1.50 to $2.00 an hour are being relocated to China where workers are paid 25 cents to $1.00 an hour. An additional benefit is that Asian women and children, who earn less than what men earn, are usually employed in these low- or semi-skilled jobs. This exploitation of cheap labor ensures a constant flow of affordable goods for mass consumption in industrialized nations.

In the first half of 2002, direct foreign investment in Mexico dropped by 15 percent ($6.1 billion) while investment in China rose by 19 percent ($24.6 billion).[9] According to the U.S. Census Bureau, U.S. imports from China have been steadily rising, from $4 billion in 1986 to $114 billion in 2002. At the same time Mexico's exports to the U.S. have begun to decline. During the first two years of the new millennium, more than 500 plants along the border have either shut down or moved their operations to China, reducing the number of jobs in Mexico by 256,000.[10] For example, in 2000, the *maquila* city of Chihuahua, which specializes in automotive parts and electronics, led Mexico in employment. By the close of 2002, Chihuahua led in unemployment. Companies like General Electric, which over the years moved many jobs from the U.S. to Mexico, are now relocating those jobs to China and recently opened a plant to produce mini-bar refrigerators.

Yet China's entry into the global market has not translated into an economic boom for China's working class. China, like Russia, had an economy completely controlled by the state. Such a system guaranteed jobs for life and then retirement, but guaranteed jobs and retirement were the first casualties of privatization. Entire cities were built around huge mills, mines, and factories that provided a multitude of social benefits, from subsidized housing, to hospitals and childcare. Privatization has brought an end to these

---

[9] Elisabeth Malkin, "Manufacturing Jobs Are Exiting Mexico," *The New York Times*, November 5, 2002.

[10] Ricardo Castillo Mireles, "Chinese Maquiladoras Threaten Mexico," *Transportation and Distribution*, Vol. 43, No. 11 (Nov., 2002): 26, 28.

guarantees and social benefits as plants close, leaving retirees to go hungry and workers to face a bleak future. Chinese society today is also plagued by corruption, crime, and inequality.[11]

In the race to be competitive, it is only a matter of time before Maytag follows General Electric's lead. Given that one-third of Mexico's hard-currency income and almost half of its $158 billion in exports is produced by the *maquiladoras*, the movement of jobs to China could trigger a major currency crisis and a greater migration of undocumented workers north.[12] In the end, China may not long remain the capitalist's paradise: today Vietnam and Thailand are beginning to offer cheaper labor than China.

STEP 2. REFLECTING

Who are the poor? According to the 1996 United Nations report "On Human Development," we live in a world where the top 358 billionaires are wealthier than the combined annual income of countries that contain 45 percent of the world's population. This continuously growing income gap has led J. C. Speth, general secretary of the U.N. Development Program, to conclude, "If present trends continue, the economic disparity between industrial nations and developing nations will assume proportions which are no longer merely unjust, but inhuman" (Moltmann 1998:77). And a biblical text from Proverbs reminds us that, "Those who oppress the poor curse their Maker, but those honoring God, favor [make a preferential option for] the needy" (Prv. 14:31).

The world today faces no greater global ethical dilemma than the question of poverty. The poor are understood as those deprived of the basic necessities needed to live a life of dignity. According to Clodovis Boff and George Pixley, the poor consist of three distinct groups: 1) the socio-economic poor, consisting of those outside the prevailing economic order (the unemployed, beggars, abandoned children, outcasts, prostitutes) and the exploited (industrial workers paid substandard wages, rural workers, seasonal wage-

---

[11] Jiang Xing, "Letter from China," *The Nation* (March 4, 2002): 23–25.

[12] William Greider, "A New Giant Sucking Sound," *The Nation* (December 31, 2001): 22–24; Saul Landau, "The End of the *Maquila* Era," *The Progressive* (September 2002): 24–26.

earners, tenant farmers); 2) the socio-cultural poor, consisting of blacks, indigenous people, and women; and 3) the new poor of industrial societies, consisting of the physically and mentally hand-icapped abandoned to the streets of huge cities, along with the unemployed, the homeless, the suicidally depressed, the elderly dependent on insufficient state pensions, and the young addicted to drugs (1989:3–10).

The poor of the world are not necessarily lazy, backward, or underdeveloped, as so many people believe. If so, then their only hope would rest with the generosity of the wealthy who might attempt to help them by providing food, education, or loans. The poor are made poor by economic forces that cause the prosperity of one nation to be rooted in the poverty of other nations. These forces constitute a social phenomenon that enriches the few through the impoverishment of the many.

Treating workers as objects means they are defined only by what they contribute to the profitability of the corporation. Seldom are they defined by their humanity. Human rights are first and fore-most about removing obstacles so as to engage in trade and com-merce rather than achieving human self-fulfillment (Bell 2001:126). For reasons like this, neoliberalism is incapable of incorporating the basics of Christianity. How does one reconcile the biblical man-date to forgive debts with the insistence that foreign debts be paid off at the expense of people obtaining basic human needs? Ironi-cally, toward the end of the 1970s in Latin America, as growing foreign debt was negatively impacting the lives of most people, some Catholic and Protestant clergy changed the words of the Lord's Prayer from "Forgive us our debts" to "Forgive us our offenses." Fear existed that Christians, pauperized by the policies of the World Bank and IMF might take the Lord Prayer's literally and actually demand that debts be forgiven so that they could have their daily bread. Churches succumbed to economic pressures by neutering the potency of the biblical message (Hinkelammert 1995:333–34).

STEP 3. PRAYING

The most prominent feature of the Christian worship tradition is the concept of sacrifice, which is rooted within the Jewish faith. Among the many reasons mentioned by the Hebrew Bible for offering a sacrifice (such as tribute, cleansing, thanksgiving, supplication, ordination, or peace), most crucial for Christians were the sin and guilt offerings. Spilling the blood of an unblemished animal for the atonement of sin became the basis for understanding the crucifixion of Christ.[13] For many Euroamerican Christians, the death on the cross of Jesus, "the lamb of God who takes away the sins of the world" (Jn. 1:29), becomes the ultimate sacrifice that serves to reconcile God with sinners. The death of a sinless Jesus, as a substitute for a sinful humanity that deserves God's punishment, restores fellowship between God and humans. Suffering and death become salvific.

Jesus paid by his death so that others might live. But this concept is not limited to the Christ event. For some to live in abundance, others must die. Theologian Mark Lewis Taylor explains that "Nascent capitalism of modernity is a sacrificial economy worshiping money as its fetish, and sacrificing the subjective corporeality of the [marginalized]. So necessary is the sacrifice that it is rationalized as legitimate" (2001:52).

The center of power can participate in all the riches that life has to offer because those on the periphery die producing those riches. The death of those perceived to be inferior can be viewed as a sacrifice offered to neoliberalism so that a few can enjoy their abundance. Like Christ, the marginalized of the earth die so that those with power and privilege can have life abundantly.

Those suffering on the margins of society epitomize what liberation theologians call God's "crucified people," for they bear in a very real way the brunt of the sins of today's oppressive social and economic structures. As a crucified people they provide an essential perspective on salvation. Theologians coming from the margins of power insist that God intentionally and regularly chooses the oppressed of history, and makes them the principal means of salvation. They maintain that this is done in the same fashion as God chose the "suffering servant," the crucified Christ, to bring salvation to the world (Sobrino 1993:259–60). God has always chosen the disenfranchised as agents of God's new creation. It was

---

[13] For Jews, sin offerings were not given for the atonement of sin. Sins committed against others were handled with an appropriate punishment or restitution formula, while deliberate sins against God were beyond redemption (Nm. 15:30–31).

not to the court of Pharaoh that God's will was made known, but, instead, God chose their Hebrew slaves, the Jews, to reveal God's movement in history. It was not Rome, the most powerful city of the known world, where God chose to perform the miracle of the incarnation, nor was it Jerusalem, the center of Yahweh worship; it was impoverished Galilee where God chose to proclaim first the message of the gospels. Nazareth, Jesus' hometown, was so insignificant to the religious life of Judaism that the Hebrew Bible never mentions it (De La Torre and Aponte 2001:78). This theme of solidarity between the crucified Christ and the victims of oppression permeates scripture.

Still, liberative ethicists insist that there is nothing salvific about suffering itself, for it tends to reinforce domination. Ethicists like Delores Williams find the image of Christ as surrogate victim too painful to incorporate into the black woman's experience, who during and after slavery was forced and coerced into a similar role (1991:8–13). Other black feminist theologians (known as womanist theologians) such as Stephanie Mitchem remind us:

> Suffering in itself is not salvific. It is redemptive only in that it may lead to critical rethinking of meaning or purpose, as might any life crisis. Such reexamination is part of the process of human maturation. However, suffering is a distinctive starting place for thinking about salvation as it brings into sharp focus human experience in relation to God. (2002:109)

Forgetting that the cross is a symbol of evil allows for the easy romanticization of those who are marginalized as some sort of hyper-Christians for the "cross" they are forced to bear. Such views tend to offer honor to those suffering, encouraging a form of quietism where suffering is stoically borne instead of encouraging praxis that can lead toward the end of suffering. If salvation exists in the life and resurrection of Jesus Christ as well as in his death, then his crucifixion can be seen for what it was—the unjust repression of a just man by the dominant culture of his time. The crucifixion becomes an act of solidarity with those relegated to exist on the underside of our present economic structure. Ethicists from the margins maintain that the importance of the crucifixion lies in Christ's solidarity with the oppressed, Christ's understanding of how those who are oppressed suffer, reassurance for the disenfranchised that Christ understands their sufferings, and finally, the hope that because of the resurrection, final victory exists.

STEP 4. CASE STUDIES

- 1. Rukkibai and her husband, Lakshman Ratohre, are among the wretched of the earth. They live in Omla Naik, India, where he toils in someone else's fields for $1.00 to $1.50 a day. His wife, who works by his side doing the same work, earns 60 cents a day. When Rukkibai gave birth to their fifth daughter, she sold the baby for 1,100 rupees, roughly $20. Chances are the child was eventually sold into the sex trade or to an orphanage that would offer the child for adoption, most likely to Westerners. Rukkibai is again pregnant. If she has a son, they will keep him, for he will be able to work the fields with his father; if she has a daughter, more likely than not they will again sell the child.[14]

  — What are the ethical implications in selling one's children so that the whole family can survive?
  — If adopted by Westerners, the child will have a more secure financial future. What importance does this have?
  — It is possible that the daughter might be raised to be a prostitute. Is it still worth taking a chance she might be adopted by Westerners?
  — Some argue that poor women should be sterilized to prevent these dilemmas. How ethically valid is this solution? Why?
  — Do first world nations have any obligations toward Rukkibai's family? If so, what kind? If not, why?

- 2. In 2001, the United States spent over $6.9 billion on plastic surgery.[15] For some (particularly women), looking younger is deemed a necessity for social or employment reasons. For some people of color, operations to thin noses or reduce lip size

---

[14] Raymond Bonner, "Poor Families Selling Baby Girls Was Economic Boon," *The New York Times*, June 17, 2001.

[15] The $6.9 billion figure was obtained during an interview with LaSandra Cooper, the media relations officer for the American Society of Plastic Surgeons (ASPS).

have been performed to create a more "European" look. Michael Jackson, who in 1982 produced the most popular record in history ("Thriller"), epitomizes the great lengths some will go to assimilate. The world witnessed his African American features flatten and his skin turn paler. From 1997 to 2002, the number of non-white patients seeking plastic surgery quadrupled. Dr. Julius Few commented on his patients of color: "Programs that are on TV or in magazines are making people of color realize that they are also able to enjoy improvement without wiping out their ethnic identity." Still, she notes that for most of these patients, "improvements" are euroamerican features.[16] Others have participated in painful procedures to straighten hair or lighten skin coloration through the use of chemicals. Still others wishing to avoid such drastic actions suppress their own culture and heritage by learning to dress, speak, and behave like white "euroamericans."

— Are such actions ethically defensible when engaged to maximize employability?
— If an individual is from the margins (a person of color), what are the ethical implications of viewing oneself through the eyes of white people?
— What are the moral issues, if any, that underlie these actions in which some people of color willingly participate?

• 3. Twenty-nine-year-old Carlos Roberto Rivera was a bricklayer in Los Vázquez, a working-class neighborhood in Argentina. With eight children to care for, he struggled to make ends meet on his $100-a-week salary. Still, he was able to put aside enough money to eventually build his own home. When the IMF cut off Argentina's credit line toward the end of 2001 for not imposing sufficient fiscal austerity, the country responded by freezing all bank accounts, plunging the nation into an economic crisis. By 2003, Rivera was lucky if he could bring home

---

[16] Tavis Smiley, "Dr. Julius Few Discusses Why Plastic Surgery among People of Color Has Become More Popular," *National Public Radio*, aired August 22, 2003.

$10-a-week from foraging in the dump. Children in his once middle-class neighborhood now need treatment for *kwashiorkor*, a disease caused by lack of protein and characterized by swollen bellies and a reddening of the hair.[17] Regardless of the misery faced by the Argentine people, IMF insists that such steps, while unfortunate, will eventually make Argentina an economically stronger nation. The IMF generally demands that debtor nations pay 20 to 25 percent of their export earnings toward debt reduction, leaving some nations, especially African nations, with debt-service-to-GNP ratios well above 100 percent. It is then mathematically impossible to repay the principle — although the interest paid in some cases has already exceeded it. At the end of World War II European nations were treated more favorably. Germany, for example, paid only 3 to 5 percent of export earnings in debt reduction and 80 percent of its war debt was forgiven. More recently, similarly favorable terms were granted to countries emerging from the former Soviet bloc.

— Is the plight faced by Carlos Roberto Rivera a necessary though unfortunate consequence of development? Does the world community, through financial institutions like the IMF, have any obligation to ease the suffering of Rivera, and others like him? Why or why not? If so, then how?

— Why is there different treatment among debtor nations? Should non-European nations be granted terms similar to those offered European nations?

— Should most of Argentina's remaining debt be forgiven?[18] Voiding such debts can negatively economically impact first-world nations. Is this fair?

— Should the limited resources of an impoverished nation be earmarked to repay the debt of the debtor-nation or to pro-

---

[17] Larry Rohter, "Once Secure, Argentina See Jobs, Food, and Hope Shrivel," *The New York Times*, March 2, 2003.

[18] Since 1995, the World Bank has initiated various forms of debt forgiveness. By 2001, twenty-two countries (eighteen of which are African) began to receive some form of debt relief under the Heavily Indebted Poor Country (HIPC) initiative. The total external debt of these countries was scheduled to be reduced by two-thirds. See Wolfen-

vide basic services like food, medicine, clean water, or sanitation? Why or why not?

- 4. For four days, Zara Fatimé, a 15-year-old girl from N'djamena, Chad, was in labor. By the time her parents took her to the dilapidated national hospital, her blood pressure was 170/80. Soon after, she lapsed into a coma. Her child arrived stillborn. The oxygen desperately needed by Fatimé could not be spared by the hospital. Fatimé is but one of the 500,000 women who die each year during pregnancy and child-birthing throughout the two-thirds world countries. That's about one woman per minute. Nevertheless, the entire $34 million contribution from the United States to the U.N. Population Fund—a fund that organizes programs like the training of midwives —was totally eliminated from the 2003 budget. Additionally, all funds were eliminated for the Reproductive Health Response and Conflict Consortium. These programs designed to improve African maternal health were eliminated because these organizations supposedly cooperated with China's pro-abortion policies.[19] Even when the U.S. provides development assistance to two-thirds world nations, its aid lags behind most other countries. According to the United Nations, during the 1990s, the U.S., the richest nation the world has ever witnessed, ranked 22 among donors with 0.1 percent of its gross domestic product (GDP) devoted to aid.[20] By 2002, the U.S. ranked last among the 28 top foreign aid donor countries. Yet Washington, D.C., maintains that free trade, not foreign aid, is the best way to help underdeveloped nations, hence the Congressional mantra: "Trade, not aid."[21]

---

sohn, "The Challenge of Globalization," April 2, 2001, World Bank's Official Web Site.

[19] Nicholas D. Kristof, "Terror of Childbirth," *The New York Times*, March 20, 2004.

[20] Sengupta, "U.N. Prepares for a Debate," *The New York Times*, May 8, 2002.

[21] Andres Oppenheimer, "America's Foreign Aid Contributions," *The Miami Herald*, July 27, 2002.

—What obligation does the U.S. have toward Zara Fatimé, or the 500,000 other women who die each year?

— Should women in Africa be denied medical assistance because of China's pro-abortion policies? Should abortion be the litmus test on deciding which maternal health programs should be funded? Why or why not?

—What form should U.S. ethical praxis take, if any, in dealing with the "Trade, not aid"?

— Does the U.S. have any obligation toward two-third nations? Explain?

—When we provide financial assistance to these nations, should it be viewed as charity, or giving back what was taken from them through protectionist policies? Why or why not?

- 5. Lisa Rahman is a nineteen-year-old who used to work at the Shah Makhdum garment factory in Dhaka, Bangladesh, assembling "Winnie the Pooh" shirts. She was paid an equivalent of five cents to assemble Pooh shirts that the Walt Disney Company retails at $17.99. In 2002, when workers united to publically complain of poor working conditions, Disney canceled all future work orders, leaving workers like Lisa Rahman with few options.[22] Meanwhile, most stockholders of Disney do not take responsibility for the behavior of the corporation in which they are invested.

— The former makers of "Winnie the Pooh" shirts demanded that Disney return to the factory, but this time around Disney would have to work with the contractor to clean up the factory and respect basic working rights. Does Disney have any responsibility to these workers? Should Disney abide by worker demands? Which is more important: the basic rights of the workers or the profit margin of Disney?

— Is it ethical for a Christian to own stocks in a company such as Disney or mutual funds (even in the form of a retirement fund) when the profits earned by that Christian stem from the impoverishment of the world's most vulnerable members?

---

[22] Gary Gentile, "Group Slams Disney for Sweatshop Conditions in Bangladesh," *The Associated Press State & Local Wire*, October 7, 2002.

Table 1
Comparison of High-Paying Manufacturing Jobs
to Lower-Paying Jobs
(All figures represent millions of jobs)

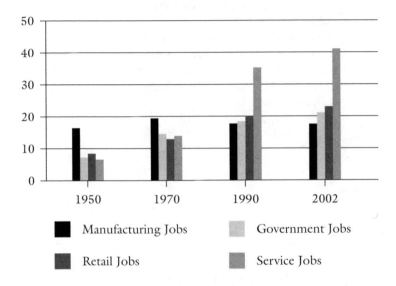

Exporting manufacturing jobs overseas has led to an economic shift from high-paying to low-paying wages within the United States. In the 1950s, most jobs were in the high-paying manufacturing sector. After peaking at 19.6 million jobs in 1970, manufacturing jobs today have dropped to 16.7 million, to just 5 percent of all U.S. jobs. Meanwhile, retail and service jobs have skyrocketed to represent 59 percent of all jobs. (Source: The U.S. Department of Labor, Bureau of Labor Statistics)

— Can a Christian profit from stock dividends paid out by companies, such as Maytag or General Electric, whose race to the bottom is responsible for creating underpaid workers in Mexico or China and unemployed workers in the U.S.? Why or why not? Commenting on the closing of the 52-year-old Galesburg, Illinois, Maytag plant, former employee Aaron Kemp said, "This is one of the most unpatriotic, most un-

American things I can imagine a company doing. They want Americans to buy their products, but they don't want to put Americans to work making those products."[23] Is Kemp correct? Should multinational corporations have any obligations toward any particular nation-state? If so, what type of obligations?

— What ethical responsibilities, if any, do dividend earners have in how transnational corporations operate? Does a moral connection exist between the person forced into poverty to increase dividend earnings on stocks and the person receiving those dividends?

---

[23] Greenhouse, "City Feels," *The New York Times*, December 26, 2002.

CHAPTER 6

War

STEP 1. OBSERVING

War is the attempt of one nation to dominate another by superior military power, usually to procure or protect property rights, which can include both resources and labor. To this end, the United States, the prime expansionist power since 1945, insures its peace and security through the freedom of the open market. Peace is crucial to achieving and maintaining prosperity for the dominant culture. To protect this *Pax Americana*, a superior military force must be maintained to ensure that a nation with only 6 percent of the world's population can continue to benefit from 50 percent of the world's resources. When President George W. Bush announced his National Security Strategy in September, 2002, he committed the United States to lead other nations toward "the single sustainable model for national success," meaning the model of the open market through free trade, or, we might say, the preservation of neoliberalism through economic or military force.

The expansion and preservation of a new economic world order will at times require a regime change in nations that refuse to succumb to neoliberalism. The wake of the 9/11 terrorist attack ushered in a new doctrine for engaging nations hostile to U.S. supremacy, granting the United States the right to start a war through a pre-emptive attack on any nation that might pose a possible future danger. In effect, the U.S. reserved for itself the right to engage in military action against any hypothetical threat before any and all other avenues for conflict resolution (such as the United Nations) have been exhausted. "First strike" to bring about "regime change" replaces the "containment"[1] and "deterrent"[2] strategies of the latter part of the last century. In reality, this new doctrine is but a repackaging of the U.S. foreign policy toward Latin America during the first half of the twentieth century—a policy that reserved the right to determine what constituted a threat to U.S. interests and security, and then to act unilaterally.

Under President Theodore Roosevelt (1858–1919), the nexus of the "first strike" and "regime change" doctrines took place. At that time, "gunboat diplomacy," as it was known, went by the slogan, "Speak softly but carry a big stick." During the last century, every country bordering the Caribbean and several countries in South America were invaded by U.S. forces (or covertly subverted by the CIA) to bring about regime change when those countries chose to follow their own destinies in ways not seen favorable to the United States. In some cases, brutal dictatorships and military juntas were installed after the United States deposed democratically elected presidents. Millions of peasants, students, church leaders, and intellectuals were abducted, tortured, or killed while opposing the U.S.-backed installed government. It can be argued, given this background, that the 2003 attack on Iraq can be better understood as a preventive measure rather than a preemptive strategy.

Any discussion of the issues of war among people at the margins takes on a quite different tone. The argument moves from a just-war debate to a discussion of racism and classism, as military violence usually stimulates and is stimulated by race, class, and gender oppressions. The margins of society raise issues of 1) the re-creation of the other's history (racism), and 2) the spoils of war (classism). These concerns played themselves out during the 2003 war on Iraq.

For violence to occur, history must be re-created, usually to the disadvantage of those who will become the victims of war. The nation initiating the military conflict must reconstruct itself as the defender of virtue and appear to have no ulterior motive for gain-

---

[1] The policy of co-existing with the threat of the Soviet Union while preventing the expansion of communism.

[2] The policy of building U.S. defenses to assure a devastating response if attacked, thus keeping the Soviet Union from aggressively acting.

ing from the military conflict.[3] Actions undertaken that may have
made the war inevitable are conveniently forgotten. In the case of
the 2003 war on Iraq, the CIA, forty years earlier (1963), had conducted a "regime change" by collaborating with the relatively small
but anti-Communist Baath Party to overthrow Abel Karim Kassem.
Once in power, the Baath Party unleashed a bloodbath, murdering leftist sympathizers on lists of suspected Communists provided
by the CIA. The "house cleaning" allowed Western corporations
like Mobil, Bechtel, and British Petroleum to conduct business
with Baghdad for the first time. By 1968, in-fighting among Baath
leaders threatened business interests, so with CIA backing Saddam
Hussein seized power.

Even though the United States knew Saddam Hussein supported terrorists, killed his own people, and was attempting to
build nuclear weapons, Donald Rumsfeld traveled in 1983 to meet
Hussein in hopes of establishing warmer relations. Iraq was seen
as strategic to U.S. attempts to thwart Iran's growing influence in
the crucial oil-producing states along the Persian Gulf. During the
Iran-Iraq war, the U.S. provided Hussein with satellite photogra-
phy of the battleground. The U.S. Commerce Department reports
that during the early 1980s the U.S. provided Iraq with numerous shipments of "bacteria/fungi/protozoa" that could be used
to create biological weapons (such as anthrax), along with 1.5

---

[3] Take, for example, the comments made by Colin Powell, the Secretary of State, during a September 8, 2002, interview with *The New York
Times*. Powell made a case for the moral right to attack Iraq:

> Our record and our history is not one of going out looking for con-
> flict, it is not one of undertaking pre-emptive acts for the purpose
> of seizing another person's territory, another people's territory, or
> to impose our will on someone else. Our history and our tradition
> is always one of defending our interest.

But history is usually the mega-narrative of the dominant culture. Conveniently forgotten by Powell was the history concerning the U.S. invasion of Mexico. The justification of this massive land acquisition was based
on a theology that conceived the dominant Euroamerican culture as chosen by God. This concept of "Manifest Destiny" taught that God had
intended Euroamericans to acquire the entire continent. The expansionist war against Mexico was then masked by the re-creation of the nation's
historical mega-narrative.

million atropine injections to be used against the effects of chemical weapons. When Hussein used chemical weapons against the Kurdish rebels in 1988, the Reagan administration responded by blaming Iran, only later relenting when mounting evidence pointed to Iraq.[4] Until the eve of the 1991 Gulf War, the U.S. had been providing Iraq with billions of dollars in financing and millions of dollars in equipment to build Iraq's missiles, conventional bombs, and nuclear, chemical, and biological weapons—all to stem the influence of Iran.[5] Most damning was the proposed mid-1990 sale of "skull furnaces"—approved by the U.S. Department of Commerce—used to produce the components of nuclear weapons (Hartung 1994:222, 232).[6]

In addition to the need to re-create the past, there is the desire to profit from the present. "To the victors of war go the spoils." In the case of Iraq, the spoils included a proven reserve of 112 billion barrels of crude oil, the largest in the world outside Saudi Arabia. The first major contract for the reconstruction of Iraq, worth $680 million, was awarded to Bechtel, with only token competition. Bechtel's chief executive serves on the U.S. Commander in Chief's Export Council and a Bechtel director, George Shultz, served as the first secretary of state in the first Bush administration, raising serious issues of impropriety. More questionable are

---

[4] See Christopher Dickey and Evan Thomas, "How Saddam Happened," *Newsweek* (September 23, 2002), 35–37; and Patrick E. Tyler, "Officers Say U.S. Aided Iraq in War Despite Use of Gas," *The New York Times*, August 18, 2002.

[5] Iraq, after being removed in 1983 from the list of terrorist-supporting nations, became the largest recipient of the U.S. Department of Agriculture's Commodity Credit Corporation (CCC) credits, acquiring 20 percent of all guarantees granted between 1984 and 1989. By 1989, the senior President Bush signed National Security Directive 26 calling for "improved economic and political ties with Iraq." This improved relationship meant an approval of $1 billion in CCC credits. When the Gulf War broke out shortly afterwards, Hussein reneged on a total of $2 billion in CCC loans leaving the U.S. taxpayer to foot the bill (Hartung 1994:238, 241).

[6] The sale was called off after Stephen Bryen of *The Philadelphia Inquirer* wrote about the transaction, bringing pressure upon the first Bush administration to cancel the agreement two weeks before Iraq invaded Kuwait.

contracts estimated to reach $60 billion that were initially awarded with no public bids or discussion—and sometimes secretly—to politically connected firms like Halliburton, directed by Vice President Dick Cheney from 1995 until 2000.

In one of these contracts, Halliburton subsidiary Kellogg Brown & Root was given control of the entire Iraqi oil operation, including distribution. Such acts violate international law. The World Trade Organization forbids discrimination against companies of WTO member nations in the awarding of contracts. Ironically, Halliburton conducted business with Iraq (as well as with two other members of the "axis of evil," Iran and North Korea) during Cheney's term as the head of the corporation. In addition to being fined $3.8 million in 1995 for re-exporting U.S. goods through a foreign subsidiary to Libya in clear violation of U.S. sanctions, Halliburton has been accused of overcharging the U.S. government for work conducted during the 1990s, resulting in a $2 million settlement to ward off criminal prosecution for price gouging.[7]

Both Bechtel and Halliburton have also received big loan guarantees ($481.4 million for Halliburton, $178.1 million for Bechtel, $675 million for Enron) from the Export-Import Bank, a federal agency, thanks to legislation signed by President George W. Bush, to provide up to $100 billion in international trade assistance, with taxpayers, in effect, subsidizing these foreign ventures.[8] Other transnational corporations have also benefitted from the war in Iraq. The executives and/or political action committees of the seventy companies to receive lucrative government contracts for billions of dollars in reconstruction work in either Iraq or

---

[7] Bob Herbert, "Dancing with the Devil," *The New York Times*, May, 22, 2003; Michael Kinsley, "To the Victors Go the Spoils," *The New York Times*, April 20, 2003; Neela Banerjee, "2 in House Question Halliburton's Iraq Fuel Prices,' *The New York Times*, October 16, 2003; Don Van Natta, Jr, "High Payments to Halliburton for Fuel in Iraq," December 10, 2003; Douglas Jehl, "Evidence Is Cited of Overcharging in Iraq Contract," December 12, 2003; Joel Brinkley and Eric Schmitt, "Halliburton Will Repay U.S. Excess Charges for Troops' Meals," *The New York Times*, February 3, 2004.

[8] Leslie Wayne, "A Guardian of Jobs or a 'Reverse Robin Hood'?" *The New York Times*, September 1, 2002.

Afghanistan contributed at least $500,000 to the 2000 election campaign of Bush-Cheney. Nine of the ten biggest contract recipients (Bechtel and Halliburton were at the top of the list) employed senior governmental officials or had close ties to government agencies and Congress.[9] And, as already mentioned, most of the contracts awarded were conducted secretively and without competitive bidding.

STEP 2. REFLECTING

Most societies create systems designed to define what is good and what is evil. Such binary systems also define what is legal and illegal, acceptable and unacceptable, criminal and noncriminal, and so on. What one society determines to be proper may be viewed with horror by another. Political assassinations, restriction of free expression, or brute intimidation could be construed as necessary evils for the advancement of a sacred cause. While all persons within that society might agree on the ultimate end, not all would necessarily subscribe or acquiesce to such tactics to achieve the goal.

The question becomes, then, how do such violent tactics become an acceptable procedure within the eyes of the society at large? French philosopher Michel Foucault maintains that it can be done only by reducing what is good to "normal" and what is evil to "abnormal" or pathological (1965:73). By extension, when engaged in a just war, war-like activities such as killing, bombing, and censorship must be employed to insure the final victory of good. Terror, then, is understood as the legitimate use of violence to enforce justice. Terror, the spilling of blood, and other acts of war become "normal," regardless as to how distasteful they may be. In fact, they become an inevitable moral imperative. The "enemies of freedom and democracy" (read those opposed to the neoliberalism of today's Western capitalism or globalization) are a threat to "truth," and, as such, must be silenced at all cost.

---

9 Edmund L. Andrews and Elizabeth Becker, "Bush Got $500,000 from Companies That Got Contracts, Study Finds," *The New York Times*, October 31, 2003; and Douglas Jehl, "Insiders' New Firm Consults on Iraq," *The New York Times*, September 30, 2003.

Many unjust attempts at power can be concealed in a holy war that rallies the people around the concepts of freedom, democracy, and justice.

War is inevitable because we choose to maintain international structures that make war possible and profitable. Still, can any war be considered "just"? Just-war theory, a medieval concept embedded in international law, was formulated by St. Augustine in the early fifth century (and expanded by Thomas Aquinas in the thirteenth century) to provide guidelines for "Christian" rulers of empire to determine when the presence of evil and injustice justified the use of violence to stamp it out.[10] Under certain circumstances, it was believed that God condoned wars conducted to destroy evil and rectify injustices.[11]

Can just-war guidelines impartially help people decide if the use of military force within a given conflict is just? Or is the determination to conduct a war simply the subjective views of those applying the just-war theory? Take, for example, the early debate in 2003 over the possible U.S. entry into a war with Iraq. The majority of religious leaders and denominations, using the principles of just-war theory, conclusively determined prior to hostilities that the U.S. preventive attack on Iraq did not meet the criteria for a just war.[12] One hundred Christian scholars of ethical theory issued the following statement: "As Christian ethicists, we share a common

---

[10]   Traditional just-war theory is based on six *jus ad bellum* principles that are concerned with establishing the moral justification for engaging in violence. They are 1) just cause, 2) legitimate authority to declare hostilities, 3) just intention, 4) reasonable chance of success, 5) proper announcement of beginning hostilities, and 6) the means used being proportional to the desired objective. In addition, two *jus in bello* principles apply for how violence is to be morally conducted. These principles are 1) determining legitimate targets, and 2) how much force is morally appropriate.

[11]   Pope Gregory VII (1073–1085) assured combatants engaged in "holy" war that they would be forgiven from the consequences of their sins.

[12]   The notable exception was Richard Land, president of the Ethics and Religious Liberty Commission of the Southern Baptist Convention. The Convention, as a whole, supported the war in Iraq. Its decision was greatly influenced by its unwavering support for Israel.

moral presumption against a pre-emptive war on Iraq by the United States."[13] Likewise, the United States Conference of Catholic Bishops issued a statement on November 13, 2002, urging the president not to engage in a preventive attack on Iraq.

Nonetheless, other ethicists believed that the conflict in Iraq met the demands of Christianity's just-war doctrine, most notably, Jean Bethke Elshtain and Michael Novak.[14] While it would not be appropriate to question the sincerity of these ethicists in arriving at their conclusions, it is reasonable to explore if just-war theory can conclusively indicate the correct ethical path. Why were two different conclusions reached after following the same precepts of just war theory? One significant observation that can be made is that even though ethicists employed the same just-war theory, they still arrived at different conclusions, partly because they approached the dilemma from diverse social locations. All had a certain prior bias that prevented them from being completely objective. In addition, even if some sort of objectivity could have been achieved by those employing the just-war theory, history has demonstrated that clerics are often used by politicians or governments to manipulate believers to either support or oppose war.

Can violence ever be harnessed for good and/or declared just? Violence is not a political tool that can be picked up and used, and then put down later, never to be used again. The use of violence forever changes a person and a society. Generally, those engaged in violence and the hate it unleashes become unfit for the process of creating a new, just social order. The biblical text attributes the

---

[13] Shaun Casey, a just-war ethicist, and Stanley Hauerwas, a pacifist, prepared the statement and circulated it among ethicists of different theological and political leaning. I was one of the signatories.

[14] Novak, a Roman Catholic philosopher, argued that the conflict with Iraq was not a "preventative war," but the "lawful conclusion" of the 1991 Gulf War that attempted to enforce the disarmament terms Iraq accepted at the close of that conflict. Elshtain, a Protestant social ethics professor, argued that Christians have a moral duty to defend the innocent. Those brutalized by Saddam's regime and the neighboring countries threatened by the regime constituted the innocent, which requires U.S. military involvement. See Richard N. Ostling, "Against Widespread Clergy Protest, Some Lay Christians Justify War Against Iraq," *The Associated Press*, February 26, 2003.

prohibition on King David's building a temple for God in Jerusalem to his use of violence, "[shedding] abundant blood and [fighting] great wars" (1 Chr. 22:8).

At times is violence the only option? Thomas Schubeck provides the example of a homeowner who confronts a burglar in the very act of robbing the homeowner's prized possessions. The homeowner has two options: he can either recognize the humanity of the burglar as a troubled person and begin a dialogue based on a genuine interest in the burglar's well-being, or he can see the burglar as a thief who needs to be physically expelled from the premises by whatever means necessary. While the former may be closer to the gospel call to turn the other cheek or forgo the spare cloak, the latter takes into account other considerations, specifically, protecting one's family or one's self from the possible violence the burglar may inflict (1993:70).

Nevertheless, while those of the dominant culture continue to struggle with the issue of whether violence can be ethically employed, for the maginalized violence is a reality. Internationally, violence continues to be used to secure financial markets and financial gain, and the United States has engaged in violence for this purpose. For example, ethicist Charles Kammer reminds us that when the former Soviet Union invaded Afghanistan, it was viewed as a savage act depriving Afghans of their right to self-determination. However, when the United States has overthrown governments, some of which have been democratically elected, it has been labeled an act of liberation, even when the end result was the installation of a brutal, undemocratic, unpopular regime (1988:27, 143). It seems that the primary difference between the actions of the Soviet Union and the U.S. is that the aggressive international acts of the latter were cloaked in moral rhetoric, sometimes justified by the use of just-war theory.

Aggressive acts can also entail lopsided trade agreements in which, as purchasers of the world's resources and labor, the U.S. sets deflated prices or engages in war when what is considered the U.S. birthright to those resources is jeopardized by other nation-states. If "our" oil supplies are threatened, we have no qualms about sending military forces to protect the continuous flow of oil, all the while claiming to engage in a crusade to uproot Islamic terrorism.

Can any war be just, if war represents Satan's triumph over the love called for by Christ? Are all wars morally reprehensible, but pardonable? Can the conditions for a just war ever be obtained? Regardless of moral discussions that take place within the dominant culture, one fact remains constant: those on the periphery of power are seldom consulted, even though they are disproportionately on the receiving end of the violence of war. It also seems today that while pacifism is an ethical option, absolute pacifism may be unattainable. There are differences between killing someone as an offensive strategy, defending oneself from violence inflicted by an oppressor, or protecting the most vulnerable from certain death at the hands of an oppressor. If forced to engage in violence, is it better to recognize it for the evil it is and rely on God's grace for forgiveness than to try to reason through the gospel message in order to justify war-like actions by using just-war type theory?

Can non-violence ever succeed as a strategy in the international arena? At the close of the first World War, the Versailles Peace Treaty sought revenge from Germany, creating an atmosphere that eventually led to the second World War. By the close of World War II, the lesson had been learned. Rather than punish Germany and Japan for the violence they unleashed, the United States embraced their enemies by re-building their nations. The result was strong allies that continue to stand the test of time.

Yet, at the close of the first Gulf War, the United States imposed an embargo on Iraq that brought the death of thousands of Iraqis, mostly children. How then can we convince an Iraqi mother and her starving child of the moral superiority of Christianity? How can we convince her not to hate us? The *imago Dei* of the enemy must be recognized at all levels of conflict, for the enemy is also created in the image of God and thus has dignity and worth. This is as true for the Afghan or Iraqi populations as it is for people in the United States.

Generally less value is given to those who are marginalized within an empire. As noted above, those who live on the margins of society are never consulted in the decision process about going to war. To go or not to go to war is determined in the halls of power, with an eye toward the geo-political gains of such an encounter. It is not the Amerindian living on a reservation, the African American relegated to the urban ghetto, or the Latina/o of this country's borderlands who is calling for more missiles, aircraft carriers, or the latest fighter jet. Ethical debates concerning what makes a war just may have validity among ethicists of the dominant culture, but for the masses who live under the strain of racism and classism, such debates are irrelevant.

Although some multinational corporations such as Bechtel and Halliburton stand to benefit financially from the war, others, specifically those who are economically disenfranchised, suffer during the preparation for war. Increases in military spending are directly related to increases in the poverty rate. Increased military spending during peacetime has a direct relationship to increased unemployment, which is clearly linked to increased poverty.[15] High military spending in advanced industrial economies diverts capital to non-growth-producing sectors, crowding out investments, reducing productivity, and increasing unemployment. Additionally, the increase in defense spending, financed through deficit spending, creates an inflationary impact on the economy that disproportionately harms the poor, contributing to an increase in income inequality (Abell 1990:405–19; idem 1994:35–43; Henderson 1998:503–20). In short, while war financially benefits the nation's elite class, the preparation for war further devastates the poor.

STEP 3. PRAYING

According to the biblical text, in some cases God commands war, even against Israel, while at other times God forbids war, even to protect Israel. In the Hebrew Bible, the violence caused by war is condoned some of the time and condemned at other times. Within the New Testament Jesus abhors violence, yet he warns of the violence that will be committed against those who follow him to the cross. All too often, the commitment of the believer to follow Jesus' example leads to violence. However, violence should never be accepted as a necessary evil, nor rejected as antithetical to Jesus (he clearly used violence to cleanse the temple and prophesied the violence of the Day of Judgment).

---

[15] Yet, it is important to note that increased military spending during wartime has the reverse effect, decreasing poverty.

Violence seems to be a reality today, and often arises from challenges to the dominant culture's grip on power. Such violence can be immediate or drawn out, as in the case of institutional violence, such as the economic forces that foster ghettos and barrios. Governments act violently when they maintain social structures that inflict prolonged harm or injury upon a segment of the population and that segment is usually disenfranchised due to race or economic standing. The choice facing the believer is whether to participate in the use of violence or to advocate non-violent resistance to oppressive structures. As Gustavo Gutiérrez reminds us, it is important to distinguish between "the unjust violence of the oppressors (who maintain this despicable system) with the just violence of the oppressed (who feel obligated to use it to achieve their liberation)" (1988:64). Not only does Gutiérrez distinguish between the two types of violence, but he also questions the prevailing double standards that exist. He writes, "We cannot say that the violence is all right when the oppressor uses it to maintain or preserve 'order,' but wrong when the oppressed use it to overthrow this same 'order'" (1984:28).

To remain silent or to do nothing in the face of violence is to participate in it by complicity. At times, in the face of the violence being committed upon the marginalized, some purposely remain silent or speak their disapproval in muted voices, lest they jeopardize their privileged space. How then should disenfranchised Christians react to the constant institutional violence they face?

When asked if counter-violence is ever an option for Christians, Gustavo Gutiérrez, along with other liberation theologians, reminds us that violence already exists in the hands of the oppressor. Thus, the question is not if Christians should utilize violence, but, rather, do Christians have a right to defend themselves from the already existing violence. For example, biblical scholar George Pixley maintains that the massacre of Egypt's first born can be understood as a terrorist act, an act inspired by God (1987:80). He goes on to note Moses' violent act of killing an Egyptian, a member of the dominant culture, for striking a Hebrew slave, a member of a marginalized group (Ex. 2:11–22). This act appeared justified even though a future commandment received by Moses would state, "Thou shall not kill." Pixley suggests that certain exceptions to the fifth commandment exist, such as capital punishment or the killing of enemies in times of war. Pixley also implies that the preferential option for the oppressed may lead to the act of taking life. Moses' killing of the Egyptian could be seen as a defensive act to protect the life of the marginalized. And it appears as if God (the ultimate Defender of the oppressed) accepts Moses in later years, justifying Moses' earlier use of violence for the sake of defending the oppressed (1987:8–9).

During the period of slavery in the United States, many slave rebellions were violent and bloody, most notably the 1831 revolt in Southampton, Virginia, led by Nat Turner. As a preacher, Turner believed that God directed him to live out his faith through actions that could lead to the liberation of the slaves. Biblical authority for such action was seen in the Exodus story of slave liberation from the tyranny of Pharaoh. Slaves had a moral obligation to find liberation by whatever means possible.

Interpreting scripture in this way has led theologians like José Míguez Bonino to support violence (even revolution), when employed to protect the humanity of the marginalized (1975: 116–18). If the oppression of the marginalized is maintained through institutionalized violence, that is, through social structures designed to privilege the few at the expense of the many, then any hope of finding salvation or liberation from the status quo will inevitably confront those same social structures. History has demonstrated that denouncing unjust social structures is simply not enough, for those accustomed to power and privilege will never willingly abdicate what they consider to be a birthright. Some ethicists from the margins maintain that violence, when employed by the marginalized to overcome their own oppression, is in reality self-defense and can never be confused with the continuing violence employed by those in power.

Accordingly, some advocate a quest for liberation "by any means possible." They argue that to wash one's hands of violence is to allow violence to be done to the marginalized. Latin American theologian Juan Luís Segundo recognizes that while all violence is evil, not all decisions to use violence are unethical. *Agape* (unconditional love) for the very least among us might lead a person, in an unselfish act, to stand in solidarity with the oppressed in their battle for self-preservation. Protecting a "non-person" might invite a violent confrontation as the oppressor, feeling backed into a corner, may fight tooth and nail to maintain the status quo. Persons making a preferential option to love the oppressed may very well find themselves harming the oppressor.

Unfortunately, the call for non-violence may come from those who wish to maintain the unjust status quo. Writing in 1969 during the height of racial unrest and the Vietnam War, James Cone astutely observed:

> It is interesting that so many advocates of nonviolence as the only possible Christian response of black people to white domination are also the most ardent defenders of the right of the police to put down black rebellion through violence. Another interesting corollary is their defense of America's right to defend violently the government of South Vietnam against the North. Somehow, I am unable to follow the reasoning. (1969:138–39)

For Cone, African Americans, along with other "unwanted minorities," were placed in a situation in which only one option was made available to them, "deciding whose violence [will be] supported—that of the oppressors or the oppressed. . . . Either we side with the oppressed . . . in a dehumanized society, or we stand with the President or whoever is defending the white establishment for General Motors and U.S. Steel" (1975:219). No middle ground, Cone insisted, was available.

Can the renouncement of violence to bring about liberation only lead to greater injustices? Daniel Bell argues:

> The offer of redemption that comes to humanity in Christ is an offer that is unmerited, undeserved. . . . In this sense, . . . redemption is an act of injustice. God is patently unjust, refusing to deal with humanity in the manner it deserves. What is due fallen humanity is death, yet God in God's grace gives life. . . . One could argue that God redeems humanity *from* justice. (2001:131)

Forgiveness does not come after the sinner repents, rather, forgiveness makes repentance possible. "While we were still sinners," Paul reminds us, "Christ died for us" (Rom. 5:8). It should not, therefore, be surprising that the early Christian community (pre-

Constantine) maintained an absolute prohibition on violence, even to the point of refusing to fight the Romans when Jerusalem was burned and sacked in 70 C.E. Warfare was understood to be a denial of Jesus' message to love one's enemies and a rejection of the life he asked his disciples to follow. For the early church, while Jesus Christ may not have been a zealot, he was a revolutionary leading a revolution to be won through his crucifixion. Not until 313 C.E., when Christianity became the state religion and took on political power under Constantine, was it necessary to develop concepts for just war to maintain the empire.

For Martin Luther King, Jr., the aim of non-violence was the creation of a relationship with the oppressors in the hopes that they too could be redeemed by God's grace. He rejected Niebuhr's understanding of pacifism as an unrealistic submission to evil power, insisting instead that it is better to be the recipient of violence than the inflicter of it (1958:98).[16] King did not advocate passivity, rather he called for an active confrontation with injustice. Nonviolence was the embodiment of the Christian ideal of *agape*, an unconditional love that confronts the aggressor so that he or she can also learn the gospel demand for *agape*.

Pragmatically, Martin Luther King, Jr., insisted that the use of violence by the marginalized only encourages the oppressor (who controls the tools of torture) to unleash even greater violence, leading to a never-ending spiral of hatred. He maintained that violence only provokes greater retribution, and those without arms will find themselves at a greater disadvantage. Rather than continuing the cycle of violence, King looked toward the radical love advocated by Christ as the solution to oppression. He wrote: "Returning hate for hate multiplies hate, adding deeper darkness to a night already devoid of stars. Darkness cannot drive out darkness; only light can do that. Hate cannot drive out hate; only love can do that. Hate multiplies hate, violence multiples violence, and toughness multiplies toughness in a descending spiral of destruction" (1963:37).

---

[16] There are basically two types of pacifists. The "absolute" pacifist renounces violence under every circumstance, and the "contextual" pacifist looks for acts of nonviolent resistance, reserving the option that under exceptional circumstances, violence may be a necessary alternative.

1980 Nobel Peace laureate Adolfo Pérez Esquivel pointed to the Plaza de Mayo mothers as a paragon that best illustrated the responsibilities of Christians.[17] For Esquivel, Christians, using Jesus as model, must refuse to carry out violence, even though seeking to transform humanity will probably lead to violent upheaval. He was adamant that terrorism, despite its source, is an attack on a human being, thus on humanity and thus on God. He questioned armed liberation movements, fearing that today's oppressed would become tomorrow's oppressors. For him, revolutions that programmatically embraced violence risk their own undoing (1983:71–72).

For social activist César Chávez, those involved in something constructive tend to refrain from violence, while those not committed to the rebuilding of a more just order tend to advocate the more destructive path of violence. Chávez insisted that non-violence requires greater courage and militancy. He once said, "I am not a nonviolent man. I am a violent man who is trying to be nonviolent" (Dalton 2003:120).

In short, those who are familiar with the violence of the oppressor must seriously consider the admonition of ethicist Major J. Jones, who wrote: "Every Christian who accepts Jesus Christ as [their] example will have to deal with the ultimate question as to whether [to take] the principle of the sanctity of life so seriously that [they] would rather give [their] own life than take the life of another, even when the other is the aggressor" (1974:171).

STEP 4. CASE STUDIES

- 1. Camilo Mejia is a permanent U.S. resident who joined the armed forces eight years ago but is now facing deportation because he sought conscientious objector status. With the rank of staff sergeant, Camilio Mejia served for five months in the

---

[17] Argentine mothers of those who "disappeared" during that country's "dirty war" would gather regularly in the early 1980s at the Plaza de Mayo across from the federal complex in Buenos Aires in a silent demonstration. They silently held a family picture with the caption "Where is my child?" Many of them also disappeared; however, they are credited with turning the tide and ushering in a new Argentina.

2003 war in Iraq. During his tour of duty he and others were ambushed and innocent civilians were hit in the ensuing gunfire. After a leave of absence, he refused to report for duty. Instead he turned himself in to military authorities, refusing to fight anymore. "This is an oil-driven war, and I don't think any soldier signs up to fight for oil. . . . There's no such thing as a fair war, no such thing as a just war," said Mejia.[18]

Some forty years before, Martin Luther King, Jr., proclaimed that the United States was the "greatest purveyor of violence in the world today" (1986:636). Since 1980, the United States has been involved in at least ten military conflicts throughout the world: 1) the war in Lebanon, 1982–1983; 2) Nicaragua: the Contra Wars, 1982–1990; 3) Grenada: Operation Urgent Fury, 1983; 4) Panama: Operation Just Cause, 1989; 5) Iraq: the Gulf War, 1991; 6) Yugoslav Wars, 1992–1999; 7) the Somalia War, 1993; 8) Haiti: Operation Uphold Democracy, 1994; 9) Afghanistan, 2002; and, 10) Iraq, 2003.

— Does Camilo Mejia have the right to renounce his military oath? Does he have an obligation to complete his military duty?
— Can soldiers choose in what wars they will participate? Why or why not?
— Is Mejia's decision not to fight, even at the cost of possible deportation, morally correct for him?
— Was Martin Luther King, Jr., correct in his characterization of the United States? Why or why not?
— Which of these ten wars can be considered "just wars?" Who was the aggressor?

• 2. Rufina Amaya is a poor, middle-aged woman who lived in El Mozote, a small village in El Salvador. On December 11, 1981, government soldiers entered the village and ordered all inhabitants into the streets. Roughly nine hundred civilians, composed mostly of women and children, were shot at point blank. Amaya, who witnessed the event, survived because she was able to hide among some bushes. Recounting her experi-

---

[18] Erik Schelzig, "Soldier: 'I Have Not Committed a Crime,'" *The Grand Rapids Press*, March 16, 2004.

ence, she says, "I heard the screams of the children, and I knew which ones were mine, they were crying, 'Mommy, they're killing us!'"[19] Ten of the twelve officers responsible for the massacre of El Mozote, were trained by the U.S. military. Located in Fort Benning, Georgia, the Western Hemisphere Institute on Security Cooperation (WHISC, formerly known as the School of the Americas) has trained over sixty thousand Latin American soldiers in commando operations, psychological warfare, and counter-insurgency techniques. In the past, training manuals produced by the Pentagon for WHISC and made public through the Freedom of Information Act advocated executions, torture, false arrest, blackmail, censorship, payment of bounty for murders, and other forms of physical abuse against enemies.[20] Among the graduates of the school were two of the three officers cited for the assassination of Archbishop Romero, three of the four officers cited in the rape and murder of the four U.S. church women, the founder of El Salvador's death squads (D'Aubuisson), nineteen of the twenty-six officers cited in the murder of six Jesuit priests, their housekeeper and her teenage daughter; and the brutal military dictators that formerly ruled Bolivia, Argentina, Guatemala, Panama, El Salvador, and Honduras. Rufina Amaya, the lone survivor of the massacre of El Mozote, concludes, "The only thing the School of the Americas has accomplished is the destruction of our countries in Latin America."

— What responsibility, if any, does the U.S. have toward Rufina Amaya? Can the U.S. government be held responsible for

---

[19] *School of Assassins*, a documentary produced by Maryknoll World Productions, 1995.

[20] A U.S. Congressional Task Force, headed by Representative Joseph Moakley, concluded that those responsible for many of the government-led massacres in Latin America had been trained by the U.S. Army at Fort Benning, Georgia. According to Representative Joseph Kennedy, "The Pentagon revealed [through these training manuals] what activists opposed to the school have been alleging for years — that foreign military officers were taught to torture and murder, [in order] to achieve their political objective" (Nelson-Pallmeyer 2001:2–5).

the actions of Latin American soldiers, trained by the U.S. military, who commit atrocities against humanity? Why or why not?

— What, if any, are the ethical ramifications of supporting this institution through U.S. tax dollars?

— Is it ethical for the U.S. to maintain a school with a history of conducting terrorist acts in Latin America even though leaders at the school insist that they are no longer engaged in such activities? Why or why not?

- 3. Abdul Hakim Murad, a Pakistani, was arrested in 1995 in his Manila apartment. Police found gallons of sulfuric and nitric acid, along with beakers, filters, funnels and fuses — in short, a bomb-making factory. On his home computer were El Qaeda plans to blow up eleven commercial airliners, one of which was to fly into CIA headquarters. Murad divulged names, dates, and places after extensive and brutal torture.

  Some ethicists allow for torture to obtain information. For example in *The City of God*, Augustine, the original author of just-war theory, condones torturing the innocent in order to obtain information (6:19:6). Generally, there are two types of torture. The first encompasses psychological techniques to disorient and wear down the prisoner, such as sleep deprivation, exposure to extreme temperatures, withholding medical treatment, or sitting in painful and uncomfortable positions for long periods of time. The second includes physical violence.

  Although the first form is employed with prisoners held by the U.S. on its naval base at Guantanamo, military and government officials denied the use of hard torture, until the Abu Ghraib prison photos became public. Still, Kenneth Roth, executive director of Human Rights Watch, noted that the United States has been handing over some suspects to countries like Egypt, Saudi Arabia, and Jordan that were not averse to employing physical torture to gain information that could be passed along to the U.S.[21] These transfers are a clear violation of American laws and the 1984 international convention that bans such transfers.

---

[21] Ibid.; see also Peter Maass, "Torture, Tough or Lite," *The New York Times*, March 9, 2003.

— Is it ethical to participate in physical torture to safeguard national security? What about psychological torture?

— Is it ethical for the U.S. to obtain vital information obtained through physical torture conducted by other countries? Why or why not?

— Are the acts of torture which took place at the Abu Ghraib prison justifiable if they lead to valuable information? Is torture to obtain information that can lead to less U.S. casualties a necessary evil of war? Is the punishment being meted out to those who participated in the acts of torture necessary or sufficient?

- 4. Just-war theorists condone the use of violence on behalf of people who are suffering from unjust violence. In the event of injustices resulting in death of a group of people, an outside state can justly intervene, or the oppressed can band together and wage a just revolution. Consider the history of the United States, specifically in its treatment of African Americans during slavery, the genocide of Native Americans during territorial expansion, and the pauperization of Latino/as during the U.S. wars of conquest (the Mexican-American War of 1846 and the Spanish American War of 1898).

    — Can an argument be made that acts of violence against euroamericans, such as Nat Turner's Rebellion, the Indian uprising at Little Big Horn, or Pancho Villa's border raids, were sanctioned by God under just war theory?

    — Given the disastrous consequences of the institutional violence of racism, is Malcolm X justified in calling for liberation by "any means possible?" Are the race riots in Miami, Los Angeles, Cincinnati, and Benton Harbor, Michigan, justified? If so, why? If not, why not?

- 5. During 2003, the Liberian government of President Charles Taylor was overthrown by the forces of Liberians United for Reconciliation and Democracy (LURD). Both sides in the conflict gave military weapons to children. Up to 60 percent of the armed fighters were under the age of eighteen, with several soldiers being as young as nine. While boys were plied with drugs and alcohol to take away the fear of fighting, young girls were forced to provide these soldiers with sex.[22] Most of the weapons used by these children are made in the United States. According to a study conducted by the Congressional Research Service, an arm of the Library of Congress, in 2001 the United States ranked first in arms sales, totaling $9.7 billion worldwide. The U.S. share of all arms deliveries worldwide in 2001 was 45.6 percent, up from 41.6 percent in 2000. Additionally, the U.S. led in arms transfer agreements, which were valued at $12.1 billion, representing 45.8 percent of all such transfers (Grimmett 2002:70–78). The United States is the major exporter of lethal weapons, selling the mechanisms by which so many of the world's marginalized die.

— Does the U.S., or any other country for that matter, have an ethical responsibility if it provides weapons to nations, specifically nations that inflict violence on its people?
— Do concerns for national security or the "war against terrorism" override concerns for the marginalized's human rights?
— Is the selling of arms simply a business transaction between a producer and a consumer? If so, do ethical responsibilities for the use of those arms rest solely with those who purchase the merchandise? Why or why not?

[22] "Use of Child Soldiers on the Rise," *CNN News*, broadcast August 5, 2003.

CHAPTER 7

Environment

STEP 1. OBSERVING

Lawrence H. Summers was the World Bank's chief economist and vice president for development economics from 1990 until 1993. He left the World Bank to serve as under-secretary of the U.S. Treasury Department during the Clinton administration. He was the Bank's "high priest" responsible for supervising all economic publications, including the pace-setting *World Development Report*. Commenting on the topic of "dirty industries," the theme discussed in one of the publications he oversaw, he wrote a memo to six highly placed colleagues. This private memo was eventually leaked to the press. In it, he wrote:

> Just between you and me, shouldn't the World Bank be encouraging *more* migration of the dirty industries to LDCs (Less Developed Countries)? . . . The measure of the costs of health impairing pollution depends on the foregone earnings from increased morbidity and mortality. From this point of view a given amount of health impairing pollution should be done in the country with the lowest cost, which will be the country with the lowest wages. I think the economic logic behind dumping a load of toxic waste in the lowest wage country is impeccable and we should face up to that. . . . I've always thought that underpopulated countries in Africa are vastly *under*polluted, their air quality is probably vastly inefficiently low compared to Los Angeles or Mexico City. (George and Sabelli 1994:98–100)

In other words, if "a load of toxic waste" is dumped in a rich country, it would cause the infirmity and death of high wage earners with normally long life expectancies. According to Summers's own publication, $20,000 per year of potential earnings for a forty-year-old with an estimated twenty-five more years of productivity can contribute $500,000 to the global economy. By contrast, if the "load of toxic waste" is dumped in a poor country with a GNP of $360 and average life expectancy of fifty-five years, the contribution of a worker to the global economy could be figured at a measly $5,400 (ibid.). Such an approach reduces humans to their economic value; people of eurocentric origins nearly always possess economic privilege that are worth more than the disenfranchised. The sacredness of profits replaces the sacredness of life. Death-causing pollutants, therefore, should be "dumped" in poor countries, perpetuating the old patterns of colonialism and imperialism. This link between the domination of the earth and the domination of the disenfranchised has been termed environmental racism.[1] Concerns for the environment include groundwater pollution, acid rain, deforestation, global warming, ozone depletion, toxic and chemical spills, strip mining, and a host of other calamities.

Most affected by environmental blight are people living on the margins of privilege. As transnational corporations race for the lowest wage (Chapter 5), they also compete to identify locations with few or no regulations governing pollution or safe working environments. Energy production is one striking example. Within the United States, energy companies face intense pressure to produce power safely with a minimum of negative effects on the environment.

Across the Mexican border few environmental regulations or oversight exist. On the edge of the city of Mexicali, a few miles from the California border, two huge power plants were constructed in 2002. One was built by InterGen, which is owned by Bechtel Corporation and Shell. The two plants are expected to generate billions of watts of electricity for millions of Californians.

---

[1] The term "environmental racism" was first coined in the 1980s by Benjamin Chavis, a minister and chair of the Committee on Racial Justice for the United Church of Christ (Baker-Fletcher 1998:4).

Ironically, as its need for energy increases and electricity bills double, Mexico will witness the power produced at its expense being exported to California. In return, Mexico can expect to gain a few jobs (paying about $2 an hour on a monthly contract) and a great deal of pollution. The plant is expected to pollute the air and water of Mexicali, as well as the neighboring Imperial Valley of California that lies across the border. Not surprisingly, California's Imperial Valley is a heavily Latino/a region.[2] These energy *maquiladoras* represent a new form of environmental imperialism where energy is literally generated for the U.S. by capitalizing on lax environmental regulations on the other side of the border.

An increase in environmental pollution is also seen in the growing energy needs and industrialization of China. Figures released in 2003 by the Chinese government confirm that coal use has climbed faster in China (the world's largest coal consumer) than anywhere else in the world. Coupled with soaring car sales,[3] China's emission of greenhouse gases (the second largest emitter of such gases after the U.S.) is threatening international efforts to curb global warming. The International Energy Agency in Paris predicts that the greenhouse gas emissions from 2000 to 2030 in China alone will nearly equal the increase from the entire industrialized world.[4]

A good part of China's growth in energy consumption is due to China's emergence as a leading exporter of manufacturing goods to the United States. A desire to minimize labor costs, along with the cost of adhering to basic environmental regulations makes China attractive to multinational corporations. One of the many exports of China is inexpensive jewelry made from iridescent stones like opals. Working for less than a dollar an hour for twelve to eighteen hours a day, with no health-care benefits, employment contracts, or union representatives, workers inhale more quartz dust

---

[2] Tim Weiner, "U.S. Will Get Power, and Pollution, from Mexico," *The New York Times*, September 17, 2002.

[3] General Motors predicts China will represent 18 percent of the world's growth in new car sales from 2002 to 2012. The U.S. will represent 11 percent and India 9 percent of said growth.

[4] Keith Bradsher, "China's Boom Adds to Global Warming Problem," *The New York Times*, October 22, 2003.

in ten years than China's safety standards allow over a thousand-year period. As a result, jewelry workers in Shuang Tu, a small town in the rugged hill country of China, experience a surge in fatal respiratory, circulatory, neurological, and digestive illnesses. According to official Chinese statistics, more deaths from such work-related diseases occur in China than in the industrialized economies of Europe and the United States combined.[5] The producers of today's neoliberalism are beginning to equal the horrors suffered by workers during the dawn of the industrial age.

Not all of what is wrong with the environment can be blamed on industrialization. World poverty also has a negative effect on the environment. Take Africa as an example. During the 1990s, Africa had the world's highest rate of deforestation as the poor cut down trees for firewood, their only source of fuel. As poor Africans burned firewood and coal to keep warm and cook, the level of air pollutants rose to three times the health standard. 30 percent of sub-Saharan children in 2002 died or were disabled by acute respiratory infections caused by the reliance on coal and firewood. The situation is aggravated as migration to urban shantytowns from rural villages increases. A direct link exists between poverty and the environment. Nations that suffer from massive poverty are simply unable to safeguard their natural resources.[6]

The United States is not immune to the negative ecological effects of environmental racism, here defined as the link between the degradation of the environment and the racial composition of the areas where degradation takes place. Within the U.S., race is the most significant variable in determining the location of commercial, industrial, and military hazardous-waste sites. A growing body of empirical evidence suggests the existence of environmental racism within the United States. An analysis of data that correlates census data (1990) with the number of toxic sites within each county reveals a consistent relationship between the presence of toxic waste sites and/or generators and the race or ethnicity of people living in those counties (Maher 1998:363). The poorer the

---

[5] Joseph Kahn, "Making Trinkets in China, and a Deadly Dust," *The New York Times*, June 18, 2003.

[6] Rachel L. Swarns, "Poverty and Environment on Agenda," *The New York Times*, August 26, 2002.

community, the greater the risk of environmental abuse. The economically able move away from such sites, a privilege not available to the poor, who are mostly people of color. The three sites that account for more than 40 percent of U.S. disposal capacity are situated in Latino and African American communities. Consequently, three out of every five Hispanics or African Americans live in an environment polluted with uncontrolled toxic waste (Hamilton 1993:67). In addition, about half of all Asian/Pacific Islanders and Native Americans live in communities with uncontrolled waste sites (Bouma-Prediger 2004:Chap.23). Black ethicist Emilie Townes has said that the effects of toxic waste on the lives of people of color who are relegated due to their poverty to live on ecologically hazardous lands are akin to a contemporary version of lynching a whole people (1995:55).

Environmental racism is not limited to the dumping of hazardous waste. A comprehensive study conducted by the *National Law Journal* during the early 1990s showed that violators of pollution laws received less stringent punishments when violations occurred in non-white neighborhoods than when they occurred in white neighborhoods; fines were often 500 percent higher in white communities than in marginalized communities. The study also discovered that when violations occurred in minority communities, the government was slower to act, taking as much as 20 percent more time, than when violations occurred in white communities.[7] And when a lawsuit was brought before the Eastern District Federal Court of Virginia about the placement of landfills in predominantly black King and Queen counties (*RISE v. Kay*), the U.S. judge acknowledged the historical trend of disproportionately placing landfills in African American areas but still ruled that the case failed to prove discrimination (Bullard 1993:28).

Environmental racism takes a heavy toll among children of color. For example, lead poisoning affects four million children in the U.S., most of whom are African Americans and Latina/os. African American children are two to three times more likely to suffer from lead poisoning than their white counterparts. Although ingesting paint chips is a major cause of lead poisoning among children whose

---

[7] Marianne Lavelle, "Discrimination Probe Planned," *National Law Journal*, September 28, 1992.

parents are too poor to afford to move, even when parents laboriously remove all paint chips, the lead dust remaining in the air is sufficient to continue the poisoning process. Lead poisoning results in behavioral difficulties, low attention span, and limited verbal skills (Bullard 1993:26).

It is no coincidence that the predominantly black neighborhood of central Harlem in New York City has the highest percentage of documented cases of asthma in the United States. One out of every four children suffers from asthma, an inflammation and constriction of the airways that makes breathing difficult. The worst triggers of asthma are found in abundance in central Harlem (and the South Bronx), specifically insect droppings, mold, mildew, diesel exhaust, and cigarette smoke.[8]

The military is also a major threat to the environment where people of color reside. Of the 651 nuclear weapons or devices exploded on the U.S. mainland by the military, all test sites occurred in Native American territories (Seager 1993:63). The vast majority of these detonations occurred on the lands of the Shoshone nation (LaDuke 1993:99). Uranium, used for atomic weapons, is mined mostly in Navajo territory. Worldwide, 70 percent of all uranium resources are located on indigenous lands. Even though most U.S. uranium mines are presently abandoned, they can still emit high levels of radioactive gases. One of the ingredients of the solid waste from uranium milling is radium 226, which remains radioactive for at least 16,000 years (LaDuke 1993:99, 102). It is reported that Navajo teenagers have a rate of organ cancer seventeen times the national average (Hamilton 1993:71).

People of color also suffer from environmental hazards in the workplace; because of discrimination, they are often relegated to the most perilous of jobs. The myth that people with darker skin have a greater ability to withstand heat was used to justify assigning African Americans to work at the extremely dangerous coke ovens in the iron and steel industry. Similarly, within the electronic industries, "darker" workers have been regularly assigned jobs dealing with caustic chemicals. The rationale used is that skin

---

8 Richard Pérez-Peña, "Study Finds Asthma in 25% of Children in Central Harlem," *The New York Times*, April 19, 2003.

irritations caused by chemical exposure are less pronounced on dark skin than on white skin (Wright & Bullard 1993:155, 157).

Finally, since stress is known to be a major cause of illnesses, the environment and work assignments delegated to people of color contribute to lower life expectancies. Such social factors as poverty and the environmental hazards it attracts are beyond the control of individuals. They certainly contribute to hypertension (elevated blood pressure), a major cause of organ damage and heart disease, within the African American community, resulting in hypertension rates in the black community twice as high as within the white community. And hypertension is not a genetic given among African Americans; in some other countries, hypertension rates are lower among blacks than among whites (ibid.:156–57).

In the final analysis, Lawrence H. Summers, the former chief economist of the World Bank, enunciated the neoliberal position when he said, "Promoting development is the best way to protect the environment" (George & Sabelli 1994:170). Those from the margins of society who experience "a load of toxic waste" dumped upon them in the name of development might have a different opinion.

STEP 2. REFLECTING

Generally speaking, eurocentric theology has concerned itself with the relationship between the Deity and humans, as well as with relationships among humans. The prominent eurocentric thread within Christianity, as practiced by the powerful and privileged, has created a faith with little connection to or understanding of a collective or communal spirituality. Nor has much attention been given to the relationship between humans and creaturekind.[9] For the most part, the environment has been seen as a means of satisfying the wants and desires of human beings. Human beings, viewing themselves as the center of the created order, have historically perceived the environment as an unlimited storehouse

---

[9] I am influenced by Carter Heyward who uses the term "creaturekind" to refer to all that God has created that is other than human, meaning animals, plants, and minerals. While the term encompasses humans, Heyward struggles for language that avoids defining all God created that is not human as "other-than-human" (2004:Chap.2).

of raw materials provided by God for human convenience. Thus, the resources of the earth have often been sacrificed in the quest for economic growth.

Yet all that has life is sacred before the Creator of life, making it difficult to limit spiritual worthiness and well-being only to human beings. Native Americans remind us that within the circle of creation, all are equal in value to the Creator. Tink Tinker expresses this view when he writes, "A chief is not valued above the people; nor are two-legged valued above the animal nations, the birds, or even trees and rocks" (1994:126). Human beings' relationships to creation become a matter of life and death, balancing one's needs and place within the world with preserving the world for one's descendants who will live "seven generations from now." While one takes from the plenty of creation, something must always be returned to maintain balance (Kidwell et al. 2001:33). Others, such as Indian scholar Aruna Gnanadason, totally reject the dualism intrinsic in Western theological thought, which sees an opposition between the spirit and flesh, men and women, or mind and body. She instead avers a cosmology that affirms the interdependence and harmony of all life forms (1996:77). Instead of a binary opposition, many Asian theologians like Kwok Pui-lan emphasize the balance of "heaven and earth, yang and ying, sun and moon, and father and mother" where they are "complementally, mutually reinforcing and interplaying with one other" (2000:90).

The earth's resources, as we are slowly learning, are not everlasting. Proper stewardship requires creating a harmonious relationship with nature, as with other human beings. Poor care of the environment creates pollution, lowers life expectancy, and is a major source of many illnesses and diseases for those living close by. The exploitation of the earth's resources, and the exploitation of the earth's marginalized are interconnected, making it difficult, if not impossible, to speak of one without mentioning the other. Brazilian theologian Leonardo Boff has given voice to the cry of the oppressed, connecting it with the very cry of the earth. He insists that the logic and justification that lead the powerful and privileged to exploit and subjugate the world's marginalized are the same logic and justification that plunder the earth's wealth and lead to its devastation (1997:xi).

Some women ethicists such as Karen Warren advocate ecofeminism, an environmental theology that seeks to overcome the hierarchy and dualism imposed upon nature. She claims ecofeminism is based on four central claims: 1) there are important connections between the oppression of women and the oppression of nature; 2) there is a need to understand the nature of these connections in order to understand the oppression of women and oppression of nature; 3) feminist theory and practice must include an ecological perspective; and 4) solutions to ecological problems must include a feminist perspective (1987:4–5). The interconnectedness between women and nature has always existed. Wilderness or virgin land awaits insemination with man's seed of progress and civilization, for nature as feminine (Mother Nature) has always required its domination and domestication (De La Torre 2003b:96) or, in the words of Vandana Shiva, "a woman to be raped" (1996:69).

For Lois Daly, the ethical goal is to reconceptualize the links between oppressor and oppressed in nonhierarchical and nonpatriarchal ways. Stress is placed in living in the world as co-members of the ecological community (1994:300). While ecofeminism unmasks the interconnectedness between the oppression of women and the oppression of nature, unfortunately feminists often fail to develop fully the need to expand the paradigm to encompass marginalized groups of color. Eurocentric women, with the privilege of not living in toxic, infested neighborhoods, at times fail to consider how race and ethnicity, more so than gender, remain the main indicators of who live in ecologically hazardous areas and who do not. Karen Baker-Fletcher makes a similar observation when she writes:

> There is a tendency among middle-class eco-feminist and mainstream eco-theologians to enjoy the privilege of extensive international travel which informs their spirituality. Such a privilege enables them to have the luxury of providing a global analysis. In contrast, there are many within the U.S. environmental justice movement who would find it a luxury to leave their own neighborhoods. This is the cause of a credibility gap between theologians in the academy

and the grassroots from which liberation spirituality emerges. (2004:Chap.10)

While environmentalists from the dominant culture concern themselves mainly with issues of clean air and water and the protection of habitats of endangered species, Robert Bullard observes:

> The environmental-equity movement is an extension of the social justice movement. Environmentalists may be concerned about clean air, but may have opposing views on the construction of low-income housing in white, middle-class, suburban neighborhoods. . . . It is not surprising that mainstream environmental organizations have not been active on issues that disproportionately impact minority communities. . . . Yet, minorities are the ones accused of being ill-informed, unconcerned, and inactive on environmental issues. (1994: 128–29)

When those racially and ethnically marginalized compare the environmental quality of life of where they live with that of the larger white society, it becomes all too obvious that a link exists between polluted sites and disenfranchisement. Few white environmentalists seriously consider this link and consequently they fail to understand a major reason why pollution occurs disproportionately in certain areas. The failure of the environmental justice movement to come to terms with the inherent racism that relegates those on the margins to the greatest ecological health risks, prevents fostering a truly global, holistic approach to the environment.

Environmentalists benefitting from white privilege cannot continue to isolate ecological concerns from environmental racism. Continuing to mask environmental racism limits, if not frustrates, any attempt or hope for the liberation of humans and creaturekind alike.[10]

---

[10] Few white ethicists are attempting to learn from the margins. However, an excellent example of an effort to understand environmental problems at the margins can be found in Rosemary Radford Ruether's book *Women Healing Earth* (Orbis Books, 1996).

STEP 3. PRAYING

If the creation story describes humanity's appointment as stewards of the earth's resources, then as caretakers, human beings are called to protect, preserve, and safeguard those resources so that all can benefit and enjoy their fruits. Creation as gift means that all living creatures have a basic right to its products and no group has the right to hoard its resources. Hoarding the earth's resources upsets the delicate balance between life and the resources needed to sustain life. We in the United States, as part of the world's richest 20 percent, own 85 percent of the world's income, yet are responsible for producing 66 percent of the world's greenhouse gases, and consuming 70 percent of the world's energy. But when the global community gathered to address the collective world impact of heat-trapping gases, the United States refused to participate, walking away from the Kyoto Protocol, an international agreement to protect our planet from the effects of global warming.

Ironically, Christianity, to some degree, has encouraged the destruction of God's creation. The first creation story ends with God saying, "And God said to [human beings], be fruitful and multiply, and fill the earth, and subdue it, and have dominion over the fish of the sea, over the birds of the heavens, and over the beasts creeping on the land" (Gen. 1:28). Biblical passages such as these have led to human domination of nature. Western Christianity's understanding of stewardship and domination as the subjugating of nature has contributed to the present ecological challenges facing humanity. The belief that the destiny of human beings is to reside with God in heaven, and that the earth is but a place of sojourn until we reach that destiny, has encouraged, at the very least, neglect of our environment.

The greatest Christian threat to the environment comes from those who hold a view of the future or the end of time (an "eschatological" view) like that made popular by the LaHaye and Jenkins novels (twelve were published between 1995 and 2003). These stories focus on the tribulations faced by those unfortunate souls "left behind" during the "last days" of Armageddon (Judgment Day) when they must face the Antichrist. Many Christians who have read these novels accept the futuristic events more as prophe-

cies than fiction. These Christians may well welcome the destruction of the earth for it indicates Jesus' "second coming" when he
raptures (takes away from the earth) those destined to be saved.
If the world ends in a conflagration and such an end is close at
hand, why then worry about the environment?

This view was best articulated by James G. Watt, secretary of
the Interior under the Reagan administration and the cabinet member officially responsible for protecting the environment. He
explained that his responsibility "is to follow the Scriptures which
call upon us to occupy the land until Jesus returns."[11] Additionally, during a Congressional committee meeting in 1981, he tes-
tified, "I don't know how many future generations we can count
on until the Lord returns."[12] In short, Jesus is coming soon to res-
cue the faithful from an earth destined to total destruction. Any
attempt to preserve or safeguard the earth is a waste of time.

It seems, though, that our refusal to recognize the damage being
committed to the environment constitutes the ultimate form of
oppression, for it brings destruction to life (including human life)
on this planet. If liberation is to come to the earth's marginalized,
then it must also come to the earth. The earth needs to be saved
in order for individuals also to receive salvation. If nature is wasted,
depleted, and destroyed, then individuals will not be able to control their destiny. Such a sin cannot be easily atoned for, for we
cannot resurrect extinct species.

Scripture articulates that the earth belongs to God. The psalmist
boldly proclaims, "The earth is the Lord's, and the fullness of the
world and those who live in it" (Ps. 24:1). The God who takes
notice of the least of creation, the falling sparrow, is concerned
with all of creation. "Man" is not called to dominate the earth;
rather, human beings are called to be stewards of the earth's
resources, insuring that each person has sufficient resources to
meet his or her needs. Baker-Fletcher insists that the incarnation,
God becoming flesh, is the act of Divinity joining the dust of the

---

[11] Bill Prochnau, "The Watt Controversy," *The Washington Post*, June
30, 1981.

[12] F. Ron Wolf, "God, James Watt, and the Public Lands," *Audubon*,
Vol. 83, No. 3 (May 1981): 58–65.

earth, the very dust from which human beings were created, in order to reconcile the broken relationship between God and creation (1998:19). The abundant life Christ came to give cannot be accomplished within a depleted earth. Survival is a key requirement for any form of abundant living.

Most indigenous religions from Africa and the Americas maintain a sacred respect for creation, a respect that has been lost and historically abused by many Western Christian groups. Earth-centered religions, rooted in the abode of ancestors, are unlike Western religions that emphasize a heavenly place or stress the placement of the stars and planets to determine the course of human events. For example, in the religion of the Yoruba people in West Africa as practiced by Caribbean blacks, whites, and bi-racial Hispanics, the earth is believed to provide all that is needed to live a full and abundant life. Like the oceans that are able to support and sustain all life that exists in its waters, so too is the land able to support and sustain all life that exists upon it. This abundance becomes evident as human beings learn to live in harmony with nature. Shortages occur when humans attempt to impose their own will upon the fair and natural distribution of nature's resources according to the needs of the people (De La Torre 2004:14).

STEP 4. CASE STUDIES

- 1. In 1982, Reverend Benjamin Chavis, who served as executive director of the United Church of Christ Commission for Racial Justice (CRJ) was arrested (along with five hundred other protestors) for blocking the path of trucks carrying toxic PCBs (polychlorinated biphenyls). The toxic pollutants were on their way to a newly designated hazardous-waste landfill in Warren County, North Carolina. The landfill was located near a small southern town of predominately black residents.

  — Were Reverend Chavis's actions ethical?
  — Is his methodology in combating what he perceives to be environmental racism effective?
  — What type of ethical actions should Christians take on the placement of hazardous waste sites near predominant neighborhoods of color? Is this a black or Latina/o issue only?

— Should euroamericans, who probably live far away from such sites, be concerned with this issue? Where then should land-fills be placed?

- 2. Nguyen Van Quy, who suffers from cancer, has had two children born with birth defects. Nguyen Thi Phi Phi has suffered through four miscarriages, while Duong Quynh Hoa suffers from breast cancer and has high levels of dioxin in her blood system. The three women worked in areas sprayed with Agent Orange during the height of the Vietnam War. They blame their physical disorders on the U.S. military.[13]

The military is a large, if not the largest, threat to the environment. During the Vietnam War, the U.S. military dumped about twenty-five million gallons of assorted noxious chemicals, herbicides, and defoliants. Dioxin, a major teratogenic (birth-deforming) contaminant, persists in the food chain for decades. Today, Vietnamese women have the highest rate of spontaneous abortions in the world with 70 to 80 percent of these women suffering from vaginal infections. Additionally, they have the world's highest rate of cervical cancer. From 1950 to 1980, fetal death rates during pregnancy increased forty times for these women (Seager 1993:64).

According to a 2002 Vietnamese government study, a total of 622,043 individuals have been negatively affected by the chemicals, including 169,693 children and 4,505 grandchildren who suffer from high rates of deformities and mental handicaps.[14] On January 30, 2004, Quy, Phi, and Hoa filed a lawsuit at the U.S. District Court in Brooklyn, N.Y. against ten U.S. companies that produced the defoliant.

— During war, actions must be taken to protect the lives of the soldiers. In Vietnam, the use of Agent Orange defoliated the heavy jungles, exposing enemy troops—hence saving U.S.

---

[13] Tini Tran, "Vietnam's Agent Orange Victims File Suit," *The Associated Press*, February 4, 2004.

[14] "More than 620,000 Vietnamese Victims of War Hebicides," *The Associated Press*, October 23, 2002.

lives. Does war justify the usage of toxic chemicals to pro-
tect our troops?
— Is preserving the lives of U.S. soldiers of greater value than the
lives of future generations of Vietnamese? Why or why not?
— Two of the primary producers of Agent Orange were Dow
Chemical Company and Monsanto. What responsibility, if any,
does the U.S. government have toward the people of Vietnam?
— Are these multinational companies liable? Do Quy, Phi, and
Hoa have any legal or moral rights to bring suits against such
corporations? Against the U.S. government? Why or why not?
— The dumping of toxic chemicals was conducted secretly,
under the cover of national security. Do citizens have a right
to know what actions their military has taken, especially
when the consequences of those actions have a generational
impact on the environment? Or does national security,
specifically in the midst of conducting a war, trump environmental concerns?

• 3. César Chávez told of Miriam Robles, Jimmy Caudillo, and
Monica Tovar, three children who died from leukemia. Their
parents had two things in common: they were farm workers
who picked grapes, and they were constantly exposed to pesticides at the vineyards where they worked, at home where the
surrounding fields were constantly sprayed, and in the polluted
irrigation water and groundwater (1993:163). Although contracts with migrant workers (through the United Farm Workers) provide protection from dangerous pesticides, farm workers
remain unprotected.

Corporate agribusinesses gave millions of dollars to the successful California gubernatorial campaigns of George Deuk-
mejian and Pete Wilson. During their administrations, charges
filed by farm workers against growers were routinely dismissed
without investigations. When the courts and the state Agricultural Labor Relations Board ordered growers to pay farm workers millions of dollars in damages, they instead settled for paying
as little as ten cents on the dollar. When state officials aggressively attempted to enforce the legal rights of farm workers, they
found themselves intimidated by the governor's political
appointees (ibid.:166).

— Is Chávez correct in stating, "pesticide poisoning of our children is perhaps the ultimate form of oppression"? Are the grapes we buy at the local market for less than $2 a pound washed in the blood of migrant workers? If so, what are our ethical responsibilities?

— If we stop buying grapes will these migrant workers be worse off if they lose their jobs?

— What are the ethical ramifications of using pesticides? Of children working in agriculture?

— What responsibility do we have in paying migrant workers a living wage so that their children need not work?

— What connections exist between politicians and the privileged, in this case the Caliafornia growers? How are these connections maintained? Are they ethical? If not, how can migrant workers be protected from the powerful buying support from potential candidates?

- 4. A super mosquito (Wyeomyia smithii) has been identified as the first genetic adaptation to global warming in the North. Modern mosquitoes wait nine days more than their ancestors of thirty years ago before they begin their winter dormancy. These mosquito survival rates, population growth, and incidence of biting can increase the risk of disease transmission. According to Republican Senator John McCain, who chairs the Science, Commerce and Transportation Committee, it is time for the U.S. government to do its part to address the consequences of greenhouse gas emissions and to discuss mandatory reductions.[15]

One of the first acts of the George W. Bush administration was to decline joining the Kyoto treaty (ratified by one hundred countries). The Kyoto treaty is aimed at reducing actual emissions to 1990 levels. Maintaining that more research was needed to determine if environmental risks warrant taking strong measures, President Bush set a policy that relies on voluntary reductions in the emission of heat-trapping gases like carbon

---

[15] Katharine Q. Seelye, "McCain and Lieberman Offer Bill to Require Cuts in Gases," *The New York Times*, January 9, 2003.

dioxide until 2012.[16] Critics charge this will have profound effects upon life on this planet.

— Is Bush correct in calling for more research? Is more research into the possible risks of global warming needed?
— Does industry have an ethical responsibility to the environment? If so, should that responsibility be carried out voluntarily or through governmental regulations?
— Should those regulations be set by the United States, or agreed to through collaboration with other nations?

- 5. On April 19, 1999, two FA-18 Hornet jets took off the aircraft carrier *USS John F. Kennedy* during the course of conducting war games in the Viéques Passage off the coast of Puerto Rico. The pilots, training for deployment to the Balkans, flew off course releasing two 500-pound Mark 82 bombs that detonated near an observation post. Four civilians were wounded, and a security guard, David Sanes Rodriguez, was killed. His death galvanized the islanders to demand an end to the military exercises on the island, whose nine thousand inhabitants had endured naval bombing exercises for sixty years. Protesters trespassed onto the Navy base and refused to move. These "People's Zone" encampments were denounced by the Navy, which warned of the danger of camping on dangerously contaminated land. At one time, over a thousand protesters gathered on the island to support the encampments, some defiantly sailing into "forbidden waters" to challenge the Navy's claim to the seas surrounding Puerto Rico.

  Although the bombing stopped in May 2003, the Navy left behind tens of thousands of unexploded bombs spewed over a nine-hundred-acre firing range. The fish, soil, crabs, seagrass, and soil are contaminated with toxins. According to Tara Thornton of the Military Toxics Project (MTP), "[The Navy] fired enough to poison every man, woman, and child on [Viéques] 420 times over." No wonder the island's inhabitants have a 27

---

16 Andrew C. Revkin, "Climate Changing, U.S. Says in Report," *The New York Times*, June 3, 2002; and idem, "Bush's Plan on Warming Needs Work and Monety, Expert Says," *The New York Times*, December 6, 2002.

percent higher incident of cancer than the rest of Puerto Rico.[17]
Rather than cleaning the tract, it will be closed to the public
and declared a "wilderness area."

— Why are war-simulated exercises, using live ammunition, not
  conducted in the United States mainland, i.e. New England?
— What ethical responsibilities does the Navy have to the inhabitants of Viéques?
— Are such acts (the protest against the death of Rodriguez)
  of civil disobedience ethical? Even if they disrupt "law and
  order"?
— Are such protests during a time when the military is engaged
  battle, in effect, an act of treason? Why or why not?
— Military and civilian programs compete for the same national
  resources. What ethical ramifications exist concerning military spending?

---

[17] Dana Canedy, "Navy Leaves a Battered Island, and Puerto Ricans
Cheer," *The New York Times*, May 2, 2003; and Rick Kearns, "U.S. Navy
Tests Create Health Risks in Viéques," *Hispanic* 12:9 (September, 1999):
12–16.

PART III

CASE STUDIES
OF NATIONAL RELATIONSHIPS

CHAPTER 8

Introduction to National Relationships

When patriotism ("my country right or wrong") replaces justice, a people are in danger of idolatry. Because the United States can be a strong force for good in the world it must be confronted and challenged when it fails to live up to its potential. Unfortunately, this nation's quest for economic dominance in the world has usually led down a path that not only creates poverty abroad, but also within our own boundaries.

What is lavished abroad to maintain the neoliberal economic order is not available to spend at home to improve social services. Every empire in history has faced diametrically opposed choices: to wield awesome power abroad by strengthening and increasing their military capabilities, or to improve the living standards of citizens at home. They must choose between guns or butter.

GUNS VS. BUTTER

Historians such as Paul M. Kennedy have used this zero-sum rule to explain how empires function. The wealth required for military domination stagnates the domestic economy because financial investment in the military is less effective in producing long-term economic growth than such investing in industries geared to meet consumers' needs and desires. In other words, the money spent on "guns" leaves less money for "butter"; it creates a drain on investment capital and raw materials, as well as on the scientist and engineers who would otherwise be engaged in commercial, export-oriented growth (1987:444–45).

Kennedy's point can be illustrated by an exchange between U.S. governors and the president that occurred on the eve of the 2003

143

war with Iraq. Due partly to national tax policies and also the weak U.S. economy, most states found themselves in the most serious financial predicament since World War II. Mounting deficits in state budgets negatively impacted all state services, especially education. For example, the governor of Missouri ordered every third light bulb unscrewed to save money; teachers in Oklahoma doubled as janitors, cafeteria help, and school bus drivers; some Colorado school districts moved to a four-day week; Nebraska state college raised its tuition by 20 percent; and teachers in Oregon worked two weeks without pay. Schools, libraries, and parks were closed, college scholarships eliminated, bus routes dropped, state troopers dismissed, and health care for the poor and mentally ill withdrawn.[1] Many of these measures still remain in place at the time of this writing in 2004.

So severe was the national dilemma that during their annual 2003 winter meeting, governors from both political parties pressed the president for fiscal assistance, particularly in the area of education. President George W. Bush told the governors that there were no additional funds.

President Bush then proposed a tax cut that appears to benefit the wealthiest Americans. The tax cut of $1.46 trillion over the next ten years is over and above the $1.35 trillion in tax cuts passed in 2001. The president specifically lobbied the governors to support his latest tax-cut proposals, which, if enacted, would cost states an additional $64 billion over the next decade. This would add to the deficit projected for 2003 of $50 billion, and the 2004 estimated $80 billion shortfall.[2]

THE COST OF EMPIRE

Empire building costs money. As the governors met in early 2003, the Pentagon stated that defeating Iraq and occupying the coun-

---

[1] Timothy Egan, "States, Facing Budget Shortfalls, Cut the Major and the Mundane," *The New York Times*, April 21, 2003.

[2] Robert Pear, "Governors, Hurting Financially, Ask Washington for Assistance," *The New York Times*, February 23, 2003; "Governors Get Sympathy from Bush But No More Money," *The New York Times*, February 25, 2003; and "Statehouse Pain and the President," *The New York Times*, February, 26, 2003.

try for six months could cost as much as $85 billion; at the same time, some White House economic advisors estimated that the "police action" could run between $100 to $200 billion.[3] This did not include payments to other nations to join the coalition. Even while the governors were expressing a need for funds to underwrite education, the president was busy negotiating an estimated $15 billion aid package to Turkey in exchange for allowing the military to use Turkey as a staging area in the upcoming war with Iraq.[4]

Because what occurs in the domestic sphere impacts the foreign sphere, and vice versa, ethics transcends national borders. White supremacy and class exploitation at home are usually linked to aggressive military attacks throughout the two-thirds world as neoliberalism is established. According to Mexican ethicist Enrique Dussel, "The suffering of the conquered and colonized people appears as a necessary sacrifice and the inevitable process of modernization. This logic has been applied from the conquest of America until the Gulf War, and its victims are as diverse as indigenous Americans and Iraqi citizens" (1995:64).

The global struggle for survival by what Frantz Fanon calls "the wretched of the earth" is the same struggle faced by those who live on the margins within an empire. A correlation does exist between how the United States treats the marginalized through-

---

[3] According to Donald Hepburn, advisor to the Middle East Policy Council, the Pentagon disclosed that the cost of preparation for war, aid to noncombatant allies, and the invasion totaled $45 billion. He said that an additional $1 billion a week was required to maintain the occupation (assuming a five-year occupation, the cost will be $300 billion). Not included in these figures are the interest charges for borrowing the monies to conduct the war. Additionally, $5 billion is required for initial humanitarian aid, $8 billion for Iraqi government salaries, and $7 billion to restore vital utilities for two years. An additional $350 billion is required to pay off Iraq's foreign debts and reparations to Kuwait for the earlier invasion. $3 billion will be needed to resettle nearly one million Iraqi refugees. The U.N. estimates an additional $200 billion over a decade will be required to rebuild Iraq's infrastructure. Iraq's oil rich fields are projected to produce $10 billion in revenue in 2004, at best, slowly climbing to $20 billion by 2006 and $40 billion by 2010. See Donald Hepburn, "Nice War. Here's the Bill," *The New York Times*, September 3, 2003.

[4] Dexter Filkins, "February 16–22: A Crucial Nod from Turkey," *The New York Times*, February 23, 2003.

out the underdeveloped world and how marginalized people within U.S. borders are treated. According to Albert Camus, winner of the 1957 Nobel Prize for Literature, the worth of any society is measured by how it treats its marginalized people.

If this true, what is the worth of the United States? This land of abundance that boasts of the greatest level of wealth ever known by any people throughout the history of humanity often fails to provide its most marginalized salaried workers with a living wage. In 2003, the Census Bureau reported that 34.6 million people, a third of them children, lived in poverty. The cost of a postwar Iraq, coupled with early tax cuts in 2000, will sap approximately $5 trillion from the nation's revenue flow over a ten-year period, making it difficult, if not impossible, for those sinking deeper into poverty to ever recover.[5] Can such an ethical system be called Christian? Pope John Paul II once called such capitalism "savage." Yet resources exist to end poverty in the United States. What seems to be absent is the will to do it. Could it be because those in control of economic policy benefit from maintaining these economic inequities? In the end, though, does refusing to hear the cry of the poor result in the loss of a nation's humanity or, even worse, its soul?

While a perfectly just society cannot be achieved here on earth, throughout human history some cultures have proven to be more humane than others. These successes can help track our progress toward a more ethical moral order. Unfortunately, success within the United States continues to be measured by degrees of financial independence. At any twenty-year high school reunion, those who become doctors and lawyers and have six-figure incomes are deemed more successful than those who work as hourly laborers or in other nonprofessional positions. It is no surprise, then, that poverty is often viewed as an individual problem, a consequence of laziness, lack of intelligence or self-motivation, or maybe just plain bad luck. The best and the brightest succeed, while the less than capable, through a social process of natural selection, are removed from the responsibility to govern. In order to protect and

---

5 "Boom Times on the Poverty Roll," *The New York Times*, September 30, 2003.

secure national tranquility, the "best and the brightest" attempt to keep at bay the others: the less worthy and the marginalized, who are usually people of color. Since the early years of this country, this process has become institutionalized as part of the very fabric of national life. It works to ensure power and privilege for the few.

Yet, from the margins of society, voices like that of Martin Luther King, Jr., have arisen to challenge the fairness of this perspective. King said, "Any religion that professes to be concerned about the souls of men and is not concerned about the slums that damn them, the economic conditions that strangle them and the social conditions that cripple them is a spiritually moribund religion awaiting burial" (1986:38).

The ethics of those privileged by present social structures will be explored in greater detail in this section of the book by examining poverty within the United States, how that poverty is maintained through the political system, and how death plagues those who are marginalized due to health care issues and the judicial system.

CHAPTER 9

National Poverty

STEP 1. OBSERVING

A bit of history is needed to understand poverty — and the growing distance between the poor and the wealthy — in our country today. Beginning with the Great Depression of the 1930s, this nation began a program of funneling large amounts of federal dollars into welfare initiatives. Known as the New Deal, legislation was passed to create a safety net to protect society's most vulnerable members, at that time particularly the elderly. The success of the New Deal could be measured by the return of wage levels to their pre-Depression era and the reduction of unemployment from almost 25 percent to nearly zero on the eve of World War II. By 1949, only a fifth of families were in the lowest earning quintile. .

The 1950s witnessed a drop in poverty levels from 32 percent at the start of the decade to 22 percent by decade's end. Meanwhile, median family income was 43 percent higher in 1959 than in 1950. If we ignore sexism and racism for the moment, most families could, with one income, buy a car, take a vacation, and provide a college education for their children. Two-income families were, for the most part, unnecessary. During the 1960s, with the War on Poverty and the Civil Rights movement, the income gap (difference between the richest and poorest Americans) continued to narrow as unemployment dropped to a low 4.4 percent and income rose by 38 percent over 1959. Although racial discrimination continued to exclude portions of the population from participating in the booming economy, the unemployment rates of black men still dropped twice as fast as white men. Increased employment opportunities for African Americans contributed to the poverty level falling by 50 percent, closing the 1960s at 12 percent (Cooper 1998:347–49).

By the 1970s, multiple factors began to widen the income gap. The energy crisis following the Arab-Israeli War brought income growth to a halt. By the close of the 1970s, median family income remained at 1973 levels while unemployment continued to rise, reaching 7.5 percent by 1980. With economic policies put in place after Ronald Reagan was elected in 1980, the income gap widened dramatically, while the middle class shrunk. These new economic policies radically changed the distribution of wealth in this country. During the 1980s, the top 10 percent of the population increased their family income by 16 percent, the top 5 percent increased theirs by 23 percent, while the top 1 percent increased their income by 50 percent. Meanwhile, the bottom 80 percent lost income with the bottom 10 percent down 15 percent, from $4,113 to $3,504. At the beginning of Reagan's administration, the income of the top 1 percent was 65 times greater than the bottom 10 percent. By the end of the Reagan administration, the income of the top 1 percent was 115 times greater than the bottom 10 percent (Phillips 1990:12–17).

The economic policies of the New Deal were replaced by a supply-side philosophy that consisted of cutting, if not eliminating, social services and benefits for the poor while providing tax breaks for the wealthy. The hope was that economic benefits given to the wealthy would "trickle down" to the less fortunate. According to figures published by the Census Bureau, this led to the richest among us seeing their inflation-adjusted income rise by 30 percent from the late 1970s to the mid-1990s, while the poorest saw their income decrease by 21 percent.

The so-called "Reaganomics" pushed unemployment to almost 10 percent, median family income dropped to 6 percent below pre-1973 levels, and poverty rose from 11.1 to 14.4 percent. The bottom quintile received 4.7 percent of all income, a full percentage point below the 1973 level. From 1947 through 1979, real income had risen for all segments of society. Since 1980 income has risen only for the most affluent families (Cooper 1998:338–54). (See Table 2, p. 150.)

Table 2
Income Growth 1947–1994

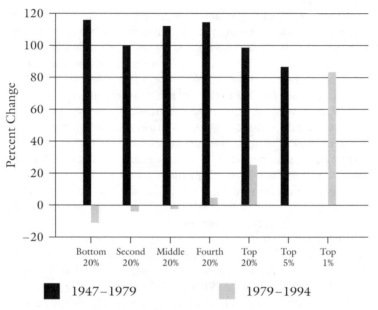

Bottom 20% | Second 20% | Middle 20% | Fourth 20% | Top 20% | Top 5% | Top 1%

■ 1947–1979   ■ 1979–1994

Note: All wages are based on 1979 dollars
Sources: Census Bureau, "Current Population Survey," March 1996;
United for a Fair Economy; and Cooper, 1998:350.

Throughout the 1990s, during the so-called economic boom, only the top quintile increased its share of the nation's income.[1] From 1979 to 2000, the Congressional Budget Office reported that the gap between rich and poor more than doubled as the U.S. experienced the greatest growth of wage inequality throughout the Western world (Wilson 1999:27). These radical economic changes within the United States have contributed to the smallest and fastest-shrinking middle class among all industrialized nations.[2]

---

[1] David Leonhardt, "In a Wealthy Country, Who Are the Truly Rich?" *The New York Times*, January 12, 2003.

[2] Keith Bradisher, "Widest Gap in Incomes? Research Points to the U.S.," *The New York Times*, October 27, 1995.

By the close of the century, the top 1 percent of taxpayers each had on average $862,700 after taxes, more than triple what they had in 1979. Meanwhile, the bottom 40 percent had $21,118 each, up by 13 percent from their average $18,695 (adjusted for inflation) in 1979. The year 2000 proved to have the greatest economic disparity since 1979, when the budget office began collecting such data. The National Bureau of Economic Research, a nonpartisan, nonprofit research group, claims that the top 1 percent enjoys the largest share of before-tax income for any year since 1929.[3] By 2002, according to Census Bureau figures, 34.8 million individuals found themselves living in poverty (compare to 25.4 million individuals in 1968), of which 12.2 million were children.[4] Further contributing to the widening income gap was the 1996 Welfare Reform Act, signed by President Bill Clinton.[5]

STEP 2. REFLECTING

Latin American liberation theologian Franz Hinkelammert insists that "the existence of the poor attests to the existence of a Godless society, whether one explicitly believes in God or not" (1997:27). Nevertheless, most people within the United States hold the assumption that anyone can succeed, if they just work

---

[3] Lynnley Browning, "U.S. Income Gap Widening, Study Says," *The New York Times*, September 25, 2003.

[4] Lynette Clemetson, "Census Shows Ranks of Poor Rose in 2002 by 1.2 Million," *The New York Times*, September 3, 2002.

[5] Although initial reports indicated that hundreds of former welfare recipients moved off the rolls into jobs, providing a substantial raise in income, more recent studies indicate a more disturbing trend. By 2003, seven years after the passage of the Welfare Reform Act, state and urban-policy researchers point to newer studies that show that a significant number of those who left the welfare rolls are unemployed and have sunk to deeper levels of poverty. The Urban Institute in Washington, D.C., estimates that one in seven families who left welfare from 2000 through 2002 have no work, spousal support, or government assistance, up from one in ten in 1999. Wade F. Horn, the assistant secretary of Families and Children within the Department of Health and Human Services, agrees with these figures. See Leslie Kaufman, "Millions Have Left Welfare, But Are They Better Off? Yes, No, and Maybe," *The New York Times*, October 20, 2003.

hard enough. That anybody can grow up to become the president is the myth we install in our little boys (sexism starts young). The only thing that might hold them back is their own lack of initiative. The "Protestant Work Ethic," a term popularized by sociologist Max Weber, undergirds American society and preaches an equality of opportunities. Hard work in the career (calling) to which God summons every person is rewarded by God with material blessings, while those who fail to work hard are punished for their laziness by poverty.

The Myth of the Work Ethic

But it seems that, generally, no matter how hard the poor work, they often continue to slip into greater poverty. The growing disparity of wealth between the poor and the rich leads us to question if it is a "work ethic" that is at stake or perhaps a "work ideology" that allows the wealthy and privileged to rationalize classism. Why is it so difficult for the poor to "get ahead"? Is wealth really a reward for hard work, and poverty a punishment for laziness? Or is there another explanation for the accumulation of even greater wealth by those at the top of the economic ladder?

Increasing poverty directly affects the well-being of our society: it leads to a rise in crime, drug and alcohol addiction, family disintegration, child abuse, mental illness, and environmental abuse. Instead of dealing with the causes of poverty and seeking a more equitable distribution of resources, those privileged with wealth seldom make the connection between their riches and the poverty of others. More often they view their wealth as something earned, a blessing from God, or a combination of both. They tend to seek to insulate themselves from the consequences of their riches, moving to gated communities and sending their children to private schools.

Ethicists from the margins argue that communities that desire a just economic base must place the humanity of their members before economic development (which can be code language for increasing corporate profits). Development today usually means short-term profit, and often at the expense of the marginalized. Yet, true development, economic as well as socio-political, takes place when society's treatment of its most vulnerable members enables them to pass from a less human existence to a more human condition. Conditions faced by the poor are caused by oppressive structures that lead to the exploitation of workers and creating material want. The ethical quest for more humane conditions requires a set of social actions — a praxis — designed to overcome extreme poverty, raise consciousness of classism, foster dignity for all people, develop an equitable distribution of the earth's resources, and secure peace — to testify to one's love for God and one's neighbor, a love that binds God with neighbor.

Regardless of how we choose to define this more human condition, it remains threatened by increasing poverty. The so-called "work ethic" is debunked when the poor work, and many full-time, simply to survive; when there are few if any options for work; and when the work is unrewarding and unfulfilling. Some full-time workers receive the legal minimum hourly wage, but their income still falls short of the official poverty line.[6] Is it any wonder that in 2001 the top quintile, the most affluent fifth of the population, possessed half of all household income, while the lowest quintile, the poorest fifth, received 3.5 percent of the total household income.[7] Furthermore, 49 percent of those who live in poverty yet worked full-time during 2002 lacked any form of health insurance and were literally an illness away from financial ruin.[8]

---

[6] According to Jared Bernstein, senior economist for the Economic Policy Institute, the official definition of poverty masks the true extent of poverty in the United States. Poverty was defined forty years ago by government statistician Mollie Orshansky, who recognizes the shortcomings of the definition. The official definition of poverty fails to consider the radical changes in consumption patterns since the early 1960s. It is based mainly on food consumption, which since then has become less expensive in relationship to housing, health care, childcare, and transportation. The National Academy of Sciences recalculated the original formula to update new consumption patterns, only to discover that the threshold can be as much as 45 percent higher. In short, millions more Americans live in actual poverty than is reported by the government. See Jared Bernstein, "Who's Poor? Don't Ask the Census Bureau," *The New York Times*, September 26, 2003.

[7] Pear, "Number of People Living in Poverty."

[8] Robert Pear, "Big Increase Seen in People Lacking Health Insurance," *The New York Times*, September, 30, 2003.

The dismantling of the New Deal has meant over the long run that working families are not able to earn a living wage. Many are forced to skip meals, forgo paying rent, or postpone needed medical care. A study conducted by the National Low Income Housing Coalition titled "Out of Reach 2003," found that rises in housing costs outpaced wages. In 2003, no state in the Union made it possible for a low-income worker to afford a modest one- or two-bedroom rental unit. Most real estate professionals calculate that rents or mortgage payments must be less than 30 percent of total family income to consider housing expenses affordable. In at least forty states, renters needed an income greater than twice the minimum wage to afford the most basic of housing (in states designated as the most expensive to live, the figure was closer to three times minimum wage).[9] Not surprisingly, the population groups more likely to live in poverty are children, African Americans and Latino/as, women living alone, non-citizens, single mothers, and those living in central cities.[10] Those more likely to be affluent are white non-Hispanics, native born, suburban, aged 35 to 59, and married (Becker 2002:65, 67).

Hardest hit are the children. Of the industrial countries, the richest nation in the world has the highest percentage of its residents living in poverty, and 14.5 million of them are children. Among all industrial nations, the United States has the largest percentage of children living in poverty. In 2000, one out of every six children under the age of six lived at or below the poverty line (ibid.). Among Latino/a and black children, the poverty rate in 2001 was an unconscionable 28 percent and 30 percent, respectively.[11] The infant mortality of the U.S. was thirty-third in the

---

9 Lynette Clemetson, "Poor Workers Finding Modest Housing Unaffordable, Study Says," *The New York Times*, September 9, 2003.

10 Native Americans are not included in this group because they are considered a separate people rather than a U.S. ethnic group. Nevertheless, more than a fourth of Amerindians live in poverty, with unemployment rates reaching 14 percent (double the national average) on reservations. See "Indian Leader Cites Poverty and Pleads for Aid," *The New York Times*, February 1, 2002.

11 In 1995, 41.5 percent of black children lived in poverty, so 30 percent in 2001 may seem like a major improvement. However, a closer look at the data reveals that more of today's poor black children live in extreme

world, behind that of several two-thirds world countries. Eighteen percent of American women have minimal or no prenatal care, again, the highest among industrial nations. Meanwhile, 11.6 percent of children, or 8.5 million, under eighteen had no health insurance in 2002.[12]

The dismantling of safety nets has had devastating effects on the family. A presentation at Harvard by welfare experts showed a rising number of children, specifically black children in metropolitan areas, live in no-parent households. The lack of adequate childcare has forced parents, specifically single parents, to leave their children with relatives, friends, or foster families. Since the Welfare Act of 1996 was enacted, the number of black children living without parents has more than doubled (from 7.5 percent to 16.1 percent). Their parents may be working in retail and service industries that pay a fraction of what they used to earn at manufacturing jobs. While these parents put in long hours to earn a poverty-line wage, their children are growing up without a parent present. These children, according to welfare experts, will perform significantly worse in school than children in single-parent homes. They will experience higher rates of school failure, mental health problems, and delinquency, thus contributing to the downward spiral of despair.[13]

The Rich Get Richer

Who then benefits from the present economic system? Why does the income gap continue to widen? First, the pay schedule of CEOs has increased at the expense of workers' wages. In 1975 corporate

poverty. If the poverty line for a family of three is $14,100, then a family of three at $7,060 or below is recognized to exist at extreme poverty. The gradual disappearance of safety net programs in the wake of the 1996 overhaul of welfare has driven the country's poorest families into greater destitution. See Sam Dillion, "Report Finds Deep Poverty Is on the Rise," *The New York Times*, April 30, 2003.

[12] Jeff Madrick, "Economic Scene," *The New York Times*, June 13, 2002; Pear, "Big Increase Seen in People Lacking Health Insurance," *The New York Times*, September, 30, 2003.

[13] Nina Bernstein, "Side Effect of Welfare Law: The No-Parent Family," *The New York Times*, July, 29, 2002.

leaders made forty-four times as much as the average factory worker. During the early 1980s, corporate leaders such as Roberto Goizueta of Coca Cola and Michael Eisner of Disney convinced stockholders to link their compensation to company stock prices. As a result, by 1985, the average CEO salary rose to seventy times that of the average worker.[14] A 2001 report published by the Institute for Policy Studies revealed that corporate leaders were earning 531 times as much as the average factory worker, a 571 percent increase (before adjusting for inflation) since 1990. Meanwhile, workers' pay, which grew at 37 percent, barely outpaced inflation at 32 percent (Anderson et al. 2001:1–6). Compare the chief executive pay in the U.S. of 531 times the average employee with the pay gap of other industrial nations: Britain at 25 times; Canada at 21 times; France at 16 times; Germany at 11 times; or Japan at 10 times.[15]

The average pay for top executives at 365 major corporations is $13.1 million a year, while the average factory worker makes $24,668 a year. If workers' annual pay during the 1990s would have grown at the same rate as CEOs', workers' annual earnings in 2000 would have been $120,491. Or if the minimum wage of $3.80 an hour would have grown at the same rate as CEOs' earnings, the 2000 minimum wage would have been $25.50 an hour rather than $5.15.[16]

CEO salaries also outpaced the stock market and corporate profits. From 1985 through 2001, the average worker saw his or her pay increase by 63 percent, while the S&P 500 index rose by 443 percent. Over the same period of time, CEOs enjoyed a pay increase of 866 percent.[17] One would have expected CEO incomes to drop as the market took a downturn in 2000. However, this did not occur because of the nature of our economy, one that privatizes profits while it socializes losses (Teninty 1991:115).

---

[14] David Leonhardt, "The Imperial Chief Executive Is Suddenly in the Cross Hairs," *The New York Times*, June 24, 2002.

[15] Gretchen Morgenson, "Explaining (or Not) Why the Boss Is Paid So Much," *The New York Times*, January 25, 2004.

[16] Ibid.

[17] Ibid.

At the start of the down market, compensation rules were rewritten once it became obvious that production goals were not going to be met. For example, at the close of the fiscal year that ended on April 30, 2003, the CEO of H. J. Heinz, the ketchup maker, received a pay package valued at $8.8 million, a 47 percent rise over $6 million in the previous year, even though the performance of Heinz stock fell by about 20 percent.[18]

Those CEOs who announced layoffs of 1,000 or more workers between January 1 and August 1, 2001, earned 80 percent higher compensation than CEOs of 365 top U.S. firms that did not announce layoffs (Anderson et al., 2001:6–7). For example, the CEO of WorldCom announced layoffs for 6,000 workers while collecting a $10 million bonus. The CEO of Disney earned $72.8 million in 2000, while announcing layoffs for 4,000 people. Such executive raises and worker layoffs took place at a range of companies, including American Express and Cisco Systems (ibid., 7–8).

Workers suffered in other ways as well. The 1938 Fair Labor Standards Act established a forty-hour week, discouraging employers from assigning longer hours by forcing them to pay time-and-a-half on any hours worked above forty. By 1975 exemptions were added by excluding "highly paid executives" who could work up to seventy hours a week with no additional pay. The problem is that "highly paid executive" was defined as anyone who supervises two other employees and is being paid as little as $13,000 a year. This loophole, exploited by the service and retail industries, has meant longer work hours for the average American without an increase in wages.[19]

The Unfair Tax Burden

Changes in the tax code have also harmed the poor. Neoliberal doctrine believes that entrepreneurs and business owners should control the economy. Because the rich supposedly have entrepreneurial

---

[18] Patrick McGeehan, "At Heinz, a Novel Way to Say the Boss Is Worth It," *The New York Times*, August 10, 2003.

[19] Rose Eisenbrey, "Just What the Worker Needs — Longer Days, No Overtime," *The Los Angeles Times*, February 14, 2003.

skills and experience, they receive greater disposable income through tax cuts and by keeping wages depressed. A "trickle down" effect is supposed to result. Unfortunately, during the last ten years, this has not happened. From 1980 to 1990, the poorest 20 percent of the population saw their tax liability increase by 10 percent while the richest 5 percent of the population enjoyed a 12.5 percent reduction in taxes (Cooper 1998:345). By 2000, the top four hundred wealthiest taxpayers in the U.S. represented 1 percent of all income obtained, a figure that had quadrupled in the eight years since 1992. Yet their tax burden dropped from 26.4 in 1992 to 22.3 percent by 2000.[20]

By 2010 when the tax cuts passed in 2001 are fully in place, the top 1 percent of taxpayers will receive more than half (52 percent) of all the tax benefits (half a trillion dollars, or $342,000 on average), more than the other 99 percent of taxpayers combined. The 2001 tax cut will transfer more wealth to the top 1 percent than virtually any act of fiscal policy in history. Meanwhile, millions of American children face substandard housing or homelessness, inadequate health care and crumbling schools. To bring about a more equitable society, instead of implementing such an inequitable tax cut, the government could have invested in the future by spending the money on education and other services for children. For the same amount of money, the government could have, among other things, established a comprehensive health care for all uninsured children, fully funded Head Start for all eligible children, provided child care for all eligible children, and hired 100,000 new teachers.[21]

---

[20] David Cay Johnston, "Very Rich's Share of Wealth Grew Even Bigger, Data Show," *The New York Times*, June 26, 2003.

[21] Bob Herbert, "Suffer the Children," *The New York Times*, July 11, 2002; *Tax Cut Basics*, Washington, D.C.: Movement to Leave No Child Behind, 2003; and *Year-by-Year Analysis of the Bush Tax Cuts Shows Growing Tilt to the Very Rich*, Washington, D.C.: Citizens for Tax Justice, 2002. In addition, it is estimated that the implementation of the 2001 tax cuts will contribute to the increase of the national debt, conservatively estimated to become $5.8 trillion by 2013. See Edmund L. Andrews, "Leap in Deficit Instead of Fall Is Seen for U.S.," *The New York Times*, August 27, 2003.

Some corporations eliminate paying portions of their taxes by registering their companies in tax havens like Bermuda or the Cayman Islands while keeping their working headquarters in the United States. For example, Tyco International, with working headquarters in Exeter, North Hampshire, saved more than $400 million in taxes by incorporating and establishing a nominal office in Bermuda. Stanley Works, who recently became incorporated in Bermuda, expects to save $30 million of its $80 million tax bill. Since Bermuda charges companies like Ingersoll-Rand only $27,653 to establish a nominal office on the island, Ingersoll-Rand can avoid at least $40 million a year in corporate taxes.[22] In 2002, the commissioner of the IRS identified 82,100 taxpayers who used off-shore accounts to evade paying taxes. The loss of offshore evasion is estimated at $70 billion annually, a burden that eventually comes to rest on the nation's average taxpayers. Ironically, the IRS scaled back enforcement for the very wealthy and off-shore corporations who engage in tax evasion maneuvers. Meanwhile, the IRS required extensive new documentation for those who claiming an earned-income tax credit, affecting the 19 million recipients with total household income under $35,000.

Racism

And the discrimination caused by racism continues to harm people of color. Contrary to popular opinion, the Census Bureau has revealed that the income gap between whites and people of color has increased with each passing year (Velasquez 1998:375–76). People of color are relegated to inner city poverty and are segregated from the middle class, making it difficult for them to break through barriers that foster and maintain their poverty. Last to be hired, they are also among the first to lose their jobs during downsizing. During the recession of the early 2000s, unemployment among blacks rose at a rate twice as fast as that of whites. The loss of 2.6 million jobs in manufacturing between 2001 and 2003 (many of which made their way to China and India) has disproportionately impacted African Americans, affecting 15 percent of

---

[22] David Cay Johnston, "U.S. Corporations Are Using Bermuda to Slash Tax Bill," *The New York Times*, February 18, 2002.

black manufacturing workers as opposed to the 10 percent of white workers who also lost their jobs.[23]

Although a large number of studies demonstrate the reality of racism, for our purposes it suffices to acknowledge that racism leads toward lower wages, greater financial burdens, and fewer opportunities to transcend the consequences of poverty. How relevant are the words of the prophet Jeremiah, who said "Woe to those who build their palace on anything but integrity, their upper rooms by injustice, making their compatriots work for nothing, not paying them for their labor" (22:13).

STEP 3. PRAYING

Historically, individuals who commit themselves to a life of Christian service would renounce all earthly possessions so as to be used by God. But are today's Christians required to renounce their riches to become disciples of Jesus? The early church wrestled with issues of wealth, concluding that any riches possessed by Christians were to be used for the betterment of the community.[24] Yet this concept is not well accepted within a capitalist economic structure. Individuals pursue their own economic self-interests, believing that an "invisible hand" will insure economic benefits for all of society. Perhaps Adam Smith's economic theories of supply and demand may be relevant in a society dominated by small businesses and petty merchants where no one seller can control the market but must compete with others. But in today's economy, Smith's theories are outdated: in the United States today the corporation controls the means of production, sets the price for the merchandise or service, and determines the wage for producing the merchandise or service. Prices are often kept artificially high and wages artificially low.[25]

---

[23] Louis Uchitelle, "Blacks Lose Better Jobs Faster as Middle-class Work Drops," *The New York Times*, July 12, 2003.

[24] An excellent text dealing with how the early church dealt with the issue of riches is Justo González, *Faith and Wealth*, 1990a.

[25] Karl Marx did predict that with the passage of time, small businesses and petty merchants would gradually be absorbed by larger industries until a concentration of industrial power rests in the hands of a few capitalists.

Defenders of our present system of capitalism see no inherent conflict between Christian morality and the pursuit of profit. It is assumed that each person has an absolute right, if not a moral obligation, to follow economic self-interest as a duty in creating a more just society. Yet the biblical text calls us to "Be subject to one another in the fear of the Lord" (Eph. 5:21). We are called to put the needs of the other before our own. How than can these two opposing views be reconciled within a rich Christian community?

Some televangelists have begun to proclaim a "name it and claim it theology," and some ministers, including Benny Hinn, preach that God wants God's children to be rich. Hinn has actually proclaimed: "Poverty is from the devil and God wants all Christians prosperous."[26] During several of his sermons he has led his congregation in repeating the phrase: "The wealth of the wicked is mine." Another, Kenneth Hagin, the founder of Rhema, The World of Faith Bible School, teaches that "[God] wants His children to eat the best, He wants them to wear the best clothing, He wants them to drive the best cars, and He wants them to have the best of everything" (McConnell 1995:175). Poverty, then, is the consequence of a lack of faith on the part of the disenfranchised. Should it be surprising that such a theology finds fertile soil within a capitalist "Christian" culture? It even explains why the poor are still with us — obviously they lack faith in God. Nonetheless, throughout the Gospel of Luke we read the opposite of what today's prophets of wealth proclaim. Not only is it the poor who inherit the reign of God, but they become the instrument by which the rich can discover their own salvation.

In Luke 16:19–31, Jesus tells the story of a poor man named Lazarus. According to the biblical text, there once was a very wealthy man who was accustomed to feasting on only the best. At the gate of his mansion lay Lazarus, a poor man covered with sores, dreaming of a future that provided him with scraps that fell from the rich man's table. When both men died, Lazarus was carried by the angels to the bosom of Abraham while the prosperous man was sent to hell to be tormented for all eternity.[27] The rich man,

---

[26] Sermon of Benny Hinn broadcast on the Trinity Broadcasting Network, November, 6, 1990.

[27] It is interesting to note that while the text provides us with the name

seeing Lazarus held in Abraham's arms, pleaded for mercy. He begged to have a few drops of water placed on his tongue to cool the agony of the flames. But Abraham refused, for a great gulf separated heaven from hell. The rich man then asked to have Lazarus go back to his family to warn them of the danger of their "mammon," their wealth. This too was denied, for as Abraham stated, "If they were not willing to hear Moses and the prophets, even if one from the dead should rise, they will not be persuaded."

Nowhere in the text does it tell us that the rich man's wealth was accumulated unjustly or that he was directly oppressing Lazarus. His judgment and condemnation to hell were based on the fact that he failed to share his resources with those such as Lazarus who lacked the basics for survival. To ignore the plight of the marginalized is to deny one's humanity. In this case, God's judgment was not based on anything the rich man did, or any belief system he confessed, or any particular church he attended. He was condemned for failing to give to the very least of God's children. He failed to use his resources so that others could also enjoy an abundant life. If we are truly to love our neighbor and if this commandment is to be the biblical basis that informs our ethics, then it is immoral to ignore our neighbor's hunger as we continue to store away our riches. To do so is to be called a fool by Christ (Lk. 12:16–21).

Although the Lazarus story condemns the rich, we must ask then, who in our time will proclaim the good news of salvation from materialism? While an analysis of this text and others that focus on the plight of the rich has become commonplace, all too often our gaze remains fixed on the wealthy man and not others. Perhaps this is because most of us read the text from the social location of the middle-class and the message of this story in Luke is reduced to a charitable act demanded of the wealthy.

But what happens if we read the text from the perspective of Lazarus? We may discover that it wasn't a sin of commission that resulted in the eternal condemnation of the rich man but a sin of omission. What if Lazarus had been the subject instead of the object

---

of Lazarus, the one from the margins, it does not name the rich man who, no doubt, was known and honored by the community at large.

of the story? What if instead of sitting by the gate dreaming about the scraps that might fall from the rich man's table, Lazarus had been proactive? What if Lazarus had demanded food, shelter, and clothes, not out of a sense of pity, but based on his human right to survive? What if Lazarus had sought solidarity with others made poor by the prevailing economic structures, and joined forces with them to demand structural changes within society? What if Lazarus had confronted the rich man with his sin of greed and hoarding? What if the rich man, upon hearing Lazarus' demands, had repented? Then salvation as liberation from sin would have also come to the rich man and he, too, could have found comfort in the arms of Abraham. Even though the rich man forfeited salvation by refusing to fulfill his ethical responsibility to the poor man, the poor are still responsible for acting as moral agents to create a just society. Those who are privileged by the way society is constructed are in need of liberation and salvation because they too are created in the image of God. God desires all, the rich and the poor, to enter into a saving knowledge of God's grace. When the marginalized seek out the liberation of the oppressors, they verify the humanity of both the privileged and themselves (De La Torre 2003a:99–100).

Jesus of Galilee, coming from the margins, challenged the rich in the hope that they would find their own salvation through solidarity with the poor. To commit one's life to Christ is to commit one's life to those without — those Christ opted for. Such a commitment to the poor is not ideological, but an expression of faith. In the gospel accounts, some wealthy persons did find God's salvation, as in the case of Zacchaeus (Lk. 19:8–10), who, when confronted with his sin of hoarding wealth, pledged to repay back four times over what he received through fraudulent means; he then split the remainder of his wealth between himself and the poor. These actions led Jesus to proclaim that on that day, salvation had come to the house of Zacchaeus. For others, the path to heaven was impossible to achieve, as in the case of the rich young ruler (Lk. 18:24–25) who, while pious and virtuous in keeping the commandments, still walked away from salvation out of reluctance to share his wealth with the poor.

Jesus incarnated himself into the lives and plight of the poor. For the church to discover its own salvation, it must do likewise.

If not, those who refuse to walk in solidarity with "the least of these," the marginalized, renounce, like the young ruler, a basic principle of Christianity, regardless of how moral they may appear to be. Simply stated, one cannot be a Christian and remain complicit with social structures that privilege whiteness, wealth, and maleness. The gospel message says that it is the people on the margins who are the salvific agents for the recipients of society's power and privilege.

Perhaps the rich man's salvation did not occur because Lazarus failed to demand a place at the banquet table. Those who exist on the margins of society also bear a burden in that they have a sacred trust and ethical responsibility to evangelize the dominant culture about the danger of power and privilege. But how? By coming together, organizing, and demanding that those in power obey God's command not to sell the poor "for a pair of sandals" (Amos 8:6). Not only will the rich find their salvation through their solidarity with the poor, the poor will facilitate this process by demanding from the rich their rightful share, working out their own salvation in "fear and trembling." Additionally, the humanity of the dispossessed is regained as they actively seek the humanity of their oppressors. Through repentance can come salvation.

STEP 4. CASE STUDIES

- 1. According to a March 2002 survey conducted by the Census Bureau, women are less likely than men to reach the highest salary brackets and more likely to live in poverty.[28] A survey released by the General Accounting Office showed that in a study of ten industries that employed women from 1995 to 2000, the gap in salary between men and women had increased in seven of those industries. By 2002, women earned 62 cents for every dollar made by male managers, down from 83 cents in 1995.[29] Heather Killen, a senior vice president of Yahoo was the highest-paid woman in the United States, with a total com-

---

[28] "Census Study Finds That Men Earn the Most," *The New York Times*, March 25, 2003.

[29] Seglin, Jeffrey, "How to Get a Company's Attention on Women's Pay," *The New York Times*, March 17, 2002.

pensation package of $32.7 million for the year 2000. Mean-
while the highest-paid male, John Reed of Citigroup, earned
$293 million. In fact, the thirty highest-paid women in corpo-
rate America, with an average total compensation of $8.7 mil-
lion, fell short when compared with the average income of the
thirty highest-paid men at $112.9 million (Anderson et al.
2001:13).

— Is this just? Why or why not?
— Is increasing these thirty women's income to $112.9 million
   to equal the wages of men the ethical praxis to engage in?
— Should Killen's wages be more compatible with Reed's?
   Although having equal access to the socioeconomic resources
   of our society is desirable, is the goal simply surmounting
   the present existing structures that cause oppression? Should
   justice be defined as equality with white men's salaries?

• 2. Nelly Kwamboka of Kenya wailed, cursed, and collapsed in
anguish at the foot of the bed where her young son had just
died of malaria. Next to her, three other children are battling
for their lives.[30] These children are included in the 2.7 million
individuals who die each year (mostly in Africa) from malaria.
Bill Gates, the CEO of Microsoft, was listed by *Forbes* in 2002
as the richest individual living in the U.S., with an estimated
worth of $51 billion, greater than the gross national product
of several countries. His net worth is equivalent to the combined net worth of the bottom 40 percent of U.S. households.
In 1999, Gates started the Bill & Melinda Gates Foundation
with $32.8 billion in assets. In its first four years, the Founda-
tion distributed $6.2 billion, of which more than half ($3.2 billion) was earmarked for improving health in two-thirds world
nations.[31] In 2003, the Gates foundation pledged $168 million
for malaria research. Some people have criticized Gates for

---

[30] "Kenya: A Predictable and Preventable Killer," *Africa News*, August
11, 2002.

[31] Stephanie Strom, "Gates Billions Reshape Health of World's Poor,"
The New York Times, July 13, 2003.

participating in a public relations campaign to polish the image of a ruthless monopolist. Others are quick to point out that the IRS rewards philanthropy by allowing tax deductions for donated funds. Yet, the generosity of the Foundation has contributed to rising vaccination rates in some of the poorest countries of the world.

— Are the criticisms of Gates justified?
— Is he being generous with money obtained through Microsoft's monopoly of a computer operating system?
— For the Kwambokas of the world, does it matter why he is donating money if its outcome is saving lives?

• 3. Anna Brown, a seventy-five-year-old woman, lives on the West Side of Chicago. Because she is unable to afford the price of natural gas, she had no heat for most of two years.[32] She is among the millions who are unable to afford decent housing in this nation due to rising costs and federal cuts in assistance to low-income people. In 2003, for the first time in thirty years, the U.S. House passed a spending bill that failed to renew existing housing vouchers. Section 8 is a federal program that benefits the poor by paying the difference between the market value of an apartment and 30 percent of a household's income. The program subsidizes more than two million families who earn less than $20,000 a year. Because the House appropriated only $11.7 billion for vouchers, only 1.78 million vouchers could be funded. Funding was eliminated for more than 114,000 low-income families who relied on rent subsidies to survive. The Congressional Budget Office predicted that an additional $900 million was needed to renew all vouchers.[33]

— What response should be given to Anna Brown, who must choose between heating her home through the winter, or eating?

---

[32] John W. Fountain, "More Families Face Loss of Heat with Public Aid Scarce," *The New York Times*, December 5, 2002.

[33] David Firestone, "100,000 Could Lose Housing Subsidies, Advocates Warn," *The New York Times*, September 5, 2003.

— Does the government have an obligation or responsibility to subsidize the rent of the poor?

— Are rent subsidies a viable solution, or do they simply deal with the consequences of poverty?

— What other possible solutions should the government consider? Rent control? A living wage?

— Should any federal program exist for the homeless? If so, who will pay for it?

• 4. Tex G. Hall, president of the National Congress of American Indians, which represents more than 250 nations, traveled to Washington, D.C., in January 2003 to deliver the first State of the Indian Nations address and to ask Washington to help create 100,000 jobs for Native Americans by 2010. He declared that "seven generations ago, the United States was engaged in forced removal of tribes to the lands west of the Mississippi. . . . Today we carry the wounds of that legacy." Amerindians, the fastest-growing segment of the population, manifest these wounds with a significantly shorter life expectancy than any U.S. ethnic group; with more than one-fourth of its people living in poverty; and with unemployment rates at double the national rate. Not to mention millions of dollars earned on tribal lands through oil, mineral, timber, and grazing leases that have been "lost" by the Interior Department.[34]

Paradoxically, investors are pouring millions into "helping" Indians receive federal recognition as tribes. Why? Gambling. As of April 2004, 291 groups seeking federal recognition signed contracts with investors wanting a slice of the $15 billion-a-year gambling industry.[35] Yet, of the 560 federally recognized tribes, a little over 200 have gambling, and less than 20 of those have generated sufficient wealth to transform their reservation's economy.

— Should legal gambling be the means by which to improve the living conditions of Amerindians? Why or why not?

---

[34] "Indian Leader Cites Poverty and Pleads for Aid," *The New York Times*, February 1, 2003.

[35] Iver Peterson, "Would-Be Tribes Entice Investors," *The New York Times*, March 29, 2004.

—What about those nations like the Mohegan of Norwich, Connecticut, who are not considering gambling? This 600-member tribe is having difficulty coming up with the millions of dollars it costs to obtain federal recognition. Should a people's identity depend on the ability to pay?

— If the federal government signed treaties with Native Americans providing them with the right to govern their own affairs, why then is recognition of a people dependent on the federal government?

• 5. At the Potomac Mills Mall in Woodbridge, Virginia, Rebecca Michalski, a sixth-grade teacher, is untroubled by America's consumer culture. "I don't see anything wrong with it," she says. "Look, people spend their time the way they want to and that's no one else's business" (Masci, 1999:1003). For example, if you received a substantial promotion at work, you might move up to the next economic level. You expect that your income will continue to rise substantially each year. You decide to buy a new house in an exclusive gated community and trade in your vehicle for a luxury car. You find that because of your increase in salary, you are now liable to pay more taxes. You then visit to a tax consultant who shows you ways to avoid most of your taxes.

—What ethical considerations do you face?

— Is Rebecca Michalski correct in saying that it is nobody's business how you spend your earnings? Why or why not? What responsibilities, if any, do you owe others?

— Is it ethical to participate in the practices recommended by the tax consultant?

— Do tax payers have any moral obligation to pay more than what the law demands?

CHAPTER 10

Political Campaigns

STEP 1. OBSERVING

Since the early 1900s, corporations have been banned from making campaign contributions to federal candidates in an attempt to prevent their "deep pockets" from subverting the democratic process. However, individuals within those corporations, and/or their families, were still allowed to make individual donations. In many cases, this was, and continues to be, accomplished through a process known as "bundling," where a multitude of individual checks written by executives and their families within a corporation are bundled together and presented to the candidate.

In addition to bundling, the Federal Election Campaign Act in 1974 allowed large corporations to form Political Action Committees (PACs) for the express purpose of pooling funds from a group of individuals who voluntarily join together to support a candidate. The express purpose of PACS was to influence the political sphere by helping elect public officials friendly to the PAC's ideology.[1] PAC contributions are made to those aligned with the interest of the corporation, or as a reward to incumbents who have continuously acted in the best interest of the corporation. Although somewhat eclipsed in the 1990s by direct contributions to candidates' campaigns through "soft money," PACs are still an important component in influencing political officials.

---

[1] The law does not allow PAC contributions for federal candidates to exceed $5,000 per candidate per election ($15,000 in the event of a primary, a run-off, and a final election). However, no limits exist in spending as long as the PAC operates independently from the candidate's campaign organization.

PAC monies do not necessarily mean that the recipients will vote a specific way, although how they vote on public issues can determine how much PAC monies they will receive during the next electoral cycle. Besides PACs, candidates can benefit from "soft money." During the 2002 midterm elections, ninety-year-old television icon Art Linkletter, of "Kids Say the Darndest Things" fame, informed the public, in thirty-second spots, that their representative to Congress "has been fighting for real prescription drug coverage." These ads ran in nineteen congressional districts where the incumbent faced stiff opposition. This ad campaign cost about $12 million, and was sponsored by a so-called grass-roots organization called the United Seniors Association, which received most of its funds from pharmaceutical companies. Because the ads said nothing about whom to vote for, but only instructed viewers to "call" their representative and encourage them to "keep standing up for America," no laws were broken because these ads were not considered campaign ads, even though they ran during the election cycle. Although most of the funding came directly from the general treasuries of corporations, the "soft money" used to run such ads, usually in increments of $100,000 or more, was deemed unregulated political donations. Soft-money giving increased from $86 million during the 1992 presidential election to $495 million during the 2000 presidential election (Jost 2002:971).

A beneficiary of PACs or soft money might choose to abstain from voting altogether if the corporation and the political official disagree on how they were originally planning to vote on the proposed legislation. The beholden politician can, behind the scenes, encourage certain witnesses to testify at a committee hearing or block those whose testimony may be perceived as harmful. Corporations can greatly benefit when public officials they support encourage or block someone's appointment to a post that oversees or regulates the benefactor's industry. In effect, the corporation transforms the relationship from regulator and regulated to a more symbiotic one between parties with mutual interests.[2]

---

[2] During the mid-1980s I served as chairperson of the Real Estate Political Action Committee for the Miami Board of Realtors. My job was to serve as a pseudo-lobbyist, traveling to both the state and nation's cap-

Although laws do exist to prevent corporations from unfairly influencing elected officials, enough loopholes exist to weaken such regulations. One example, the pharmaceutical industry, indicates how most other corporate and special interest groups subvert the democratic process to the detriment of the poor. The United States is the only industrial country in the world that does not regulate the price of medicine. To keep it this way, top executives of Bristol-Myers Squibb, one of the nation's largest pharmaceutical firms, pressured its managers to donate $1,000 in their own name and an additional $1,000 in their spouse's name to the Bush campaign during the 2000 election. Records were kept of donations. Even though election laws bar such types of coercion, the pharmaceutical industry succeeded in preserving the status quo.

The forty million recipients of Medicare form a large block of consumers of prescription drugs. In 2003, Congress passed legislation that allows only private health plans to deliver Medicare prescription drug benefits. Medicare is thus preventing from directly negotiating steep discounts on the prices of medicine. If the government was allowed to negotiate the price its beneficiaries pay for medicine, the cost of prescription drugs would substantially drop. Since the new regulations bar Medicare from any form of negotiation, higher prices for medicine can be expected.[3]

---

itals, to relay our organization's positions on specific legislation and target candidate whom we would support and provide funding. It was very common to "hedge one's bets" by giving monies to both candidates. Regardless who won, we would be on the winning team. When there was a particular candidate we really liked, we were always able to funnel additional monies to them through "bundling." Our support bought us access. I always had a direct line to the representatives we supported with a phone call or visit, access which I lost when I was no longer representing the PAC. It was common for me to hear, in my position, candidates state, "Just tell me what you guys want and I'll support it." One candidate in particular who was running for reelection once threatened to vote against a measure we supported because he had not yet received our organization's financial endorsement. We quickly stated that an oversight was made and cut a check to his reelection committee. While this was not the norm, still, it is the way the system legally operates.

[3] Sheryl Gay Stolberg and Gardiner Harris, "Industry Fights to Put Imprint on Drug Bill," *The New York Times*, September 5, 2003.

Obtaining support for candidates who would give the drug companies what they wanted was brazenly simple. Jim Nicholson, then chairperson of the Republican National Committee, wrote an April 9, 1999, letter to Bristol-Myers chief executive Charles A. Heimbold, stating:

> We must keep the lines of communication open if we want to continue passing legislation that will benefit your industry. . . . Your expertise in health care and involvement in Republican politics are of great benefit to me, and I would like to get your opinion on what we have proposed. . . . I welcome any suggestions you may have on how we can make it an even stronger plan.[4]

The lines of communication were indeed kept open. In fact, the entire pharmaceutical industry contributed $26.6 million dollars to political candidates ($8.3 million to Democrats and $18.3 million to Republicans) in 2000. For the 2002 mid-term elections, the industry gave $26.9 million ($6.6 million to Democrats and $20.3 million to Republicans), a substantial increase over the contribution of $3.2 million, divided between both parties, in 1990. In addition, during 2002, the industry spent $500 million for lobbying, employing six hundred lobbyists, of whom about two dozen were former members of Congress.[5]

A more crass example of how these "lines of communication" were kept open is found in a recent amendment to a homeland security bill. Congress gave an unexpected surprise to the pharmaceutical giant Eli Lilly & Company. Lilly has developed a preservative in vaccines called thimerosal. Parents claim that the mercury content in thimerosal is responsible for causing autism and other neurological ailments in their children. Thousands of legal cases were filed seeking damages. Nevertheless, as part of a domestic security bill signed by the president, thimerosal was placed into a "vaccine court," leading to the possible dismissal of all legal

---

4 Richard A. Oppel, Jr., "Documents Show Parties Often Mixed Fund-Raising and Policy," *The New York Times*, November 7, 2002.

5 Ibid.; and Robert Pear and Richard A. Oppel, Jr., "Election Gives Drug Industry New Influence," *The New York Times*, November 21, 2002.

suits that are filed against Lilly over its negative effects. How did this provision get written into the domestic security bill? No one knows. What is known is that Lilly, a major Republican donor, contributed more than $1.6 million to candidates for office, more than any other pharmaceutical company.[6]

It appears that the words to public officials found in the book of Deuteronomy remain relevant for our times: "You shall not pervert justice, nor show partiality, nor take bribes, for a bribe blinds the eyes of the wise and perverts the words of justice" (16:19).

STEP 2. REFLECTING

The ability of incumbents to raise great sums of money for a "war chest" sufficiently large to scare off potential rivals, coupled with sophisticated gerrymandering designed to create safe district seats for the party in power, has contributed to a 98 percent reelection rate for incumbents. Most members of Congress are beholden, more or less, to those responsible for raising the funds needed to mount successful campaigns. Once elected, most politicians indebted to the corporate leaders who placed them in power advocate the neoliberal policies favorable to the corporations, policies that usually maintain the status quo and safeguard privilege.

As discussed in the previous chapter, neoliberalism has succeeded greatly in transferring wealth from the bottom of society to the top, as witnessed by the growing income disparity between the poor and the rich — a process brought about by reducing available social services (such as welfare, support for education, and health care) and increasing tax breaks for the wealthiest. Neoliberalism poses a distinct threat to democracy. When concentrated wealth influences legislation, it is only a matter of time until political inequality follows. True democracy is replaced with a democratic

---

[6] It is known that the senior Bush sat on Lilly's board of directors in the late 1970s, and that the present White House budget director, Mitchell E. Daniels, was a former Lilly executive. Also, Lilly's CEO, Sidney Taurel, was appointed by the second Bush in June 2003 to serve on the presidential advisory council on domestic security. Sheryl Gay Stolberg, "A Capitol Hill Mystery: Who Aided Drug Maker? Security Bill Amendment Slipped in Unseen." *The New York Times*, November 29, 2003.

façade and the public is led to believe that it is exercising its right to choose leaders. Because corporations funnel large sums of money to candidates from both parties, the corporations win regardless of who wins the election.

We have created a social structure where politicians, with a keen eye on special interests, determine what is ethical. We allow politicians to construct the social order in which we live when we are politically irresponsible. This happens when 1) we call politics dirty and flee from it and/or 2) we concentrate solely on supporting politicians who learn to expound certain "Christian" jargon without seriously considering the ramifications of their political actions. Yet, throughout the Bible God shows concern and love for the disenfranchised. God cares about the political order.

Given the continuing influence of corporations through PACs, we are now moving away from a representative democracy to an oligarchy, a system in which unequal wealth creates political inequality. The excessive wealth enjoyed by the privileged few provides them the right, through the funneling of campaign contributions, to influence and in some cases to determine laws and regulations, often to their own benefit. Wealth funneled to political campaigns, especially through soft money, serves to hide, fuse, and confuse the will of the privileged few with the will of the majority. For example, even though the 2001 and 2003 tax cuts disproportionately benefitted the wealthiest among us, still the vast majority of people were led to believe that these cuts were good for the overall economy, even as the deficit spun out of control.

The marginalized's concept of ethics is far different from that of politicians beholden to PACs and soft money. Any law or regulation is ethical if it produces a more human existence as a response to *agape*— meaning unconditional love. Proper public policy promotes a more human existence by providing opportunities for all citizens to participate in the abundance of life promised by Christ, and specifically those citizens who are the most vulnerable within a society. PACs and soft monies, whose purpose is to have laws and regulations reflect private interests rather than public interests, prevent the societal goal of *fiat justitia, ruat coelum*— let justice be done though the heavens should fall. Although the elimination of PACs and soft money will not usher in a new dawn of justice, their continuation prevents the disenfranchised from participating equally in what society has to offer.

According to W. E. B. Du Bois, the best way to prevent the rich from controlling the political process is for democracy to be allowed to modify industry. In seeking an alternative to the present disjointedness between economics and electoral democracies, Du Bois advocated a proper relationship between the two. He wrote, "While wealth spoke and had power, the dirtiest laborers had voice and vote." Or, as restated by Dwight Hopkins, "The power of wealth submits and succumbs to the will of a collective, conscious, common folk" (2000:136). The ethical question to ponder is, how do soft money and PACs subvert and pervert the proper relationship between economics and electoral democracies? Hopkins may very well be correct in stating:

> The federal government (the presidential, judicial, and legislative branches) often appears to be a competing system of objective checks and balances. But if the national politics and economics were threatened with a reversal, that is, if the pyramidal monopoly capitalists structure in the United States began to move bottom to top, then so-called checks and balances system would rally to prevent such a movement. The present system would immediately stop the realization of genuine democracy in which the majority of the citizens — the people at the bottom in the United States — would own all the economic resources as well as the military industrial complex, and would, therefore, control the federal government. (Ibid.:187)

STEP 3. PRAYING

Speaking to the prophet Jeremiah, God said:

> Go down to the house of the king of Judah, and there speak this word — say, Hear the word of God, O king of Judah who sits on the throne of David, and also your servants and your people who enter through these gates. Thus says God — Do justice and practice righteousness; deliver the one wronged from the hands of the oppressor; do not oppress the alien, the orphan, or the widow; do no violence; and do not shed innocent blood in this place. (Jeremiah 22:1–3)

God calls political leaders to do justice by linking justice with how the disenfranchised are rescued from the oppressor's hand, with how the least in society are treated,[7] and with how those who are innocent are protected. Today it has become standard practice for special interest groups to contribute funds through PAC, and soft money to those charged with establishing justice. We seem to have become so accustomed to this form of political order that it has become normative in our eyes. Theologians from the margins of society, however, offer up a different political model, a model based on the concept of the Trinity.

For the dominant culture, the concept of Trinity is a cosmic religious mystery that explains how a monotheistic deity can be understood as three entities: Father, Son, and Holy Spirit. Although it is emphasized that these three separate entities are an equal composition of one, still, the average Christian perceives a hierarchy, with Father being first, followed by the Son, and trailed by the Spirit. For those doing ethics from the margins of society, the relationship existing within the Trinity, between Father, Son, and Holy Spirit, is not a cosmic puzzle in need of solution, but rather a paragon to be emulated by humanity. Father, Son, and Spirit do not exist in a hierarchy; rather, all three share equally in substance, power, and importance. The Trinity represents a Godhead whose very existence is that of a sharing Being, co-equal in power, awe and authority. As Justo González reminds us, the fourth-century theologians (for example, Ambrose, Jerome, Basil, and Gregory of Nazianzen) who developed the doctrine of the Trinity were staunch critics of greed and argued for economic justice (1990b:113–14).

The Triune God provides a pattern of sharing for those who claim belief in the doctrine of the Trinity, a pattern that subverts any economic system that requires an undereducated and under-skilled army of laborers so that the few can disproportionately hoard the majority of the wealth (De La Torre and Aponte 2001:91). Each person of the Trinity fully participates in divinity, sharing God's power and nature while maintaining their distinct

---

[7] The biblical phrase "alien, orphan and widow" can be understood as meaning the marginalized.

functions. This teaching of the Trinity maintains that it is God's nature to share. God invites all to share divinity and power with God and each other, or as Paul would promise, to become "co-heirs with Christ" (Rom. 8:17). Luis Pedraja writes:

> God reveals to us how to live with one another and in God's image by calling us to engage in a life of sharing. The com-munal nature of the early church as exemplified in the Book of Acts also points us in this direction. What the Trinity reveals to us is a God who exists by sharing both power and divinity. If God does not hoard power, then neither should we hoard power. If God shares the very property of divinity and the essence of the divine is in sharing with others, then should we not live in the same fashion? (2004:Chap.4)

Implementing the Trinity model significantly impacts how eco-nomics and politics should be done by a people attempting to establish a just distribution of power. The model calls for the dis-mantling of social structures that maintain economic injustices and it also calls for all power to be shared, destroying structures of dominance and oppression that foster marginalization. How, then, can those who insist on maintaining their power and privilege become part of the body of Christ?

Throughout his ministry, Jesus proclaimed that God's reign was at hand. What did he mean by this phrase? Those doing ethics from the margins believe that Jesus, and all the prophets before him, understood God's reign to mean a striving toward establishing the Trinity model as the foundation for a social order where justice prevails for all. God's reign is not limited to the other-worldly, but also exists in the here-and-now. This reign of God can best be understood by what Jesus did: he fed the hungry, he healed the sick, he proclaimed the good news to the poor. But while Jesus anchored his good news with the experience of the disenfranchised of his time he still emphasized the ethical responsibilities of those who possess power and authority over others, warning of the importance of moral diligence.

During Jesus' earthly ministry, he and his disciples lived from a common purse (Jn.13:29). The early church continued by creat-ing a church where "all the believers were together, and held all things in common, they sold their goods and possessions and distributed them to all, each according to their need" (Acts 2:44–45). Nonetheless, there were those who tried to create a façade of Christianity while holding on to the material possessions that secured their privilege. The apostle Peter challenged Ananias and his wife Sapphira, who publicly agreed to participate in the Trinity model of community, but privately attempted to secure their wealth. Their sin was not that they withheld a portion of the proceeds of the sale of their property, for, as Peter said, it was their property to keep or dispose as they saw fit (Acts 5:1–11). Their sin was to claim to be part of the faith community while attempting to maintain an uneven distribution of the power that comes from wealth. In a similar way we can conclude that our present political process that establishes an uneven distribution of power and wealth, thanks in great part to PACs and soft money funneled to politicians, is unreconcilable with the model of the Trinity.

STEP 4. CASE STUDIES

- 1. According to present campaign laws, candidates for office are allowed to spend an unlimited sum of their own money on their campaign as long as they decline federal matching funds. Wealthy individuals such as Ross Perot (1992, 1996) and Steve Forbes (1996) financed their multimillion-dollar bids for the White House from their own pockets. Ironically, during the 1996 presidential election, Elizabeth Dole and Dan Quayle both withdrew their bids for the White House, citing a lack of funds. Money is needed to mount any successful campaign, due in part to the skyrocketing costs of television politics.

    — Is this just? Are the wealthy, like Perot and Forbes, free to spend their money any way they choose?
    — Should the ability to make a bid for president be based on the ability to raise money?
    — Should limits be placed to "level the field"? Why or why not?
    — Are ordinary citizens deterred from running for elected office because of their inability to raise as much money as the financially well-connected incumbent? What about less-expensive local elections?

— Should "soft money" be allowed?
— Are the basics of democracy threatened by the current system?
— Should public funds be used to finance elections?

- 2. On January 1, 1999, ninety-year-old Doris Haddock (Granny
D) of Dublin, New Hampshire, began a walk from Los Angeles to Washington, D.C., to deliver a message to elected officials. Some three thousand miles and one year later she arrived
at the front steps of the U.S. Capitol, where she proclaimed,
"The people I met along my way have given me a message to
deliver here. Shame on you, senators and congressmen, who
have turned this headquarters of a great and self-governing people into a bawdy house." Granny D's march was to bring attention to large campaign contributions from corporations, wealthy
individuals, and special interest groups who purchase influence
within the political process (Cooper 2000:259). For example,
during the George W. Bush admnistration, Energy Secretary
Spencer Abraham wrote the *National Energy Policy* with the
assistance of over one hundred executives and lobbyists from
the energy industry. No representative of environmental organizations or consumer groups participated. When they attempted
to meet with the secretary, they were turned away. Many of the
organizations that helped create our national energy policy are
among the most generous political donors, with eighteen companies among the top fifty givers. Topping the list was Enron,
which gave about $2.5 million to Republicans and $800,000
to Democrats.[8]

    — Was Granny D's march effective? If so, why? If not, what
    other actions can people take to protest the influence of large
    political contributions from corporations?
    — Are PACs in and of themselves ethical? Why or why not?
    — Should corporations be allowed to contribute to political
    campaigns? Should limits be placed on what a corporation
    can give?

---

[8] Don Van Natta, Jr. and Neela Banerjee, "Documents Show Energy
Official Met Only with Industry Leaders," *The New York Times*, March
27, 2002.

— Some insist that the use of "soft money" for political fundraising and privately financed campaigns is protected by the First Amendment as a form of free speech, in a sense, "money-as-speech." Is this true? Why or why not?

- 3. Candidates from both parties have received contributions from companies whose executives have been arrested, indicted, or have admitted guilt for defrauding the public or their stockholders. Donations given to federal candidates and party committees during the 2001–2002 political cycle were as follows: Global Crossing gave $1.28 million, WorldCom gave $1.16 million, Qwest Communications gave $877,295, Arthur Anderson gave $758,839, Enron gave $750,350, Tyco gave $314,872, and Adelphia gave $27,250.[9] U.S. colleges were also among the recipients: there are about a half-dozen Kenneth L. Lay (of Enron)-endowed chairs, about forty Arthur Anderson professors of accounting, and several Enron centers of education.

  Some politicians, such as Republican Frank R. Wolf of Virginia, returned their contributions. Others, like Democrat James P. Moran, also of Virginia, did not.

  — Should politicians like Moran return monies from such corporations, as did his colleague Wolf?
  — What should colleges and universities do with funds they have received from corporations that have been indicted for defrauding the public and/or investors?

- 4. Many members of Congress or office holders in former administrations become lobbyists when they leave office. For example, Representative Robert L. Livingston, the former chairman of the Appropriations Committee, now heads one of the most successful lobbyist firms in Washington, D.C. Companies like Chevron-Texaco, Oracle, and Northrop Grumman typically pay him fees of $10,000 to $30,000 a month. His firm

---

[9] Ariana Eunjung Cha, "Give Back the Money? It's an Ethical Dilemma for Recipients When the Donor Has Been Tainted by Scandal." *The Washington Post National Weekly Edition*, September 23–29, 2002.

took in $8.6 million in 2002 and is expected to make over $11 million in 2003.[10]

— Should former public officials be allowed to become lobbyists? If not, is this restricting their rights to employment?
— Should limits be placed on what a lobbyist can be paid? Why or why not?
— Why are firms willing to pay lobbyists such high fees? Are these reasons ethical, even if they are detrimental to those who cannot afford lobbyists?

- 5. Governor Bob Riley of Alabama is a Bible-quoting, teetotaling businessman who as a congressman, represented a mostly rural district. Prior to his run for governor, he distinguished himself as a staunch conservative who consistently voted against any type of liberal legislation. Alabama's tax system has been and still is highly regressive, with taxation beginning on family incomes as low as $4,600 (neighboring Mississippi starts at over $19,000). Alabama also relies on a sales tax as high as 11 percent, even on groceries and infant formula. Alabamians with income under $13,000 pay about 10.9 percent of their income on taxes and those who make over $229,000 pay just 4.1 percent. Those who benefit the most from this arrangement are the state's large timber companies and mega-farms whose powerful lobby groups have maintained the status quo.[11]

Yet, surprisingly, when Riley was elected governor, he proposed a new tax plan that would shift the tax burden from the poor to the wealthy. His reasoning was based on his belief that the Alabama tax system violated biblical principles that prohibit Christians from oppressing the poor. Governor Riley's tax plan was voted down during the September 2003 election. Even John Giles, president of the Christian Coalition, spoke out against the plan.

---

[10] John Tierney, "G.O.P. Lobbyists in Demand as Business Sees Its Chance," *The New York Times*, January 6, 2003.

[11] Adam Cohen, "What Would Jesus Do? Sock It to Alabama's Corporate Landowners," *The New York Times*, June 10, 2003.

— Although Governor Riley's tax plan was voted down, was it a proper ethical stance to take? Why or why not?

— Was the governor imposing his religious views on the people of Alabama?

— Why do you think John Giles of the Christian Coalition spoke out against the plan?

— Both Governor Riley and the head of the Christian Coalition claimed the Bible as the authority for their position. Were either of them right? Why?

CHAPTER 11

Life and Death

STEP 1. OBSERVING

While disagreement exists about what actions should be taken on most political and economical issues, there is general agreement on the basic human right to good health. Nearly everyone would argue that human beings have a right not to have their well-being threatened by exterior forces. Although we may disagree as to how this might happen, still, human beings can expect not to have governments or businesses impose upon them conditions that produce illness or death. In fact, it could be argued that when this occurs, it undermines Jesus' promise to provide an abundant life. Yet, for many within the United States, the quality of health care ranges from poor to non-existent. In addition to a lack of adequate health, specifically for the poor who are disproportionately people of color, those with darker skin also face a greater risk of being incarcerated and/or executed by the state. This chapter will explore how issues of life (adequate health care) and death (capital punishment) impact marginalized communities.

The Lack of Health Care Coverage

The lack of health care coverage causes both medical and financial problems for the uninsured. Since the dismantling of the social safety net set in place by the New Deal, a decline in health coverage has occurred within all employment sectors since 1980. Those most affected are low-income wage earners (defined as having a family income below $30,000), comprising two-thirds of all uninsured people. Because they are employed, they are not eligible for public insurance. Due to their low income, they cannot afford to buy employment-based or individual health insurance. Those who are foreign-born and not offered employment-based insurance find it almost impossible to obtain public coverage because of the restrictive immigration and welfare policies enacted since 1995.

It should be noted that the lack of health care insurance is not limited to the poor and people of color. The white middle-class now also finds itself struggling to maintain an insurance plan. One New York City subway poster, sponsored by Working Today, a nonprofit agency, captures the mathematics of the situation: "After paying for health insurance, you take home less than the minimum wage."

Although the uninsured are predominately non-Hispanic U.S.-born white citizens (the largest segment of the population), race and ethnicity play a significant role in determining who is and who

Table 3
2002 Percent of Uninsured

Uninsured in 2002

Source: Census Bureau

is not insured. African Americans are twice as likely and Latina/os three times as likely as whites to lack basic health coverage. (See Table 3.) These racial and ethnic groups have higher rates of inadequate or no coverage because they receive less employment-based insurance and include more lower-income families (Institute of Medicine 2001:61–64, 82–84).

The Quality of Health Care

Even when insurance and medical treatment are available, the quality of care received varies by one's race or ethnicity. According to a study appearing in *The New England Journal of Medicine*, the race and gender of a patient complaining of chest pain affects the physician's decision about whether or not to refer the patient for cardiac catheterization (Schulman et al. 1999:623). In another study published by the same journal, pharmacies in predominantly nonwhite neighborhoods were significantly less likely to stock medication to treat patients with severe pain than those pharmacies located in predominantly white neighborhoods (Morrison et al. 2000:1026). Several articles published by *The Journal of the American Medical Association* seem to indicate that poverty, along with race and ethnicity, influence the quality of care received by acutely ill insured patients in a hospital. Even when the patient's income and insurance benefits are the same, racially and ethnically disenfranchised persons receive a lower quality of health care (Kahn et al. 1994:1174).

The first comprehensive study of racial disparities in health care was conducted by the Institute of Medicine, an independent research agency that advises Congress on health care issues. Reviewing over a hundred studies conducted from 1992 to 2002, the report concluded that the disparities in health care due to race and ethnicity contribute to higher death rates among people of color from cancer, heart disease, diabetes, and HIV infections. To illustrate the point, they cite a study conducted by Medicare that shows that blacks suffering from diabetes are 3.6 times more likely than whites to have their limbs amputated instead of receiving more sophisticated treatments.[1] The empirical evidence overwhelmingly

[1] Sheryl Gay Stolberg, "Minorities Receive Inferior Care, Even if Insured, Study Finds," *The New York Times*, March 21, 2002.

indicates that, all things being equal, those who are racially and ethnically marginalized receive a lower quality of health care than their white counterparts.

In short, the present-day health care system in the United States is structurally designed in such a way that it brings better health to the white middle and upper classes than it does to people of color. One could go so far as to say that it tends to bring ill-health or even death to poor people of color. This reality has historical roots. The most infamous example is the forty-year-long (1932–1972) Tuskegee experiment in which the U.S. Public Health Service (PHS) conducted an experiment on 412 poor black sharecroppers in the late stages of syphilis. They were told by government researchers that they were being treated, when in fact they were not. The data hoped to be obtained from the experiment was gathered from autopsies. Consequently, these poor black men were deliberately left to degenerate under the ravages of tertiary syphilis, whose symptoms included tumors, heart disease, paralysis, blindness, insanity, and finally death.

Ironically, this experiment was underway at the time white Americans were prosecuting Nazi officials at the Nuremberg trials immediately following the Second World War for carrying out medical experiments on human beings (Jews). More recently, about fifteen hundred six-month-old, predominately black and Hispanic babies in Los Angeles were used as human guinea pigs in June 1990. They were given an experimental measles vaccine developed by Kaiser Permanente. The parents of these children were never informed that the vaccine, which was used before in two-thirds world countries with devastating results, was experimental.[2]

Disparities in the Legal System

The legal system within the United States also negatively impacts marginalized communities. A disproportionate number of people of color face prison and capital punishment. At the close of the twentieth century, the United States incarcerated more than two million of its citizens, of which 70 percent were people of color.

---

[2] Marlene Cimons, "U.S. Measles Experiment Failed to Disclose Risk," *The Los Angeles Times*, June 17, 1996.

In 2000 it was estimated that 10 percent of African American men were behind bars. While African Americans represent approximately 13 percent of the U.S. population, they represent 50 percent of the prison population (Parenti 1999:xii, 167). Figures like these that indicate that prison populations are disproportionately composed of people of color should not be surprising, especially when we consider the following:

— Latino/as are likely to be found innocent in only 26 percent of their legal cases while non-Hispanics are released before trial 66 percent of the time;
— blacks who kill whites are sentenced to death 22 times more frequently than blacks who kill blacks and 7 times more frequently than whites who kill blacks;
— black youths are 6 times more likely to be imprisoned than white youths, even when charged with similar crimes and when neither has a prior record.[3]

Amnesty International has documented how the United States places a greater worth on the life of a white person than it does on the life of a person of color. Since capital punishment was reinstated in 1977, some half a million people have been murdered. The race of these victims was almost equally split between whites and nonwhites, yet 80 percent of all executions occurred for those convicted of murdering a white victim. While most murders in this country are intra-racial (the murderer and victim are of the same race), of the 845 prisoners executed from 1977 to 2002, 53 percent were whites convicted of murdering whites while 10 percent were blacks convicted of murdering blacks, thus maintaining the subconscious belief that the life of a black person is worth less than the life of a white person. When blacks are brought to trial for murder, prosecutors routinely dismiss black jurors. Hence, we should not be surprised that at least one out of every five executed African Americans was convicted by an all-white jury (Amnesty International 2003:3).

---

[3] Paul Shepard, "Rights Group's Study Links Justice and Race; Want Lawmakers to Act," *The Grand Rapids Press*, May 7, 2000.

The U.S. Department of Justice's own statisticians show that of the 3,581 individuals awaiting execution in the United States at the start of 2002, 55 percent were white while 45 percent were nonwhite, of which 11.2 percent were Hispanic (Snell and Maruschak 2002:8). Statistics such as these have led Amnesty International to conclude that "Beyond any reasonable doubt, the U.S. death penalty continues to reflect the deep-rooted prejudices of the society that condones its use. Amnesty International cannot find any evidence that current legal safeguards eliminate racial bias in the application of the death penalty" (2003:2). Other studies have concluded that the race of the murder victim plays a significant role in determining whether the victim's murderer will be executed.[4] Black leaders, like Jesse Jackson, declare:

> Who receives the death penalty has less to do with the violence of the crime than the color of the criminal's skin or, more often, the color of the victim's skin. . . . The death penalty is essentially an arbitrary punishment. There are no objective rules or guidelines for when a prosecutor should seek the death penalty, when a jury should recommend it, and when a judge should give it. This lack of objective, measurable standards ensures that the application of the death penalty will be discriminatory against racial, gender, and ethnic groups. (1996:96–97)

Not only is the imposition of capital punishment dependent on a person's race or ethnicity, but it is also highly dependent on a person's economic class. The economically privileged are simply not executed. U.S. Supreme Court Associate Justice William O. Douglas bemoaned the fact that "one searches our chronicles in vain for the execution of any member of the affluent strata of this society" (Costanzo 2002:174). Why have people of color, specifically blacks, been historically over-represented in our prison system and most specifically on death row? Mark Lewis Taylor suggests that our present judicial system is rooted in the former

---

[4] Adam Liptak, "Death Row Numbers Decline as Challenges to System Rise," *The New York Times*, January 11, 2003.

institution of slavery, thus explaining its apartheid character. He writes:

> Especially after the Civil War and the announced abolition of slavery, the prisons became the major locus for the continual enforcement of slave conditions for black Americans. In short, today's prison is enmeshed in the legacy of slavery just as today's capital punishment is in the legacy of lynching. (2001:45)

Whether considering the health system or the legal system, the underlying assumption is that life can be reduced to a commodity whose value can be determined. But in this country not all human life has equal value. The life of a white person has historically been more valuable than that of a dark-skinned person, the life of a wealthy person more valuable than that of a poor person, and the life of a heterosexual man more valuable than the life of a woman or gay person. A quick perusal of life insurance rates indicates the differentiating worth of individuals. In the past, nonwhites were charged about 25 percent higher premiums for the same coverage of life insurance paid by white people. Companies like MetLife have been ordered by a U.S. district court judge to respond to accusations of consistently charging African Americans higher premiums than whites. Other companies, like Prudential and American General, chose to settle, refunding up to $206 million to policyholders. Numerous studies exist showing that people of color also pay higher auto and house insurance.[5]

This nation's judicial system seems to be rooted in the violent birth of the country, influencing how the very definition of justice is determined. For Mark Lewis Taylor, the very foundation of the

---

[5] Scott J. Paltrow, "In Relic of '50s and '60s, Blacks Still Pay More for a Type of Insurance," *The Wall Street Journal*, April 27, 2000; "MetLife Ordered to Respond to Rate Discrimination Suit," *Insurance Journal*, June 27, 2001. See also an interesting report on how people of color pay higher insurance rates, specifically in housing (U.S. Department of Housing and Urban Development, *Testing for Discrimination in Home Insurance* at www.huduser.org/publication/fairhsg/homeown/discrim. html).

United States and the forging of its economic life designed to benefit a small segment of the dominant culture was achieved through the violent appropriation of the land of the indigenous people and the cultivation of that land by the imposition of African slavery (Taylor 2001:50–51). Thus, those who have suffered under the unjust U.S. justice system cannot rely on or look toward the dominant culture for guidance on defining justice. The persistence of discriminatory social structures like the health care system or American legal system is an indictment of the dominant culture.

STEP 2. REFLECTING

One of the consequences of the economic structure of the United States is the subjugation of its own citizens, particularly the marginalized, to social structures such as our health care and legal systems that do not foster abundant life. The social structures of a society are established around or to support certain social and moral values. But the question must be asked: whose or what social and moral values are the foundation of these structures? Is the morality of any given society whatever the dominant culture of that society decides is correct social behavior? To a great extent, any judicial system that is established by the dominant culture exists to legitimize the social and moral values of that culture, which is usually privileged by whiteness and economic class. These values are then imposed upon the marginalized, who may well perceive them to be unjust and oppressive.

We should therefore not be surprised when ethical issues concerning health care or the legal system represent the perspectives of the dominant culture. Seldom explored are the perspectives of the disenfranchised, usually those ill treated by the present systems. A clear example lies within the field of bioethics, where the roles played by racism, classism, and sexism within the medical establishment are rarely discussed. When bioethicists focus on the ethical issues raised by scientific and technological advances, advances that may prolong or secure a richer quality of life, little attention is given to how or why those on the margins fail to benefit.

Generally the marginalized are excluded from the benefits of medical advances, or the fair application of justice within the legal system, mainly because of how they are seen. "Seeing" can transform human beings into things, into objects. Once social structures adopt this form of seeing, it becomes normalized and legitimized within society. Seeing (or defining) dark-skinned bodies as dangerous occurs unconsciously. This is demonstrated by simply consulting a dictionary for a definition of the word "black." When the dominant culture gazes upon a dark-skinned male body, that body is automatically defined as something evil, wicked, harmful, and dangerous. If the act of "seeing" is used to mask the power and privilege of those who benefit from how reality is constructed, then seeing dark bodies as dangerous is the first crucial step in maintaining a system that continuously seeks to punish or confine those dangerous dark bodies.

Actions taken upon people of color based solely on appearance are illustrated by a study conducted at the Department of Psychology of the University of Colorado, whose findings were published in the *Journal of Experimental Social Psychology*. The research was inspired by the shooting of Amadou Diallo, an unarmed 22-year-old West African immigrant killed in the Bronx in 1999 by police officers who mistook his wallet for a gun. The subjects of the study played a video game where they were instructed to shoot human targets that were armed. Some of the targets were white, others were black. The subjects, who in all but one sample were primarily white, were more likely to mistakenly conclude black men were armed and shoot them. When confronted by blacks holding cell phones, wallets, soft-drink cans, or cameras, the subjects were more likely to shoot than when confronted by whites. When confronted by white targets with guns, subjects were less likely to fire than if the targets were blacks with guns. The study concluded that:

> Ethnicity influences the shoot/don't shoot decision primarily because traits associated with African Americans, namely "violent" or "dangerous," can act as a schema to influence perceptions of an ambiguously threatening target . . . [hence] participants showed a bias to shoot African American targets more rapidly and/or more frequently than White targets. The implications of this bias are clear and disturbing. (Correll et al. 2002:1325, 1327)

How our culture teaches us to "see" dark bodies shapes the behavior of people responding quickly and automatically when confronted by those from the margins who are dark-skinned.

STEP 3. PRAYING

The *imago Dei* (the image of God) in every person created by God establishes the infinite worth of each human being. To ignore this *imago Dei* violates the inherited rights of all humans. Because the spark of the Absolute exists within every human, all possess dignity. Even so, social structures are constructed to deny the worth of those who are relegated to the margins or, worse, cause the oppressed to question if they even possess the *imago Dei*. As Desmond Tutu observed, "The ultimate evil is not the suffering . . . which is meted out to those who are God's children. The ultimate evil of oppression . . . is when it succeeds in making a child of God begin to doubt that he or she is a child of God" (1991:131).

How is the *imago Dei* denied? By assigning more worth to one human life than to another human life because of race, class, or gender. To ignore the *imago Dei* of the least among us is to reject the God of life.

Taking capital punishment as an example, we can note that biblical texts, specifically in Leviticus, prescribe capital punishment for such crimes as murder and rape. But Leviticus also prescribes that a disobedient, stubborn child who curses his or her parent is subject to the death penalty (20:9). So is the adulterer (20:10), the homosexual (20:13), the person who curses (24:16), and the Sabbath breaker (Ex. 31:14–15). Still, biblical texts also provide examples of murderers and rapists who were not condemned for their transgressions. Moses, who killed an Egyptian (Ex. 2:11), is chosen to lead his people to liberation. King David, a man chosen by God, uses his power as king to force himself on Bathsheba and then, to cover his transgression, has her husband murdered (2 Sam. 11). In this particular case, not only is David acquitted (2 Sam. 12:13), but the ancestry of Jesus can be traced back to this adulterous union (Mt. 1:6). Such apparent contradictions between God's law and how those chosen by God fell short of the law, yet were greatly used by God, can be understood through the affirmation of the basic principle of the sacredness of human life due to its reflection of the *imago Dei*.

The *imago Dei* finds fullest expression in the personhood of Jesus as he turned many "rules" upside down. For example, Jesus said, "You have heard that it was said, an eye for an eye and a tooth for a tooth, but I say to unto you, do not resist evil" (Mt. 5:38–39). It could be argued that Jesus was "unjust" as that term is defined by our present culture, for he refused to punish the wrong doer. Rather than accommodating the current definition of justice by meting out deserved punishment, he was quick to provide undeserved mercy. In John 8 he is confronted with an adulterous woman caught in the very act (where was the man?), a capital offense. Asked to judge her, he instead balanced justice and mercy with the famous line, "Whoever is without sin should cast the first stone." Throughout the New Testament, Jesus provides a model that should prompt us not to look toward the law for justice principles, but rather to ground moral guidance and principles upon relationships, always cognizant that all human beings contain the image of God.

STEP 4. CASE STUDIES

- 1. The Reverend Jim Holley, minister at Detroit's Little Rock Baptist Church, recalls a family who came to him seeking guidance. Their elderly father was on a respirator. The doctors respectfully suggested that it was time to let him go. Still, the family wondered if the white doctors were anxious to pull the plug on their black father to give the machine to a white person. "True enough," says Reverend Holley, "when we went back in there, the man had passed. And the machine was being used by somebody else."[6]

  Given the history of medical care in the U.S., which has devalued the life of the marginalized, we should not be surprised that ethical dilemmas such as the use of euthanasia are approached quite differently by people of color. As society debates the morality of assisted suicide, people of color cannot help but wonder if this could be used as a new opportunity to victimize the marginalized. If a person of color is being kept alive by a respirator, would doctors encourage the family to "pull the plug" because a white patient might need that respirator?

  Seven former and current members of the U.S. Commission on Civil Rights filed legal briefs with the U.S. Supreme Court

---

[6] Lori Montgomery, "Blacks Fearful of White Doctors Pulling the Plug," *The Detroit Free Press*, February 26, 1997.

arguing that the poor, the disabled, and those racially and ethnically disenfranchised would be among the first to feel substantial pressure from medical professionals to die if physician-assisted suicide were legalized.

— Is Reverend Holley and the family he ministered to being paranoid and oversensitive, or does sufficient evidence exist for them to be concerned?

— If euthanasia were legal, would insurance companies find it more cost effective to cover assisted-suicide medical procedures for people of color rather than finance aggressive, and expensive, treatment?

— Should the marginalized be concerned about assisted suicide, if it were legalized, becoming a significant form of medical treatment for people of color? Why or why not?

- 2. During the 1950s, the U.S. ranked third among all nations in its ability to prevent infant mortality.[7] By the 1990s, the U.S. had the highest infant mortality rate of all the Western European countries. In 2004, infant mortality within the U.S. rose for the first time since 1958.[8] Developing countries like Sri Lanka, Cuba, and Jamaica were among the many who had a lower infant mortality rate (Sanders & Mattson 1998:14). More disturbing is the finding that among U.S. non-euroamericans, the infant mortality rate was higher than those of many two-thirds world nations. In 2003, the infant mortality rate for white babies was 5.7 per 1,000, while for black infants the figure was more than double at 14.0 per 1,000. U.S. Hispanic infants had a higher rate, with Amerindians having the highest;[9] nevertheless, the overall gap between white and non-white infants continued to widen (Iyasu et al. 2002:826).

---

[7] The infant mortality rate indicates the number of deaths occurring among children under the age of one per 1,000 live births in a given year.

[8] Rob Stein, "U.S. Infant Mortality Rate Rises 3%: First Increase Since '58 Surprises Officials as Other Health Indicators Keep Improving," *The Washington Post*, February 12, 2004.

[9] "Disparity in Child Mortality a Complex Equation," *Albuquerque Journal*, September 15, 2003.

— Do these statistics indicate that the value of white infants'
lives is greater than that of infants of color? If not, how do
we explain the continuously growing gap between the mortality rate of white infants and infants of color?

— If women of color are unable to afford prenatal care or vaccination shots once the child is born, due to lack of insurance
or low-paying wages, should they be provided by the state?

— Should the U.S. have universal health care insurance? If so,
who would pay for it?

- 3. In 1986, Calvin Ollins, a fourteen-year-old, special-educa-
tion eighth-grader was convicted and incarcerated for life for
the rape and bludgeoning murder of Lori Roscetti, a twenty-
three-year-old medical student. Police, under community pressure to solve the case, arrested Ollins along with three others.
Authorities told Ollins that if he confessed, he could go home.
Thinking he would return to his mother, Ollins confessed, only
to recant once he realized he was instead going to prison. Mar-
cellius Bradford, also convicted of the crime, implicated Ollins
after, he says, he was beaten by police and promised a reduced
sentence. Ollins and the others charge that the police manufactured evidence, coerced confessions, and falsified lab results.

Fifteen years later, DNA tests proved Ollins was innocent.
He entered prison as a child and left as a twenty-nine-year-old
man.[10] An examination of one hundred and ten inmates whose
convictions were overturned from 1989 (when DNA tests began
to be conducted) till 2002 found 1) eleven served time on death
row, two of whom were exonerated days before their execution;
2) slightly over a third received compensation, mainly through
state claims, for their wrongful imprisonment; 3) all were
dumped back into society as abruptly as they were plucked out,
with no help entitlements (e.g., parole officers and counseling);
4) almost all were poor; 5) two-thirds were black or Hispanic.[11]

---

[10] Sharon Cohen, "Jailed at 14, Freed at 29: 'I haven't begun to live,'"
The Grand Rapids Press, June 2, 2002.

[11] Sharon Cohen and Deborah Hastings, "Freedom Often Brings Pain
after a Thousand Years in Prison," *The Grand Rapids Press*, June 2, 2002.

— What obligations does the state have toward the wrongfully convicted? Should the state providing counseling, job placement, and so on to these individuals? If so, who should pay for it?

— Should the state's legal liabilities for wrongful convictions be limited?

— Is the fact that most are poor and of color relevant or significant? Why or why not?

— Are accusations of police brutality to be taken seriously? If so, how?

— What about those who are rightfully convicted of a felony and serve their time? Upon being released, in most states, they are barred from receiving welfare or food stamps, public housing, voting, obtaining certain jobs in plumbing, education, barbering, or health care (just to name a few). Should such restrictions exist, even after they have paid their debt to society?

— Are these former prisoners simply getting what they deserve for the crimes they committed?

— What consequences, if any, exist for society if these former felons are not reintegrated into society?

— Is the fact that these ex-convicts are disproportionately black and Latino significant?

4. In 1984, David Wayne Spence was sentenced to death in Texas for killing three teenagers. His death-row appeal got the attention of a Waco businessman, who spent part of his personal fortune attempting to prove that Spence's conviction was the result of suppressed evidence and intimidated witnesses. Authorities denied these allegations. In 1997, Spence was executed, but his case was brought up again in 2000 as an example of a miscarriage of justice when the media questioned then-presidential candidate George W. Bush's record on capital punishment.[12]

During the 2000 presidential election, then-candidate Bush unapologetically proclaimed his born-again evangelical Christian faith. Simultaneously he touted his "law and order" cre-

---

[12] John Council, "Weirdness in Waco: A Rundown of Some of the Town's More Unusual Cases," *The Texas Lawyer*, July 28, 2003.

dentials while governor of Texas, where he oversaw over one hundred and fifty executions, including that of David W. Spence.

— Does a contradiction exist between being a Christian and capital punishment? Why or why not?

— Should the fact that those most likely to be executed are poor (because they lack the funds to obtain competent counsel) or black (due to institutionalized racism) make any difference in the capital punishment debate? Why or why not?

— How is the process for determining capital punishment reconciled with mainstream American values like equal protection, fairness in distributing justice, due process, or the protection of the innocent?

— The majority of nations have abolished capital punishment as a fundamental human rights violation. Are they correct? Should the U.S. do likewise? Why or why not?

— Because the commandment says "Thou shall not murder (*rāsah*)" instead of "Thou shall not kill (*hārag*)," can it be argued that the state has the right to kill an offender? Can that right be lost? How?

— Is capital punishment an effective deterrent to capital crime?

— Should justice be based on the principle of *lex talionis*, a life for a life? Can this principle be reconciled with the biblical mandate?

• 5. Madison Hobley, Stanley Howard, Leroy Orange, and Aaron Patterson awaited execution in Illinois. They had long claimed that they falsely confessed under torture overseen by Commander Jon Burge of the Chicago Police Department, who has since been fired. Although they have yet to convince judges or prosecutors that they were wrongly convicted, all four were released from prison after being pardoned by the Illinois governor.[13] Since Illinois reestablished the death penalty in 1997, thirteen death-row prisoners have been exonerated. As a result, the state conducted an extensive three-year study of the capital punishment system. The conclusions convinced Governor

---

[13] Jodi Wilgoren, "Illinois Governor Pardons Four Death Row Inmates," *The New York Times*, January 11, 2003.

George Ryan that the system was both flawed and racist, leading him on January 11, 2003, to commute the sentences of all
death row inmates (164 men and 3 women). Governor Ryan
defended his action, saying that it was correct "because our
three-year study has found only more questions about the fairness of sentencing, because of the spectacular failure to reform
the system, because we have seen justice delayed for countless
death row inmates with potentially meritorious claims, because
the Illinois death penalty system is arbitrary and capricious—
and therefore immoral."[14]

Illinois is not the only state raising such questions. The attorney general of Maryland called for the abolition of the death
penalty in his state due to the exoneration of several death-row
prisoners (via DNA evidence) and the release of that state's own
report on the system, which showed that race plays a role in the
prosecution of death penalty cases. The study conducted by the
University of Maryland concluded that blacks who kill whites
are significantly more likely to face the death penalty within
Maryland than blacks who kill blacks, or white murderers.[15] In
Pennsylvania, a committee appointed by that state's Supreme
Court recommended that the state halt all executions until the
effects of racial bias in capital cases can be better understood.
The committee concluded that, "empirical studies . . . demon-
strate that, at least in some counties, race plays a major, if not
overwhelming, role in the imposition of the death penalty."[16]

When the Illinois report was released, the study's co-chair
declared "repair or repeal . . . fix the capital punishment system
or abolish it . . . there is no other principled recourse."[17]

---

[14] Jodi Wilgoren, "Few Death Sentences or None Under Overhaul
Proposed by Illinois Panel," *The New York Times*, April 16, 2002; idem,
"Two Days Left in Term, Governor Clears Out Death Row in Illinois,"
The New York Times, January 12, 2003.

[15] Adam Liptak, "Death Penalty Found More Likely When Victim Is
White," *The New York Times*, January 8, 2003; idem, "Top Lawyer in Maryland Calls for End to Executions," *The New York Times*, January 31, 2003.

[16] Idem, "Suspension of Executions Is Urged for Pennsylvania," *The
New York Times*, March 5, 2003.

[17] Wilgoren, "Few Death Sentences," *The New York Times*, April 16,
2002.

— Even though Governor Ryan believed Madison Hobley, Stanley Howard, Leroy Orange, and Aaron Patterson were falsely convicted, the judicial system did not. Did the governor overstep his authority?

— Is the system truly flawed? Does race matter? If so, should it be fixed or abolished?

— Even if the system of capital punishment were fool-proof, should it still be abolished?

— Does the state have a right to execute its most dangerous citizens who commit heinous crimes? Why or why not?

PART IV

CASE STUDIES
OF BUSINESS RELATIONSHIPS

CHAPTER 12

Introduction to Business Relationships

Each society must determine for itself how the goods and services the community needs and/or wants are to be produced, who will be responsible for producing these goods or providing these services, where production will occur, and how the goods and services will be distributed within the community. Within the present global marketplace, the responsibility for answering these questions generally belongs to multinational corporations. In theory, an employee has a right to accept or reject employment at a given company. If a corporation treats its employees poorly or refuses to pay a living wage, the employee is free to find a job elsewhere. But what if the two parties negotiating are not equal, which is true of the average worker and the typical company? Or what if through monopolistic dealings and political connections, one company can determine how a particular good or service is to be produced, who will produce it, where it will be produced, and how it is to be distributed? What effects will this have on employees and consumers?

Corporations are recognized by society as "artificial persons"; they are able to enter into agreements and to be sued when those agreements are broken. Corporations, which are legal entities with limited liabilities, consist of three groups of people. First come the stockholders who provide capital; their liabilities are limited to the money invested. In theory, the *raison d'être* of the corporation is to create profit for these shareholders. Second are the directors and officers charged with administrating the corporation's assets and running the day-to-day activities. And, finally, there are the employees who provide the labor necessary to produce the goods or provide the services.

In effect, the corporation is a "soulless" person. Can it, then, be expected to follow moral dictates and practices? Even if it were to operate according to some moral standards, we are again forced to ask, whose or which standards? If a multinational corporation has offices in the United States, the Middle East, and Asia, should it follow Christian, Muslim, or Buddhist ethics? Should it adhere instead to a system of secular humanist ethics? How should it operate if it has a branch office in a society that believes women have a moral obligation to stay at home and raise children? Should the corporation not hire women or pay them less? Should corporate ethics be defined by what is customary or legal in the country in which it operates? Should "when in Rome do as the Romans do" be the basic rule to follow?

For example, laws regulating the disposal of corporate by-products, which are stringent in the U.S. in order to protect the environment, are lax in many two-thirds world countries. Likewise, the safety regulations in the U.S. that protect employees from physical hazards at the workplace are non-existent in some other countries. Yet, on the other hand, a practice like bribing government officials to facilitate the navigation of bureaucratic red tape, while illegal in the U.S., is considered an acceptable and necessary business procedure elsewhere. Because certain safety and environmental regulations that are mandatary within the U.S. cut into corporate profits, relocating to two-thirds world nations with less stringent laws may be desirable for a corporation. Do these practices in different countries require a system of business ethics in which what is moral depends on where one does business?

Economist Milton Friedman argues for restricting moral obligations, limiting corporate responsibilities to obeying the laws in whatever nation a corporation finds itself pursuing profit:

> There is one and only one social responsibility of business — to use its resources and engage in activities designed to increase its profits so long as it stays within the rules of the game, which is to say, engage in open and free competition, without deception or fraud. . . . Few trends could so thoroughly undermine the very foundations of our free society as the acceptance by corporate officials of a social responsibility other than to make as much money for their stockholders as possible. (1962:133)

Friedman ignores any connection between corporate profitability and the quality of life of the general public or of the corporation's employees. Corporations are legally created entities responsible for abiding by the law to insure individual legal rights, but their participation within society also subjects them to certain moral rights beyond simply making "as much money for their stockholders as possible." Corporate responsibility that goes no further than making as much money as possible can produce a vacuum in ethics and clearly lead to abuse. According to business ethicist Manuel Velasquez: "Unlike legal rights, moral rights are not limited to a particular jurisdiction. If humans have a moral right not to be tortured, for example, then this is a right that human beings of every nationality have regardless of the legal system under which they live" (1998:87).

Nonetheless, a danger exists if such moral rights are established from the perspective of the dominant culture that has a vested interest in corporate profit, in securing "as much money as possible." Moral rights must be a product that includes the disenfranchised community from which many employees are drawn. And if we speak of *Christian* moral rights, then it is the responsibility of the marginalized faith community to spearhead the formulation of what these moral rights should be.

The definition of moral rights should never be too tightly limited and it should include positive actions as well as proscriptions. As Joel Feinberg notes, moral rights mean that other agents have a positive duty to assist the holder of moral rights with what is needed to pursue freely those rights (1980:224). Conservatives generally reject the concept of positive duty, maintaining that the government should not demand that businesses become responsible for the welfare of their employees, but simply that businesses not interfere with the employees' pursuit of their rights.

For example, if it is determined that individuals who work for a corporation have a moral right to a wage that supports the basics of human existence (food, clothes, and shelter), then the concept of positive rights would insist that corporations have a duty to pay a living wage. The employer cannot simply claim the worker's right to freely choose to work elsewhere. For while workers may indeed have the right to reject a job, they cannot reject every job if they hope to survive. Because workers cannot bargain as equals with multinational corporations to arrive at mutually beneficial arrangements, they are limited to the type of wages corporations are willing to pay. When the heads of corporations increase their wealth at the expense of the labor pool because they have the power to control wages, the corporation, even though it is an artificial person, is acting immorally. By extension, those who are privileged by the actions of the corporation are also acting immorally — whether they are the officers, directors, stockholders, or the consumers.

In Part II of this book, we considered case studies that explored the impact of neoliberalism upon the global stage. Part III provided case studies that narrowed our exploration to the field of national policies. In this final part, we will consider case studies that explore the ethics of business within a global marketplace by focusing on three areas: the moral accountability of corporations, affirmative action, and private property.

CHAPTER 13

Corporate Accountability

STEP 1. OBSERVING

At the start of the twenty-first century, the American business community was rocked by corporate scandals. The business shenanigans that occurred in corporations like Enron, Arthur Anderson, Global Crossing, and Adelphia Communications (to name but a few) revealed how a privileged elite was able to amass great fortunes on the backs of shareholders, the middle-class, and the poor.

Trading Money for Influence

We begin with the example of Enron CEO Ken L. Lay, who had close ties with the Bush family. Enron hired prominent members of the first Bush administration (such as James Baker and Robert Mosbacher), and was also among the largest donors to the second Bush presidential campaign. Newly elected President George W. Bush appointed two of Ken Lay's nominations to the Federal Energy Regulatory Commission (FERC), and one, Pat Wood, was named chair of the commission. FERC has oversight of the nation's electricity and gas markets, markets in which Enron made most of its money. The Commission failed to act during the winter of 2000–2001 when Enron manipulated the price of gas and electricity during California's energy crisis. Enron's price-gouging maneuvers insured that the company made the bulk of its profits ($7 billion in net trading profits during the energy crisis) at the expense of Californians who endured rolling blackouts and higher energy prices.[1]

---

[1] David Barboza, "Despite Demand, Enron Papers Show Big Profit

Examining Enron's connections with the Bush administrations is not intended to imply that Republicans are the only ones to benefit from relationships with multinational corporations. For example, Democratic Party chairperson Terry McAuliffe made $18 million by investing $100,000 in telecommunication giant Global Crossing before it went public and he then dumped his stock (along with founder Gary Winnick and co-chairperson Lodwrick Cook) before bankruptcy made the stock worthless. Similarly, George Bush, Sr. received stock valued at $14 million, in lieu of an $80,000 fee for speaking to Global Crossing's clients in Japan.[2]

While the peddling of political favors in return for campaign support continues to plague and threaten U.S. democracy, it is important to note that corporate scandals that enrich the privileged are not limited to accounting shenanigans or trading money for influence. Another major issue is the commodification of human beings for the sake of profit, a process that at times results in the loss of human life — usually the life of the less fortunate. Practices of both the Bayer pharmaceutical company and McWane foundries illustrate this point.

The Commodification of Human Life

Cutter Biological, a division of Bayer, profited handsomely from the sale of a blood-clotting medicine for hemophiliacs. By 1982, the Center for Disease Control (CDC) warned that medicine using blood products, like the one produced by Cutter, might transmit the AIDS virus. In February 1984, as evidence mounted that the earlier version was infecting hemophiliacs with AIDS, Cutter introduced a safer medicine. By October of that year, a joint study conducted by Cutter and CDC found that the newer medicine eradicated the threat of transmitting the AIDS virus because it was heat treated. However, 74 percent of hemophiliacs who had used the older, unheated version of the medicine tested positive for HIV. Not surprisingly, the study, once made public, made the old ver-

---

on Price Bets," *The New York Times*, December 12, 2002; and Adam Zagorin, "The Trail out of Texas," *Time* (February 18, 2002): 41.

[2] Michael Weisskopf, "Equal-Opportunity Crises," *Time* (February 25, 2002): 45.

sion of the medicine unmarketable within the United States and Europe. The company, holding an overstocked inventory of the old medicine valued at $4 million, then distributed it to Asia and Latin America.[3]

In November of that same year, Cutter informed its Hong Kong distributor that "we must use up stocks" of unheated medicine before making "safer, better" heat-treated products available. Not only was the old medicine sold, but Cutter continued to produce unheated medicine for foreign distribution because it held several fixed-price contracts that made the old medicine more profitable. Hundreds of overseas hemophiliacs who used Cutter's unheated medicine have since died of AIDS. When the company raised the ethical question whether it could "in good faith continue to ship nonheated-treated coagulation products" abroad, the company's task force that studied the issue responded in the affirmative. In twenty years since then, how has Bayer, the parent company, responded to the task force's ethical decision? Bayer continues to claim that Cutter "behaved responsibly, ethically and humanely" in selling its old product abroad. Bayer was not alone in its ethical reasoning. Three other American-based companies, Armour Pharmaceutical, Baxter International, and Alpha Therapeutic, also continued to sell unheated medicine, citing the same reasoning as Bayer.[4]

It is easy to assume that Asians and Latin Americans received the life-threatening medicine because their lives were worth less than those of "Americans." While this is true to some extent, it is also true that companies like Bayer are more concerned with making a profit than with discriminating against certain groups. With mounting pressure to discontinue the unheated medicine, Bayer continued to question the study's findings although most scientists agreed with the CDC study that the heat-treated medicine prevented AIDS.

If a corporation decides that its first responsibility is to create profit for its stockholders, then it may need to redefine what is just and ethical in order to allow the maximum profit to be made. If

---

[3] Walt Bodgdanich and Eric Koli, "2 Paths of Bayer Drug in 80s: Riskier Type Went Overseas," *The New York Times*, May 22, 2003.

[4] Ibid.

people are hurt in the pursuit of profit, it matters very little whether they are white or of color or where they come from. This does not mean that racism and ethnic discrimination do not continue to play a role in deciding who benefits from corporate decisions, it just reiterates that classism can be color-blind if it means greater power and privilege for the dominant culture's elite.

McWane Corp., the world's largest manufacturer of cast-iron sewer and water pipes, provides a second example. Everything, including safety programs or environmental controls, are subordinated to production, thus making McWane the most dangerous employer in the United States.[5] High profits are maintained as long as the production line is moving, hence the motto: time equals pipe, and pipe equals money. Workers, usually poor, regardless of race or ethnicity, are prohibited from stepping away from the production line to use the restroom, are regularly disfigured by amputations and burns, and occasionally find death in the workplace. At one plant, supervisors refused to wait a few hours for federal safety inspectors to arrive before restarting the conveyor belt responsible for crushing an employee to death.

From 1995 to 2002, at least forty-six hundred injuries and nine deaths were recorded at McWane foundries, an appalling figure given that the plant only employs about 5,000 workers at any given time. Undoubtedly many injuries went unreported because of widespread disciplinary actions against injured employees for "violating safety rules." Injured employees who filed claims were routinely terminated. Nevertheless, with over four hundred federal health and safety violations in 1995 alone, McWane foundries had four times more violations than their six major competitors combined. In addition, that same year, McWane received at least four hundred and fifty violations of pollution rules and emission limits, placing it among the worst polluters in New Jersey, Alabama, and Texas.[6]

Is McWane a rogue company whose business practices are the exception? Or is McWane's vision of capitalism — cutting costs,

---

[5] David Barstow and Lowell Bergman, "At a Texas Foundry, An Indifference to Life," *The New York Times*, January 8, 2003; and "Family Profits, Wrung from Blood and Sweat," January 9, 2003.

[6] Ibid.

laying off workers and pressing those who remain to work more efficiently and longer hours — becoming the norm? We live and work in a capitalist environment where causing the death of a worker by willfully violating safety rules remains a misdemeanor under federal law, a crime punishable by a maximum of six months in prison. This crime is less serious then harassing wild burros on federal land, which is punishable by at least a year in prison. According to federal regulations, the lives of workers are less valuable than those of burros. Even though 200,000 U.S. workers perished from traumatic injuries on the job throughout corporate America from 1972 to 2001, only 151 cases were referred for criminal investigation and only eight cases resulted in prison time, with a maximum term of six months. Companies like McWane find that complying with safety and environmental regulations is more burdensome and costly than paying regulatory fines. From 1995 to 2002, McWane paid less than $10 million in fines and penalties for safety and environmental violations, a mere 1 percent of its annual revenue and less than most companies set aside for miscellaneous expenses.[7] Simply stated: it's not profitable to safeguard the lives of employees.

The corporate pursuit of profit creates an environment that allows the privileged few, with few if any repercussions, to accrue great wealth at the expense of others — at various times the stockholders, the consumers, the taxpayers, or the employees. Although a detailed analysis of how these different groups are negatively affected by corporate operations would prove beneficial, it will suffice here to concentrate on just one of these groups — the employees.

STEP 2. REFLECTING

The exploitation of labor dehumanizes workers by reducing their existence to expendable commodities. Workers become non-persons who are prevented from living the abundant life promised to them by Christ. What the economic order values is how cheaply their labor can be extracted, regardless whether their wage affords the necessities of clothing, food, and shelter. Hence, what are

---

[7] Idem, "Deaths on the Job, Slaps on the Wrist," *The New York Times*, January 10, 2003.

perceived as moral vices (stealing and lying) may appear more as virtues than vices to the marginalized when dealing with those with power and privilege. For example, since the twelfth century, theologians have recognized the rights of the poor, specifically "theft arising from necessity." The bishop of Paris, Guillaume d'Auxerre, insisted that the poor could take what they needed in order to survive. This right to steal to survive was proclaimed within the context of the famines and plagues common in that era (Boff and Pixley 1989:165).

Ethicist Cheryl Sanders continues this form of situation ethics in her analysis of slave testimonies. Slave masters would hire ministers to preach to the slaves about the virtues of speaking honestly and of not stealing from the owners of their bodies (1995:14–15). A former slave, commenting on a sermon preached against stealing, said,

> I did not regard it as stealing then, I do not regard it as such now. I hold that a slave has a moral right to eat and drink and wear all that he needs, and that it would be a sin on his part to suffer and starve in a country where there is plenty to eat and wear within his reach. I consider that I had a just right to what I took, because it was the labor of my hands. (Raboteau 1978:296)

The ethics of the slaveholder, which defined the stealing of food by slaves as a vice, was a socially constructed ethics designed to protect their privilege within the social order. The real question to ask is did the slaves have a moral right to steal from their masters? Do the oppressed, whose labor is stolen from them, have an ethical right — or one could say, duty — to take what is produced through their labor to feed themselves and their family? Updating this question leads us to ask if employees today who are not paid a living wage also have a right to "steal" from their employers for the purpose of meeting their basic needs for food, clothes, and shelter?

For former slaves, stealing items necessary for survival (food and clothing) was justified on the grounds that they had been victimized by a worse sin, namely, the theft of a human being. This is why an ethics developed among the disenfranchised of "stealing from thieves and deceiving the deceiver." But stealing and lying had their own constraints. It was understood that such actions were only to be done against those who were privileged. Stealing from a fellow slave led to the accusation of being "just as mean as white folks" (Sanders 1995:14–15). Scripture scholar Brian Blount observes that while there was agreement among slaves not to steal from each other, it was, however, "not only appropriate but also moral to 'take' from an owner . . . because owners often fed their slaves as little as possible in order to increase their margins of profit, [and had no] other means of assuaging the hunger of their children and kin" (2001:40–41).

Although one cannot compare the institution of slavery with the situation of marginalized employees, the same motivation of maximizing profit at the expense of others exists. When the economy experiences a downturn, some companies continue to grow and prosper on the backs of their employees. Not receiving a living wage contributes to individuals living a less than human existence. In effect, denying workers a living wage is stealing. Corporations steal from employees when they extract a full week of labor and refuse to compensate them with what is needed for basic necessities for the week.

Wal-Mart, the world's largest retailer with over 3,552 stores throughout the United States and employing more than 1.2 million workers (Wal-Mart likes to call them "associates"), provides a good example of these practices. With stores in nine countries,[8] Wal-Mart produced $245 billion in revenue during 2002, an amount greater than the economies of all but thirty of the world's nations. Wal-Mart has also invaded Mexico, making it that nation's largest private employer with over 100,000 workers in 633 outlets laboring for about $1.50 an hour.[9] It is also the largest retailer in Canada. The practices employed at Wal-Mart exist, in varying degrees, in other corporations that employ predominantly the marginalized.

---

[8] Besides the United States, Wal-Mart has 633 stores in Mexico; 266 in Britain; 225 in Canada; 92 in Germany; 31 in China; 25 in Brazil; 15 in South Korea; and 11 in Argentina.

[9] Tim Weiner, "Wal-Mart Invades, and Mexico Gladly Surrenders," *The New York Times*, December 6, 2003.

On December 20, 2002, a federal jury in Portland, Oregon, found Wal-Mart guilty of forcing its employees to work unpaid overtime. Employees in twenty-seven other states have similar class-action suits pending against the giant retailer. These employees were pressured to clock out after working forty hours, but to continue working, violating the Federal Labor Standards Acts that require employees receive time-and-a-half pay for all hours worked over forty within a week. According to testimony given during the Oregon trial, time cards were falsified by erasing hours worked in order to keep those hours below forty and thus avoid paying time-and-a-half. Failure to comply negatively affected promotions, raises, and employment security. This is not the first time Wal-Mart has faced such accusations. In 2000, Wal-Mart settled a class-action suit in Colorado for $50 million that asserted that its laborers were forced to work off the clock.[10]

Why would an employee willingly work off the clock? Take the example of Liberty Morales, a woman with limited job skills and only a high school diploma. She states that she routinely worked off the clock without complaining. She knew through the experience of others who did complain that if she did not comply, she would be fired, given fewer hours, demoted, or reassigned to the night shift. Compliance, on the other hand, led to desired schedules and promotions. In her own words, "I put up with it because I needed to work."[11]

In addition to this practice, the retailer is also facing a sex-discrimination lawsuit that accuses it of denying equal pay and promotions to 700,000 of its female employees from 1996 to 2001. The suit claims that female employees make $1,150 less per year than men in similar jobs, while female managers make $16,400 less. According to one of the women testifying, her department manager in South Carolina explained that Wal-Mart pays men more than women because the Bible says God made Adam before Eve.[12]

---

[10] See three *New York Times* articles by Steven Greenhouse, "Wal-Mart Faces Lawsuit Over Sex Discrimination," February 16, 2003; "Suits Say Wal-Mart Forces Workers to Toil Off the Clock," June 25, 2002; and, "U.S. Jury Cites Unpaid Work at Wal-Mart," December 20, 2002.

[11] Ibid.

[12] Ibid.

In additional to this blatant sexism, an internal audit under court seal revealed that from 2000 to 2003, employee records at 128 stores showed extensive violations of child-labor laws and state regulations requiring time for breaks and meals. Child-labor violations are estimated to be in the tens of thousand each week with more than a million violations of meals and break regulations. Walmart dismissed the audit as meaningless.[13]

When employees at Wal-Mart attempted to unionize in order to have more leverage with management, union supporters were fired, intimidated, and threatened with the loss of bonuses. A union supporter at a Jacksonville, Texas, store was fired for supposedly stealing a banana. The only successful effort at organizing Wal-Mart employees occurred in the meat department in a Texas store. Within two weeks of unionizing, the department was disbanded by the company. A former Wal-Mart store manager who now works as a union organizer summed up the company's attitude: "They go after you any way they can to discredit you, to fire you. It's almost like a neurosurgeon going after a brain tumor: We got to get that thing out before it infects the rest of the store, the rest of the body." Such actions have led to over forty complaints filed with the National Labor Relations Board from 1999 through 2002. Eight cases were settled, ten cases were decided against Wal-Mart, and the rest are pending. According to Wal-Mart's senior vice president, Jay Allen, the reason Wal-Mart remains nonunion is because the company has done a great job in keeping its employees happy and paying them competitive wages. Yet nonunionized Wal-Mart employees average $8.50 an hour compared to $13 at unionized stores.[14]

Wal-Mart's refusal to unionize negatively impacts those who work for Wal-Mart and threatens to undermine the wages being paid by other competitors like Sears, K-Mart, and Costco, who are now demanding contract concessions from unions so they can compete with Wal-Mart. They cite their inability to compete with Wal-Mart's wages and benefits, which are 20 percent below theirs.

---

[13] Idem, "In-House Audit Says Wal-Mart Violated Labor Laws," *The New York Times*, January 13, 2004.

[14] Idem, "Trying to Overcome Embarrassment, Labor Launches Drive to Organize Wal-Mart," *The New York Times*, November 8, 2002.

In effect, Wal-Mart, the nation's largest corporate employer, is lowering the living standards for everyone by aggressively and artificially keeping wages depressed for the sake of profit. Because Wal-Mart is able to cut the cost of operations by paying employees less, Wal-Mart has been able to push over two dozen national supermarket chains into bankruptcy. Since 1990, Wal-Mart prices, on average, have been 14 percent lower than its competitors, partly due to substandard wages. The list of now defunct chains includes Grand Union, Bruno's of Alabama, Homeland Stores of Oklahoma, and, more recently, F.A.O. Schwarz. In February 2004, Wal-Mart opened its first of an expected forty supercenters in California. In California, unionized stockers and clerks average $17.90 an hour, with health benefits after two years, solidly placing them within the middle-class. Wal-Mart's employees, with an average starting pay of $8.50 an hour with little or no health insurance, find themselves living in poverty.[15] The Wal-Martizing of America means that to compete, other supermarkets must race against Wal-Mart to the bottom of the labor pool or face their own demise.

In her book *Nickel and Dimed: On (Not) Getting By in America*, Barbara Ehrenreich took several jobs at wages available to the unskilled in an attempt to discover if she could live as a low-wage worker. She worked at three different jobs and failed to achieve the basic necessities: decent housing, sufficient food, basic clothing, and proper health care. She worked as a waitress in Florida, a house cleaner in Maine, and a Wal-Mart employee in Minnesota. During her orientation as a new Wal-Mart employee she was warned of the dangers of unions and why she would be worse off if they were to organize Wal-Mart employees. Even more significant was the admonition against "time theft." Time theft is doing anything other than working while on company time (2001: 144–46). While employees are guilty of the sin of "time theft" when they take a five-minute break to go to the bathroom (as defined in the supercenter where Ehrenreich worked), Wal-Mart participates in grand-scale time theft by understaffing stores while forcing employees to work off the clock. Reminiscent of sweatshops in two-thirds world countries, several Wal-Mart super-

---

[15] Ibid.; and idem, "Wal-Mart Driving Workers and Supermarkets Crazy," *The New York Times*, October 19, 2003.

centers, according to pending lawsuits, even lock the doors at closing time and force employees to work additional hours at no pay.
   Compare the plight of the marginalized working at Wal-Mart
with the situation of their top executive officer, H. Lee Scott, whose
total compensation for 2003 was $18.28 million. The connection
between the privileged elite and the poor and marginalized workers is maintained through a corporate system that enriches the former at the expense of the latter. The privilege of top executives is
protected through the creation of a professional-managerial class
that then serves as a buffer zone between top management and
those employees living in poverty due to low wages.
   The function of a professional-managerial class was ignored by
Marxist economic theorists who centered their analysis on only two
classes: the bourgeoisie and the proletariat. Barbara and John Ehrenreich have argued that the middle class, composed of technical workers, managerial workers, "culture" producers, and so on, must be
understood as comprising a distinct class in an advanced capitalist
society. They call this group the professional-managerial class
(1972:8–11). Middle-class managers, who are responsible for ensuring that employees work at the lowest possible wage, with few or
no benefits, consist of salaried employees who do not own the means
of production but function within the social division of labor as the
reproducers of capitalist culture and class relations. Not surprisingly, the relationship between this professional-managerial class
and the employees is usually antagonistic.
   This professional-managerial class is, in effect, a contradictory
class. Although, like the poor, they are excluded from owning the
means of production, their interests are still opposed to the workers because of their managerial positions within the corporate
organization. Although materially comfortable, they remain associated with the processes of exploitation (Wright 1985:285–86).
The excessive profits made by the heads of multinational corporations makes it possible to "bribe" this contradictory class, by
higher salaries, into maintaining the status quo and thus strengthening the marginalization of the disenfranchised.
   The professional-managerial class can take comfort in knowing
that while things may be economically bad, at least they are not
the marginalized. Nevertheless, the professional-managerial class
is also susceptible to unemployment, underemployment, and low

wages. Those losing jobs due to downsizing are not so much the uneducated poor, but rather today they are predominantly middle-class people with college degrees, years of experience, and seemingly impeccable credentials. A downwardly mobile professional-managerial class presents an additional problem. The distinction between them and the marginalized is being blurred. Not surprisingly, the no longer upwardly mobile are angry and "illegal" immigration or affirmative action policies easily become scapegoats for the economic conditions that have led to their joblessness.

The rise of the professional-managerial class has contributed to two sets of business ethics, both constructed to benefit the economic elite. The marginalized who work at the bottom rungs in companies like Wal-Mart are expected to be upright, honest, and loyal. They must pass drug tests to prove they are responsible, and take personality tests to ensure their submissiveness. As business ethicist Alex Michalos pragmatically points out, it is good for corporations to promote ethical behavior among its personnel, for the business cannot survive if its employees are not maintaining the company's best interests. It also becomes profitable for companies to maintain a public *persona* of being ethical; while no doubt some firms are, for others it is simply an issue of public relations (1995:54–57). The professional-managerial class is responsible for maintaining the ethical façade for the benefit of the top executives who are ultimately responsible for "the bottom line," even at the expense of those upright, honest, and loyal employees.

It would be erroneous to caricature the top executives of Wal-Mart as demonic or wicked people. In fact, many are considered virtuous, upright leading citizens and churchgoers. In his exposé of Wal-Mart culture, Bob Ortega reveals the disconnect between the Christian virtues expounded by top officials and their corporate practices. He concludes:

> David Glass [Wal-Mart's president] was considered by his friends to be a fine, upstanding, morally correct, and honest man. Don Soderquist [Wal-Mart's vice-chairman] was a devout Christian once named lay churchman of the year by a national Baptist organization. And yet these two ran a company that profited from the exploitation of children — and,

in all likelihood, from the exploitation of Chinese prisoners, too. Time and again it was put before them, by *Dateline* [NBC revealed that some Wal-Mart products made in Bangladesh used illegal child labor], by Harry Wu [former Chinese political prisoner for nineteen years who alleged some Wal-Mart products were made with slave labor], by the *Wall Street Journal*, by others. And yet their response was to do the very least they could, to hold up, time and again their feeble code, as if its mere existence — forget monitoring, forget enforcement — was enough; as if by uttering once more "our suppliers know we have strict codes" would solve any problem. And nothing would change. (1998:258–59)

It is of little comfort to the marginalized that these top officials have certain personal virtues. Just as faith without works is dead (Jas. 2:20), so too are right virtues without right praxis meaningless.

STEP 3. PRAYING

In teaching about the day of final judgment, Jesus tells a parable of two stewards in charge of the master's household — one conscientious, the other self-absorbed. The conscientious steward fulfilled his ethical obligations to both the master and his fellow servants. The self-absorbed steward instead beat those under his authority. Rather than providing his fellow servants with their fair share of profits from the work performed, the steward instead ate and drank what was stolen from the laborers. The steward's master came home unexpectedly and, seeing how both stewards had behaved, he rewarded the conscientious one while he condemned the oppressive one, casting off the latter to where there is "constant weeping and grinding of teeth" (Mt. 24:45–51). Through the parable Jesus prescribes the ethical responsibilities of those with power over workers. Increasingly, laws and government regulations tend to legitimize the power and privilege of multinational corporations — who have become the stewards of today's world. Because these new oppressive stewards "lord it" over the disenfranchised majority and contribute to their poverty, salvation becomes ever more elusive for them.

Rather than looking at the CEOs responsible for setting the wages of the employees, as well as their own compensation, our culture teaches us to blame the workers for their lot. Sometimes we justify this callousness through an ideology based on Charles Darwin's findings that argues for a natural selection that supposedly ensures the "survival of the fittest." Some economic philosophers have proposed that just as animals compete with each other to survive, so too do human beings. Social Darwinists maintain that free markets guarantee that only those who are aggressive enough will survive because they are the fittest — in effect, the best human beings. Hence, those who fail deserve to fail because they are neither the fittest nor the best. There is no reason then for the government to provide them with assistance (such as welfare, unemployment compensation, and so on) because preserving these economic "losers" would perpetuate inferior qualities in the next generation.

The Spirit of God runs counter to the exploitation of labor. When corporations create conditions that contribute to the poverty of workers — whether being disguised as a defense of democracy, open economic markets, or Christian virtues, these corporations in reality are complicit in establishing and maintaining institutionalized violence. Violence is never limited to the use of physical force, but incorporates power used to achieve wealth and privilege at the expense of others. Violence is anything that prevents an individual from fulfilling the purpose of Christ's mission, that of giving life and giving it abundantly (Jn. 10:10).

Such violence (usually manifested as racism, classism, and sexism) becomes institutionalized when it is built into the very structure of the corporation. The violence experienced by the working poor through inadequate food, clothes, health care, and shelter brings profit to those within the corporation, specifically its officers, directors, and, to a lesser extent, the stockholders. Such exploitation of workers dehumanizes them, turning them into just another resource. Contrary to such common practices, biblical texts calls for workers to be treated humanely and justly:

> You shall not oppress a poor and needy hired servant, neither among your compatriots nor an alien who is in your land or within your gates. You shall pay them for their work on

the same day. The sun shall not set upon them, for they are poor and upon these wages their heart is lifted up. Let them not cry out against you to God, and it be sin against you. (Deut. 24:14–15)

STEP 4. CASE STUDIES

- 1. On December 11, 1995, the Malden Mills textile factory, founded in 1906 in Lawrence, Massachusetts, burned to the ground. Nearly 1,400 employees found themselves unemployed two weeks before Christmas. The factory owner, Aaron Feuerstein, collected over $100 million from the insurance companies. To rebuild in Lawrence would cost Feuerstein over $300 million. Although the fire was a terrible accident, it did provide an opportunity to rebuild elsewhere.

  — To remain competitive, should Feuerstein sell any remaining assets and follow his competitors, who have already relocated to two-thirds world countries in the quest for lower wages?
  — Does the company have any ethical obligation to the town of Lawrence? To its employees?
  — Does Feuerstein owe his employees anything more than what he already paid them in the form of salaries?

  Feuerstein decided not only to rebuild in Lawrence, but to continue paying his employees their full wages including medical benefits at a cost of $20 million and he guaranteed employment once the factory was rebuilt. Feuerstein stated, "I have an equal responsibility to the community. It would have been unconscionable to put 3,000 people on the streets and deliver a death blow to the cities of Lawrence and Methuen. Maybe on paper our company is [now] worth less to Wall Street, but I can tell you it's [really] worth more" (Velasquez 1998:120–21).
  — Was Feuerstein's decision foolish or ethical? Why?

- 2. The use of immigrant labor is a way of increasing profits. For example, immigrants entering the United States on a tourist visa from Russia, Poland, Lithuania, Mongolia, and the Czech

Republic, or undocumented immigrants from Mexico and Central America end up waxing the floors of Wal-Mart department stores seven nights a week. A raid of twenty-one states in October 2003 revealed that the world's largest retailer employed, via sub-contractors, either improperly documented or undocumented immigrants in clear violation of overtime, Social Security, and workers' compensation laws. Most of the janitors arrested during the raid were from Mexico. Victor Zavala and his wife Eunice were two of those arrested. They worked at the Wal-Mart in Old Bridge, New Jersey, every night of the year, except Christmas and New Year's Eve. Victor feels that he has worked hard for the "American Dream," only to now face deportation, along with his wife and three young children.

Although Wal-Mart officials deny knowledge that their company's cleaning contractors used undocumented immigrants, federal investigators insist Wal-Mart executives knew about immigration violations; after all, similar raids were conducted in 1998 and 2001. Employing the undocumented financially benefits the company by minimizing costs. The investigation showed that janitors usually worked fifty-six hours a week and were paid approximately $6 an hour with no time-and-a-half for overtime. Not paying Social Security, taxes, or health insurance provided the subcontractors with an immediate 40 percent cost advantage.[16] In the end, consumers benefitted through lower prices.

— Should Victor and Eunice Zavala, along with there three children, be deported? Why or why not?
— Does patronizing an establishment that is able to offer cheaper goods at the expense of a marginalized labor pool make the purchaser of those goods complicit with the oppression?
— Do employees who receive substandard wages and are unable to earn enough to feed their family have a right to "steal" food from the grocery aisle to make ends meet?

---

[16] Steven Greenhouse, "For Mexican, Wal-Mart Meant Work 363 Nights a Year;" *The New York Times*, October 25, 2003; and "Illegally in U.S., and Never a Day Off at Wal-Mart," November 5, 2003.

- 3. Companies like Wal-Mart, in an effort to keep the price of popular toys like Etch-A-Sketch on the shelves for under $10, have squeezed manufacturers to further cut costs, leading many to shift their low-cost operations to China, which makes 80 percent of the toys sold within the U.S. Initially selling for $3.99 in 1960, if Etch-A-Sketch had kept pace with the consumer price index, it would have been priced at $23.69 by Christmas 2003, rather than $9.99. Originally made in Bryan, Ohio, production was moved to Shenzhen, China, in 2000 as Kin Ki Industries took over production. In Bryan, workers like Nancy Bible and Caroline Miller made Etch-A-Sketch for over thirty years. Prior to the closing of the plant, they, along with other workers, trained their Chinese counterparts who were to take over their jobs. Once Etch-A-Sketch, the anchor of Bryan, left, the community died.[17] The Chinese didn't fare much better. Kin Ki workers are mostly teenage migrants, who work about eighty-four hours a week for 24 cents an hour with no medical insurance, work contracts, or pension programs. They sleep head-to-toe in tiny, cramped rooms. One such worker, who refused to give her name for fear of repercussions, said, "I keep this job because my parents and my daughter depend on the money I earn. No one likes to work in these conditions, but I have no choice."[18]

  — Is it wrong for Wal-Mart to force suppliers to be more efficient and pass these savings to consumers in the form of lower prices?
  — Does a market reduction in clothes and food prices by 10 to 15 percent have a positive impact on the poor?
  — Do goods with lower prices, those affordable by the poor, justify the means by which those prices are achieved?
  — Do lower prices justify the end of the life-long employment of Bible and Miller, or the death of the Bryan, Ohio, community?

---

[17] Joseph Kahn, "An Ohio Town is Hard Hit as Leading Industry Moves to China," *The New York Times*, December 7, 2003.

[18] Joseph Kahn, "Ruse in Toyland: Chinese Workers' Hidden Woe," *The New York Times*, December 7, 2003.

— Are the sweatshops of China, like Kin Ki Industries, unethical, or do they provide needed employment? Why or why not? What about the concerns of the unnamed employee who finds she has no other choice?

• 4. Kim Brathwaite, a mother of two, started work as an assistant manager at a Brooklyn McDonald's restaurant. She was in charge of the night shift. However, as she prepared for work, she faced a difficult choice when her babysitter failed to show up. She had to miss work and jeopardize the job that supported her children, or leave her two children, a nine- and one-year-old, home alone. She chose the latter, a disastrous decision because her apartment caught fire, her two children perished, and she found herself arrested for reckless endangerment of children and faced up to sixteen years in prison. Yet, according to Child Trends, a nonprofit research organization in Washington, D.C., parents themselves have reported leaving more than three million children under thirteen — and some as young as five — to care for themselves on a regular basis (a few hours a week).[19] The working poor find themselves making choices similar to Kim Brathwaite's because, most of the time, no better options are available.

— Should job security be a right for parents who are unable to find childcare?
— Should wages be sufficient to pay for adequate childcare?
— What obligations, if any, do employers have toward single parents?
— If trends continue to indicate that more children are being left alone so that parents can work to support those children, does the government then have a responsibility to step in and provide some form of relief?
— Whose responsibility is it to provide adequate childcare?

• 5. More and more, churches are resembling national corporations. The mega-church phenomena has reached out to the

---

[19] Nina Bernstein, "Daily Choice Turned Deadly: Children Left on Their Own," *The New York Times*, October 19, 2003.

"unsaved" by providing a supermarket strategy isolated from the community-at-large. These walled-in villages provide members full service: twenty-four hours a day, seven days a week. Parishioners can shop, eat at name-brand restaurants, bank, enjoy arcades and amusement rides, work out, rock-climb, and attend school at these part-resort, part-shopping mall complexes where the sanctuary serves as an anchored tenant. Theology ceases to be the main draw to a particular church as amenities become more important. Still, Patty Anderson and her husband Gary claim to have found faith in the 50,000-square-foot activity center of the Southeast Christian Church in Louisville, Kentucky. "I really had no intention of being part of a church," recalls Gary Anderson, a physiology professor at the University of Louisville. But shooting hoops at this 22,000-member megachurch eventually led him to the sanctuary.[20]

— Are there any moral dilemmas with churches adopting capitalist business models?
— Are these mega-churches a testimony to God's blessings, with memberships in the tens of thousands and operating budgets that rival many relief organizations set up to deal with the physical needs of the world's disenfranchised?
— Or are these churches becoming the spiritual form of a gated community where like-minded people who long for moral values can be insulated? Why or why not?
— Is it important to note that many of these mega-churches are located in middle-class suburbia, rather than urban centers where, in most cases, the wealth of these churchgoers is created? Does that make a difference?
— What about Patty and Gary Anderson? Does their "conversion" justifies the mega-church concept? Why or why not?

---

[20] Patricia Leigh Brown, "Megachurches as Minitowns," *The New York Times*, May 9, 2002.

CHAPTER 14

Affirmative Action

STEP 1. OBSERVING

During the antebellum period (prior to the Civil War), it was illegal to teach African Americans to read. Even after the ratification of the Fourteenth Amendment to the U.S. Constitution (equal rights for all citizens), traditions, customs, and local ordinances conspired to prevent blacks from receiving an adequate education. Consequently, whites became the interpreters of reality. Those who could read were in a position of power over those who could not because those privileged with an education maintained and manipulated the flow of information. During this time, there was widespread fear, particularly in the South, of educated persons of color, so schools were segregated, job opportunities deprived, and resources to correct these injustices denied.

If knowledge is indeed power, then marginalization can be maintained by limiting, censuring, or fabricating "truth," not just for African Americans, but for any who fall short of the ideal, an ideal maintained in turn by the dominant culture. As seen by the dominant white majority, the post-Civil Rights era has corrected most of the grievances of people of color. For many of the marginalized, however, while some advances have occurred, institutionalized violence, specifically in education, continues to exist because social structures are designed to preserve the racism, sexism, and classism that has historically benefitted those privileged by the status quo.

In spite of affirmative action and some legal gains, people of color continue to be ignored by institutions. As we have already seen, statistics of the U.S. Census Bureau reveal that the vast majority of those living below the poverty level are people of color. Fetal, infant, maternal, and neonatal deaths are twice as likely to occur in nonwhite groups. Blacks and Hispanics are more likely than whites to become victims of homicide, and unemployment levels are exceptionally higher for people of color.

The presence of racism, however, does not refer *only* to those who are passed up for a job or not admitted into college; racism is also an expression of the reality of institutionalized violence in an economic and social system that fosters violence upon the disenfranchised because of the pigmentation of their skin. Racism is a system-wide phenomenon that affects employment and advancement within the society. It often decides who gets decent housing, education, and health care; who gets to live in "safe" neighborhoods; and who is stigmatized as sinful (as in Max Weber's *Rise of Capitalism*) because they are unable to "pull themselves up by their bootstraps," never realizing, as so many people of color have said, that they haven't any boots.

Racism means that people of color and women often lack the same skills as white males because they have been locked out of education and/or employment opportunities. Because of racism and sexism in the past, people of color and women are conspicuously absent from the more desirable and prestigious jobs within society today. Not surprisingly, 99 percent of the heads of the Fortune 500 companies are white males. How then can society remedy this structural flaw? One of the means used is affirmative action. Noting the inadequacy of the 1964 Civil Rights Act to remedy institutionalized racism, then President Lyndon B. Johnson signed Executive Order 11246 requiring government contractors to implement a type of affirmative action to ensure people of color get hired. Some believe President Johnson's action was itself discriminative. Ethicist Manuel Velasquez asks:

> If a racial group, for example, has been unjustly discriminated against for an extended period of time in the past and its members consequently now hold the lowest economic and social positions in society, does justice require that members of that group be compensated by being given special preference in hiring, training, and promotion procedures? Or would such special treatment itself be a violation of justice by violating the principle of equal treatment? (1998:119)

Although a thorough discussion of how affirmative action impacts employment, housing, and social services would be valuable, we will focus here on its impact within the education system, specifically higher education.

In the period of Reconstruction following the Civil War, people of color began to attend school, but in educational systems that were racially segregated: a community would have a white school and a "Negro" school. In the early 1950s, a process began to end segregation in our nation's schools. Until then racial segregation had been the norm, based on a U.S. Supreme Court ruling that justified the "separate but equal" rule. In Topeka, Kansas, a black third-grader named Linda Brown had to walk one mile to get to her black elementary school, even though a white elementary school was only seven blocks away. When her father attempted to register his daughter at the white elementary school, the principal refused to admit her. The U.S. District Court for Kansas heard the case on June 25–26, 1951. The school argued that because segregation in Topeka and elsewhere pervaded many other aspects of life within the United States, segregated schools simply prepared "colored" children for life in America. Losing the case in the District Court, it was appealed to the Supreme Court, which did not rule until 1953.

Today that ruling is known as *Brown v. Board of Education.* Although the Court did not abolish segregation in public areas, nor did it place a time limit as to when schools needed to desegregate, it did declare segregation to be unconstitutional. In spite of the Court's decision, most public schools simply ignored the ruling and continued racial segregation. It would take four years and the dispatching of federal troops to Little Rock's Central High School to provide a few black students access to a white school. Through the 1960s and 1970s a battle raged throughout our nation's public school systems, which fought tooth and nail the will of the Supreme Court.

What role did Christian churches play? Many of the same Christian churches, particularly in the South, that preached that the saving grace of God is for all people, regardless of race or ethnicity, responded to the moral crisis of segregation by establishing their own "Christian" schools. Members could now send their white children to a school where they would not have to sit next to black or brown children. Many Christian schools established during these times were founded for the sole purpose of going around the Supreme Court's mandate to desegregate. Although such schools were a response to a political situation, their motivation was religiously based. For biblical fundamentalists, Ham, Noah's son, was divinely cursed (Gn. 9:20–27), developing the inferior traits of kinky hair and dark skin. Others believed that blacks were not descendants of Adam, but of a type of animal created prior to Adam, hence lacking a soul. Still others claimed blacks were the sinful product of cross-breeding between humans and animals. Regardless, black traits have historically been attributed to Satan.

Even at the beginning of the new millennium, four decades after *Brown v. Board of Education*, there are still many "Christian" schools with a faculty, administration, and student body that are predominately white. The role played by these Christian schools to maintain the "separate but equal" mind-set raises suspicions among people of color about the moral commitment of the dominant culture to create a truly desegregated learning environment. Ironically, the students within a predominately white educational system also suffer because they acquire an education devoid of diversity, limiting their ability to function or succeed in the new global marketplace. The new global system of neoliberalism means that our present generation will have to deal with, purchase from, sell to, negotiate with, work for, and supervise people from different races, cultures, and ethnicities.

STEP 2. REFLECTING

Is it possible to be color-blind in a society where color still matters? Racism reinforces the societal belief that people of color are inferior because they lack white skin. Affirmative action initiatives were put in place to combat the mind-set that people of color, specifically blacks and Latinos, present a threat to the dominant culture. Affirmative action has little if anything to do with correcting past wrongs. Debates over affirmative action usually mask the mind-set that believes that any position "given" to a person of color is, in actuality, a position taken away from a so-called "deserving" white student. The level of intellectual acumen possessed by students of color matters little, because they are never considered as good as or as likely to succeed as a white student.

It has been charged that affirmative action is itself a form of "reverse discrimination." Yet the acceptance to a college of Latino applicant "X" does not mean that white student "Y" with a higher SAT score was not accepted because he or she was displaced by Latino "X." In reality, if Latino "X" was denied admittance, it would be more likely that another white student with a lower SAT score than white student "Y" might be accepted because he or she might belong to one of several subgroups that receive preferential consideration, such as children of parents who attended the school, athletes, or low-scoring children of possible future donors. Or, perhaps the spot going to Latino "X" may instead go to another student of color who scored higher than white student "Y," or the position might be given to a foreign student.

Affirmative action is not another form of racism (or sometimes called "reverse racism") but rather a recognition of white privilege. Whites currently have the advantage, holding a disproportionate number of more desirable jobs and attending more prestigious educational institutions than people of color. No one contends that whites are excluded from getting a college education simply because they have white skin. The same cannot be said about students of color. Affirmative action is an attempt to provide an equal opportunity for all, regardless of race, to achieve the advantage currently reserved for white males. Its purpose is not to exclude whites, but to serve the missions of colleges and universities to create diverse learning environments for the betterment of the overall student body and for the good of the general public.

Rejecting the assumption that people of color are inferior, those on the margins of society recognize that they are locked out of educational and employment opportunities because white males, the guardians of society's power structure, either consciously or unconsciously bias their decisions in favor of other white males. Numerous studies show that even when people of color and/or women are more qualified, white males in power will grant higher salaries and positions to their fellow white men (Velasquez 1998:405). This normative act of bias, whether conscious or unconscious, serves to further institutionalize racism, sexism, and classism. Affirmative action is designed as a corrective measure to restore equal opportunity.

Ironically, affirmative action is beneficial for neoliberalism, and the "Establishment" generally recognizes this fact. A record-setting sixty-six friend-of-the-court briefs were filed in support of the University of Michigan's admission policies. Those filing *amicus* briefs in the Supreme Court cases *Grutter v. Bolliger* and *Gratz v. Bollinger*[1] were not liberal or activist organizations, but rather the defenders of the present conservative establishment, such as the military, including twenty-one retired generals and admirals and three former superintendents of military academies; and some titans of corporate America such as General Motors, Viacom, Microsoft, IBM, Bank One, American Express, Boeing, Shell, General Electric, Coca-Cola and fifty-four other Fortune 500 companies. They maintained that race should be one of many factors used to achieve a more diverse student body.[2] Because selective universities train the future leaders of society, society, marred by racial and ethnic tension, will benefit from a diverse and integrated leadership corps. Ironically, again, it was a conservative U.S. Supreme Court that agreed to uphold the law school admission policies of the university. It was acknowledged that for the United States to compete aggressively on the global stage, its white students must understand and work with diversity.

Justice O'Connor expressed the hope that within twenty-five years of the decision, there would no longer be a need for affirmative

---

[1] *Grutter v. Bolliger* involves admission to the University of Michigan's law school, while *Gratz v. Bollinger* deals with admission to the university's undergraduate program. Both cases were filed in 1997 on behalf of white female applicants who were denied admission. They argued that promoting racial and ethnic diversity was not a compelling enough reason to justify the university's admission policies. They also argued that admission policies at the University of Michigan were too broad to promote diversity, hence failing to meet the compelling-interest exemption that the court applies to the Constitution's equal-protection clause.

[2] Justice Powell's written opinion in the court's landmark 1978 case *Regents of the University of California v. Bakke* allowed colleges to consider race in determining admission for the sake of diversity, as long as it did not use quotas.

action. Unfortunately, at least three obstacles prevent Justice O'Connor's vision from being realized. First, there is a reluctance to eliminate class preferences in college admissions, specifically the legacy-type programs that function as the affirmative action of privileged middle- and upper-class whites. Legacy programs, a relic of white supremacy, give admission preference to the sons and daughters of alumni. Top colleges regularly admit alumni children at two to four times the rate of their overall applicant pools.[3] In addition, many selective colleges treat applicants from very wealthy families as legacies, because the families are able to make major financial contributions to the institution. Portraying affirmative action solely as a race issue fails to consider the affirmative action, which is accepted as normative, that wealthier white students benefit from on a regular basis. Neoliberalism continues to influence all aspects of human life, where today white privilege is more than ever trumped by class privilege.

One of the major class struggles occurring today is being fought in the admission buildings of the highly selective colleges and universities. Children of the wealthy can afford the SAT tutors and top prep schools that groom their children for marquee colleges. But as the income gap continues to widen, as discussed in Chapter 9, the once protected privilege of whiteness becomes less secure for the lower and middle classes and creates a backlash of legislation, referendums, and court decisions attempting to limit affirmative action. Protection is sought for white privilege, specifically through college legacy programs. But, as North Carolina Senator John Edwards asked, does a legacy program, an eighteenth-century aristocratic birthright, have a place in a twenty-first century democracy?

During the oral arguments on the University of Michigan cases, Justice Breyer asked the attorney representing white students suing the university about the difference between legacy preference and affirmative action. According to the lawyer, the Equal Protection Clause of the U.S. Constitution prohibits race discrimination, not discrimination based on alumni affiliation. Yet, because students of color were historically discriminated against when applying to

---

[3] Jacques Steinberg, "Of Sheepskins and Greenbacks," *The New York Times*, February 13, 2003.

predominately white universities, few of today's students of color have parents who attended Ivy League institutions. Students of color are thus locked out of legacy opportunities, continuing the racism that privileges white applicants who claim legacy. In fact, five of the nine U.S. Supreme Court justices (or their children) who determined the *Grutter v. Bollinger* and *Gratz v. Bollinger* cases were themselves "affirmed" into the legacies of Ivy League schools.[4]

It is a given that students with better grades, who made the mistake of not being born white and wealthy, have difficulty entering such selective colleges. According to an analysis of the 1999 entering graduate class at leading private research universities, a considerable number of high-scoring minority students were not admitted. For example, among male students of color with SAT scores well within the top ten percent of minority test-takers and the top twenty percent of all test-takers, only 35 percent were admitted (Bowen and Levin 2003:232–39, 250). Because race and class privilege trump merit, affirmative action serves as a counterbalance to legacy preference.

A second obstacle preventing Justice O'Connor's vision from being realized is the unequal distribution of funds for K-12 education. Justice O'Connor recognized this obstacle during a rare interview with *The Chicago Tribune* in which she said: "I hope it looks as though we don't need artificial help to fill our classrooms with highly qualified students at the graduate level. . . . And if we do our job of educating young people, we can reach that goal."[5] Yet, in spite of Justice O'Connor's optimistic hope for the future, the reality is a national refusal to provide a basic public education for all its children.

---

[4] Justices Breyer and Kennedy have ties to Stanford University that span three generations; Justice O'Connor's two children benefitted from legacy at Stanford University. Stanford admits one-fourth of all legacies compared to just one-eight of the overall applicant pool. Justice Stevens attended the University of Chicago and Northwestern Law School as did his father, and Justice Ginsburg's daughter benefitted from legacy at Harvard Law School. See Daniel Golden, "For Supreme Court, Affirmative Action Isn't Just Academic," *The Wall Street Journal*, May 14, 2003.

[5] Jan Crawford Greenburg, "O'Connor Voices Hope for Day Affirmative Action Not Needed," *Chicago Tribune*, June 25, 2003.

In the early 1990s Jonathan Kozol described schools in predominately poor and non-white districts as functioning with outdated second-hand books, gaping holes in their roofs, overcrowded classrooms, inadequate climate control, non-operational restrooms, running sewage, and in one case, a classroom conducted in an abandoned pool (1991:23–37). The financial situation faced by these marginalized schools has worsened with the passage of time and has been exacerbated by how school financing continues to be distributed. According to a study conducted in 2002 by the Educational Trust, a nonpartisan group, predominately black and Hispanic school districts spent on average $902 less per student than mostly white districts.[6] In major urban centers like New York City, students of color received about $2,152 less than white students. The study showed that in thirty of the forty-seven states that submitted financial data to the federal government, those schools with the smallest representation of poor students (predominately students of color) got substantially more than districts with high concentrations of poor students.[7] Not surprisingly, schools outside of the prosperous suburbs must contend with fewer funds than their white counterparts. With limited access to computers and microscopes, non-suburban schools struggle with overcrowding, a decaying infrastructure, and outdated resources. In short, schools with the greatest financial needs get the fewest resources.

Even if the federal and state governments were committed to eliminating the financial discrepancies between white and minority schools, they would still be unable to do so. On average, state and federal governments provide less than 56 percent of the schools' revenues over the past decades. The remainder comes from local sources, specifically property taxes.[8] The financial structures created to fund K-12 education are tied to the neighbor-

---

[6] Nationally, school districts that are predominately white spent $6,684 in state and local money per student compared to $5,782 in predominately black and Latina/o school districts.

[7] Diana Jean Schemo, "Neediest Schools Receive Less Aid, Report Shows," *The New York Times*, August 9, 2002.

[8] Steven A. Holmes and Greg Winter, "Fixing the Race Gap in 25 Years or Less," *The New York Times*, June 29, 2003.

hoods, which in turn have historically been and continue to be segregated. Because the neediest schools are located in predominately poor neighborhoods where most of the residents are of color, K-12 educational funding will never be equitable unless the financial structures are radically changed. This present system of unequal educational opportunities in K-12 means that most students of color will be unable to compete with white students for college admission, not because they are intellectually inferior, but because institutionalized racism and classism in education have ill-equipped them.

A third obstacle to Justice O'Connor's vision is the recent trend of moving toward a more segregated educational system. According to the Harvard Civil Rights Project, the proportion of blacks and Hispanics in white-majority schools significantly dropped between 1988 and 2002, making them more isolated from their white counterparts than before desegregation initiatives began in the early seventies. The termination of dozens of court-ordered desegregation plans (specifically busing), along with an increase of students of color within the overall population, continuing white flight from urban centers, and redlining of real estate have all contributed to the resegregation of the nation's schools. Whites, who represent 61 percent of the population, are the most segregated group, attending schools where 80 percent of their classmates are white. But this is as much a class issue as it is a race issue, linking segregation by race with segregation by poverty. Blacks and Latino/as attend schools where about 45 percent of the students are poor, compared to 19 percent of whites (Frankenberg and Lee 2002:2–22). Nonetheless, Justice O'Connor's colleague, Anthony Kennedy best articulated the new approach to education in a seminal opinion. Writing about a Georgia school district, he said, "Racial balance is not to be achieved for its own sake. . . . Where resegregation is a product not of state action but of private choices, it does not have constitutional implications." From Missouri to Oklahoma, similar court decisions are reversing *Brown v. Board of Education*, so that once-integrated schools are again becoming segregated.[9]

---

[9] Allen G. Breed, "Separate But Equal?" *The New York Times*, September 29, 2002.

Lisa Navarette, vice president of the National Council of La Raza, commenting on Justice O'Connor's vision of affirmative action ending by 2028, said it best, "If all we do over the 25 years is affirmative action, then we will still need affirmative action."[10]

STEP 3. PRAYING

At times, the dominant culture believes that inclusion is an adequate ethical response to structural oppression. Diversity and multiculturalism do not equal justice, they equal political correctness. Even if society were to abide by some politically correct decorum and thus eliminate the appearance of bigotry and prejudices, it still could not reverse the damage of centuries of racism wrought upon those relegated to the margins. Nor could it eliminate the consequences of miseducation, which have led to poverty and all the misery, bitterness, and hatred poverty produces. Ethics, when done from the margins, attempts to move beyond political correctness, that Disney-like façade where different cultures, races, and ethnicities are presented as "a small world after all."

Affirmative action must be understood as a product of love rather than political correctness. Basing ethics upon the concept of love is not new. Many eurocentric ethicists have attempted to base their deliberations upon such a concept. However, many have fallen short because they have applied love primarily to interpersonal relations, while ignoring issues of social injustices like segregation within education. Martin Luther King, Jr., more so than any other love ethicist, made love the essential theme for both the private and public sector (Williams 1990:18–23). Nevertheless, for many ethicists of the dominant culture (Reinhold Niebuhr is one example), unconditional love (*agape*) as an essential theme for the public sector is seen as problematic as a standard for moral behavior; or as Niebuhr said, an "impossible possibility" (1943:76).

However, by failing to make love the primary motive for social actions such as affirmative action, the good intention to love remains disjointed from the action of love. The transformative power of love remains restricted to the inner soul, rather than the

---

[10] Holmes and Winter, "Fixing the Race Gap," *The New York Times*, June 29, 2003.

outer social environment. While admirable theoretical models are constructed to explain varied nuances in conceptualizing love, those on the margins complain that at times it is difficult to see the connection between the complex models and their practical application within the "everyday" of the disenfranchised. For so many who deal with the daily struggle for dignity, ethical deliberations founded upon love as an abstraction provide little help for those marginalized by the educational system.

For example, in his text *Christ and the Moral Life*, James Gustafson states "Love as a disposition needs love as an intention, as a purpose, and also love as a norm" (1968:256). This provides no help for the marginalized. Although Gustafson goes on to define intention as a "basic direction of activity," still one is hard pressed to find examples in his book of praxis for justice *based on love* in facing the greatest injustices of the time. When we consider that his book was published in 1968, during the black community's struggles for civil rights, we are left asking why he didn't connect his ethical perspectives with the moral crises unfolding before him and the Christian community. Did his silence confirm the power of those within the center to determine what is, and what is not to become a topic for moral discourse?[11] As James Cone reminds us, white ethicists (Gustafson is just one example) reflect the racism prevalent in society. The "invisibility" of racism is maintained by suggesting that the problem of racism is only one social expression of a larger ethical concern (1975:201).

If it is true that God is love (1 Jn. 4:8), then the only absolute that can be claimed is love. Therefore, love ought to be the prime motive behind every decision taken, including affirmative action. But is the biblical concept of love sufficient? Because of the prevalent racism in higher education, those from the margins remain leery of basing any ethics upon a fixed law or regulation formulated by society, specifically the dominant culture. In the end, relying on how the dominant culture defines love (either paternalistically or as "tough" love) can mask the self-interest of those with power. The basic flaw of relying solely on love as defined by

---

[11] In all fairness, Gustafson does include Martin Luther King's essay, "Letter from Birmingham Jail," in a collection of essays he co-edited with James Laney in another book published that same year (1968:256–74).

the dominant culture is one of trust. Can the dominant culture be trusted to act in love? If the past history of how people of color have been treated in the United States is to serve as a guide in answering this question, then the answer is obviously no.

In addition, love coming from the centers of power and privilege usually focuses on how "they" can love those who are marginalized. But unconditional love is never limited to one direction (in other words, love from the privileged toward the marginalized) lest it reduce the disenfranchised to objects by which those in power can express their paternalistic charity. Love must be mutual. To love the marginalized is to serve them and receive in return God's love through them. Thus, the privileged and powerful find their salvation by discovering God, through Christ, in the lives of "the least of these," their neighbors. In this way, God's love can be experienced, a love manifested in the establishment of just relationships that can lead toward just social structures like affirmative action. Only then can community be established and hope arise for a just social order.

STEP 4. CASE STUDIES

- 1. Russell Crake, a white student, graduated from Houston's Bellaire High School, an academically challenging public high school, with a 3.94 grade-point average and a 1240 SAT score. Still, he was not admitted to the University of Texas at Austin, state's flagship campus and most prestigious institution. Yet many other students, among them students of color, with lower grade-point averages and SAT scores hundreds of points lower were admitted.[12]

  In a similar situation in another part of the country, citing reverse discrimination, President George W. Bush instructed the Justice Department to file a brief with the U.S. Supreme Court stating that the admission policies at the University of Michigan were "fundamentally flawed" and "divisive, unfair, and impossible to square with the Constitution."[13] The brief

---

[12] Edward Blum and Roger Clegg, "Percent Plans: Admissions of Failure," *The Chronicle of Higher Education*, March 21, 2003.

[13] Peter Schmidt, "Bush Asks Supreme Court to Strike Down U. of

stopped short of arguing that all race-conscious admission policies are unconstitutional. The Bush administration pointed to admission policies at state universities in California, Florida, and Texas as "race-neutral" alternatives that guarantee college admission to a percentage of top graduates of each high school class, regardless of SAT scores. Yet, this is the same admission policy that prevented Russell Crake from being admitted to the University of Texas.

— Should race play a role in determining college admission?
— If colleges cannot consider race in the admission of students, how should colleges diversify their student bodies? Is a diverse student body desirable and/or necessary in the first place? Why or why not?
— Is the admission system used in California, Florida, and Texas a feasible alternative? Why or why not?
— Does it make a difference that Russell Crake's rejection by the University of Texas in Austin was based on an admission policy that excluded race rather than because of affirmative action?
— Does it make a difference that white students with lower scores than Mr. Crake were admitted to the University of Texas in Austin?
— For this type of quota system to work, shouldn't all high schools offer the same level of education? Is this possible?
— What admission policy should prevail in the case of graduate and professional schools, as well as private colleges?
— One district court judge who ruled against Michigan suggested using a lottery system, placing less emphasis on grades and LSAT scores. Is this a more ethical alternative? Why or why not?
— Where should debates over race-conscious admission policies take place: the federal courts, state referendums, state legislation, and/or acts of Congress? Why?
— Where should decisions on affirmative action be made? Why?

Michigan Affirmative-Action Policy," *The Chronicle of Higher Education*, January 24, 2003.

- 2. Sonia Gil, an "A" student, attended high school in the Bronx, New York, never doubting she would one day attend college. Her parents, a factory worker and a homemaker from the Dominican Republic, instilled in all of their eleven children the importance of an education. Some ten years later, Ms. Gil, now twenty-seven, is still attending a community college, but part-time. She wants to become one of the 16 percent of Latino/a high school graduates who go on to earn a four-year college degree (compared with 37 percent of Euroamericans and 21 percent of African Americans).[14] Like most Hispanics, she faces language and cultural barriers. Like most people of color, she must cope with inadequate urban high schools and dwindling finances.

  Most students of color who benefit from affirmative action come from the middle class. According to a study conducted by the Educational Testing Service, 74 percent of students at the 146 most prestigious institutions (where affirmative action is practiced and competition is intense) came from families in the top 25 percent of the nation's socioeconomic scale, with only 3 percent coming from the bottom 25 percent.[15] Two separate reports conducted by groups representing different views on affirmative action (the U.S. Department of Education as a critic of affirmative action and the liberal Century Foundation in favor of it) arrived at similar conclusions: There would be less need for race-conscious admission policies if more attention were given to low-income families. According to the Century Foundation, only 3 percent of students at our nation's selective colleges come from the poorest fourth of the nation's population, and just 10 percent come from the bottom half.[16]

— Does a difference exist between affirmative action that benefits primarily middle- and upper-class students of color and

---

[14] Mireya Navarro, "For Hispanics, Language and Culture Barriers Can Further Complicate College," *The New York Times*, February 10, 2003.

[15] Holmes and Winter, "Fixing the Race Gap," *The New York Times*, June 29, 2003.

[16] Peter Schmidt, "Reports Cite Alternatives to Race-Conscious Admissions," *The Chronicle of Higher Education*, April 11, 2003.

affirmative action that could benefit those students of color who are economically disenfranchised?

— Should economic class be considered when colleges or graduate schools decide which students of color to admit?

— Should a program of economic affirmative action that would consider both racial and economic diversity be adopted? Why or why not?

• 3. Erika Medina, Miguel Puente, and Rita Garcia were turned down for admission to Cal Polytechnic in San Luis Obispo, California. They have since sued the state university, contending that its admission system illegally discriminated against students of color by giving undue weight to SAT scores. The lawsuit is based on the claim that California laws prohibit discrimination by institutions that receive state funds. The plaintiffs insist that SAT scores are being used as a means by which students of color are denied higher education.[17]

The SAT is widely accepted as a measure of scholastic achievement or merit. Each question is carefully pretested by the Educational Testing Service (ETS) and, as a result, testers can determine in advance how members of one ethnic group will fare on any particular question. Whites consistently pick the correct answer to some questions; on other questions, minorities perform better. Yet, according to Jay Rosner, executive director of the Princeton Review Foundation, the only questions that appear on SAT exams are the white-preference questions.

In an article published in the *Harvard Educational Review* in the spring of 2003, a former ETS researcher charged that black students often performed better on harder verbal questions than whites because words used in common vocabulary are understood differently by members of different racial/ethnic groups. Yet, these harder questions were not incorporated into SAT exams; in fact, every one of the 138 questions on the 2000 SAT exam favored white students, with not one of the pretested questions favoring minority students appearing.[18]

---

[17] Peter Y. Hong, "Lawsuit Accuses University of Admissions Bias," *The Los Angeles Times*, January 9, 2004.

[18] Jeffrey R. Young, "Researchers Charge Racial Bias on the SAT,"

— Do merit-based scholarships, determined in most states by SAT scores, discriminate against Latino/a and black students? Against poorer students?
— If this is true, should SAT scores be the means of determining merit?
— Do Erika Medina, Miguel Puente, and Rita Garcia have a case against Cal Polytechnic? Why or why not?
— What would be an ethical way to determine admission to state colleges that are funded by the state taxpayers to serve all citizens of that state?

- 4. Shortly after the Supreme Court ruling on the University of Michigan case, Linda Chavez, president of the Center for Equal Opportunity[19] and former staff director of the U.S. Commission on Civil Rights said:

Underlying the majority opinion in the *Grutter* case is the unsettling notion that black and Latino people are incapable of succeeding on their own merit in this society — at least at the present time. Although they would never say so outright, the justices seem to believe that such minority students are incapable of perform-

---

The Chronicle of Higher Education, October 10, 2003. The reason a question chosen for the SAT favors white students is due to how "reliability" is defined by the test designers. A question intended to be difficult is considered reliable if those who score highest consistently do well on the exam, and those who score low on that particular question consistently do poorly on the exam. Thus the highest achievers among test takers, who have historically been white students, set the standards. Questions on which they do well become, by definition, reliable, and questions on which they do poorly become unreliable, and are thus eliminated from consideration, even though students of color may score higher.

[19] The Center for Equal Opportunity, with a $1 million annual operating budget, was one of the three organizations at the forefront in defending the white plaintiffs' cases against the University of Michigan. The other two organizations were the Center for Individual Rights, with a $1.7 million annual budget, and the American Civil Rights Institute, with a $1.4 million budget. It should be noted that the head of the Center for Equal Opportunity, Linda Chavez, is a Latina, and the head of the Center for Individual Rights, Ward Connerly, is black. See Peter Schmidt,

ing at the same level as white and Asian students and must, therefore, be judged by different standards. The justices have sent a very clear message to black and Latino students: "We don't expect you to measure up." Melanin, their arguments implies, must be treated as a measurable "plus factor" to make up for intellectual or academic deficiencies. It is a view that is racist at its core.[20]

— Is Ms. Chavez correct?
— How much weight do her comments have on the issue since she is a Latina?
— Whom does she speak for? Is there such a thing as a Hispanic spokesperson?
— If spokespersons of minorities disagree on issues, how are whites in the dominant culture to interpret the views of minorities who contradict each other on affirmative action, or any other issue for that matter?

• 5. Kelly Ryan, a "B" student at the University of Georgia, used her college trust fund to purchase a new car, take trips to Italy, Switzerland, and Argentina, and invest (and lose) in the stock market. Enough money may remain to purchase her first piece of real estate when she graduates. Likewise, Kristin McKenna, whose parents' income is over $200,000 a year, used her college fund to purchase a car. Rather than use their college trust funds for books and classes, the two co-eds relied on scholarships from the government.

Ms. Ryan and Ms. McKenna's windfalls are not anomalies, but rather are becoming the norm for the wealthy. At least twelve states have shifted from scholarships based on need to "merit." According to the Department of Education the percentage of students from families with annual incomes over $100,000 who received state grants between 1992 and 2000 grew seven times

---

"Behind the Fight Over Race-Conscious Admissions," *The Chronicle of Higher Education*, April 4, 2003.

[20] "In Reactions to the Michigan Rulings, Diversity Abounds," *The Chronicle of Higher Education*, July 4, 2003.

faster than the percentage of students coming from families with earnings under $20,000 a year.

In addition, university grants to the highest-income students grew twice as fast as awards given to the lowest-income students. Not surprisingly, a study conducted by Harvard's Civil Rights Project showed that students from the wealthiest high schools in Florida and Michigan were more than twice as likely to win merit scholarships than their counterparts from the poorest schools. When some states, like Florida, considered shifting more funds to need-based scholarships, they met formidable political resistance.[21]

The federal government also provides the wealthiest private universities, which serve the smallest percentage of low-income students, more financial aid dollars than colleges with a greater share of poor students. Ivy League schools received from the federal government five to eight times the median amount to pay students in work-study jobs. And, in spite of these Ivy League schools having the largest endowments in the world (Yale and Harvard have over $10 billion and Princeton $8.7 billion), they still received from the federal government five to twenty times the median amount of grant money for students' everyday needs.[22]

— Is it ethical to give scholarships to Ms. Ryan or Ms. McKenna? Why or why not? Compare their situation with that of Ms. Gil (case study #2). Is this an ethical distribution of scholarship resources?

— Should public funds be given to those with the financial means to attend college on their own?

— Should public funds be used to support private universities that have large endowments?

— Should restrictions be placed on the use of government funds for educational support?

---

[21] Greg Winter, "B's, Not Need, Are Enough for Some State Scholarships," *The New York Times*, October 31, 2002.

[22] Idem, "Rich Colleges Receiving Richest Share of U.S. Aid," *The New York Times*, November 9, 2003.

CHAPTER 15

Private Property

STEP 1. OBSERVING

Until the present day, land and its ownership were part of nearly every social, economic, or political issue. While the ownership of land is still important for creating, sustaining, and maintaining wealth, in the new world order wealth can be created apart from land. Under the present system of neoliberalism, the importance of property has diminished, as the means of production need not necessarily be owned. For example, the source of Microsoft's billions is cyberspace rather than physical space. Capital need not be connected to a particular workforce or tied to a specific physical location. With a few keystrokes on a computer, an entrepreneur in New York can transfer billions in assets from Paris to Tokyo within microseconds. In such a world, wealth tied to a particular piece of land is losing its importance. Why then explore the ethical ramifications of private property? Because it is still land that sustains all of life, and the primary obstacle in preventing the vast majority of the world's dispossessed from living a more humane existence is the lack of control over the land — physically, politically, and economically. Hence the question is before us: What are the socioeconomic consequences of land ownership upon the world's dispossessed?

For most of us, land appears to be neutral. Yet the ownership and use of land lies behind much of the political, social, and economic violence that tears apart the world today. While land, in and of itself, is not the root of evil, it has been used as an instrument to foster injustice. The commodification of land — making it into something that can be bought and sold — turn it into a source of power over others and can also turn it into an idol, something to be worshiped. How then can the use of land become a redemptive source of justice?

Historically, in Greece and Rome property did not belong to an individual; instead, individuals, grouped in families, belonged to the land. Originally, the family was attached to the family altar, and the altar was attached to the soil. Even if the family perished, the land endured. Consequently, an intimate relationship was formed between the family (not the individual) and the soil. The property was improved not for the lifetime of a single person but for all generations. The past and future were connected through the soil. Land was used *inclusively* and it represented the wealth and well-being of the overall community. How then could land be valued and exchanged in the marketplace? (de Coulanges 1980: 54–55, 62).

The modern construction of Western society, particularly a system based on neoliberalism, is based on an *exclusive* use of land. Individual self-interest remains supreme. The land is valued for its physical location and its resources rather than as the source of all life. The person with the most land or with land in the most ideal location is often the wealthiest individual in a community or the member of the community with the most power. This individual pursuit for the most profitable use of the land contributes to a negation of community and communal values and shows a lack of concern for the general welfare. This approach to land valuation is a clear obstacle to justice and the very antithesis of the biblical mandate concerning the use of land as God's stewards.

STEP 2. REFLECTING

One of the fundamental purposes of neoliberal governments — which usually operate in an individualistic and capitalist society — is to protect private property and preserve an open market economy. In many places and at different times in U.S. history, the Christian faith has been artificially linked to a laissez-faire economic philosophy. This connection has then been used to create ethical truths concerning freedom and rights, often allowing the dominant culture to prosper freely, even at the expense of others. The application of freedom and rights to human dignity has often been missing from the equation. Property rights have also become a battle cry in any serious conversation about correcting the wealth disparities within the United States. César Chávez explained how property rights can be used to mask oppression:

> When the racists and bigots, the industrialists and the corporation farmers were not shedding our blood, they were blocking our way with all kinds of stratagems. We have heard them all — "Property Rights," "States Rights," "Right to Work." All of these slogans, as you will have noticed, and as you will still notice, have been uttered in ringing tones of idealism and individual freedom. But that is the special genius of those who would deny the rights of others and hoard the fruits of democracy for themselves: They evade the problems and complex challenges of equal justice by reducing them to primitive oversimplifications that plead for nothing else but the perpetuation of their own special, exploitative interests. (Dalton 2003:67–68)

The danger in hiding behind a "Property Rights" slogan is that when wealth is concentrated in the hands of a few, democracy is threatened if the privileged few use their property to control the direction and policies of the society. And this often happens. In short, economic power leads directly to political power. The fight then waged is not for the land itself, but over who will have the right to use, enjoy, and gain from it. This is why land use should be subject to theological discussion.

American economist Henry George defined land as follows:

> The term land necessarily includes, not merely the surface of the earth as distinguished from water and the air, but the whole material universe outside of man, for it is only by having access to land, from which his very body is drawn, that man can come in contact with or use nature. The term land embraces, in short, all natural materials, forces, and opportunities, and, therefore, nothing that is freely supplied by nature can be properly classed as capital. A fertile field, a rich vein of ore, a falling stream which supplies power, may give to the possessor advantages equivalent to the possession of

capital, but to class such things as capital would be to put an
end to the distinction between land and capital, and, so far
as they relate to each other to make the two terms meaningless (1951:38–39).[1]

Our modern construction of property considers property as a
thing to be claimed and possessed. Property represents personal
liberty over against external powers and/or the means by which
one's needs are satisfied, produced, or distributed. The lure and
promise of property are liberty and security; the property holder
thus dominates the one without property, who as a result is also
without liberty or security (Meeks 1989:99–125). Or, as Frantz
Fanon wrote, "For a colonized people the most essential value,
because the most concrete, is first and foremost the land: the land
which will bring them bread and, above all, dignity" (1963:44).
Over time, land moved from being part of the natural environment to become one more commodity that could be used for domination. The misuse of land has become throughout history a
primary source of massive oppression and misery.

Mexican theologian Enrique Dussel maintains that private real
property has three origins: one either works for it, steals it, or inher-
its it. If one works for it, the amount of land acquired is relatively
small. If much property is owned, then it was undoubtedly stolen,
he says, sometimes without one's realizing it. Stealing it causes the
dispossessed to be impoverished and/or killed (1978:25). When

---

[1] Henry George (1839–1897) was a North American economist and
social philosopher who rooted a doctrine of land in ethics rather than economics. While living in San Francisco, he argued that the Western economic boom he witnessed resulted from the development of the railroads.
Nevertheless, a paradox existed. While this "boom" created an unparal-
leled increase in wealth, most people remained trapped in widespread
poverty. George concluded that the industrial development occurring during his lifetime concentrated wealth in the hands of the few who controlled land. When the value of land rose, so did their fortunes. Yet, their
wealth was not the result of their efforts but was due to the increase in
the population and the development of the economy. His teachings ceased
to be taken seriously because he did not hold any advanced degree during a time when economics was becoming a specialized profession.

property is inherited by one's children, the original sin of stealing and murder is transmitted to the next generation who, through complicity with their progenitors' acts, continue to benefit from land ownership.

Most modern principles of land ownership are based on the *laissez-faire* economics of Adam Smith. Smith argued that pursuit of economic self-interests within the context of a competitive society will benefit all persons. Thus, no restraints should be placed on the accumulation of land. Land ownership by individuals is a fundamental if not sacred building block of civilization, and to suggest the resumption of land as common property is paramount to advocating a regression toward some pre-modern, uncivilized existence.

Yet, Smith's model creates problems. For example, the privileged will be in an economic position to acquire immense portions of land. Through their holdings, they can impose laws upon those who need land for basic subsistence. In exchange for the use of the land, tenants must recognize the supreme authority of the landlord, whether the landowner is an individual, a multinational corporation, or a civil government. When society is constructed on the fundamental principle of private ownership, the state must protect property by enacting laws against trespassing and theft. Thus, to steal a loaf of bread from the wealthy, whose surplus is sufficient to feed an entire city, even for the purpose of feeding a hungry child, is a crime.

English philosopher John Locke (1632–1704), the "father of classical political liberalism," is responsible for advancing certain "self-evident natural rights," one of which is the exclusive use of real property. He viewed property as an institution of nature, not a social convention based on human laws (1952:17). Property became the third of the inalienable rights, along with "life and liberty." Locke argued for the right of each person, based on self-preservation and personal interest, to keep whatever property he or she possessed, despite the means utilized in its acquisition or an individual's ability to use all of its resources. Locke first limited the accumulation of property to what would not spoil, rust, rot, or decay (ibid. 23). However, with the introduction of a cash economy, previous limits were no longer applicable. Eventually money became the common denominator for land, as well as for labor.

While the fruits of the land might spoil, money as a commodity does not. Wealth, accumulated in the form of gold or silver (money) became unlimited (ibid. 29), and so did the accumulation of land.

The state, constructed to preserve the rights of the individual to life, liberty, and property, is duty-bound to insure these inalienable rights (ibid. 5–6). And the state is needed by the landholders to guarantee their property interest. The sacredness of property was reaffirmed in the young U.S. republic, reserving the right to participate in the political discourse to those white males owning property. Rather than the traditional right to property being derived from the power to rule, the Federalist Papers inverted this concept to reflect a right to rule in order to protect said property. Land became owned by "legal" individuals possessing a title that conferred rights protected by the state's judicial system. Still, land equality remained a seditious idea to be quashed because it created the possibility that the wealthy might lose their privilege. The goals of the young republic were fully identified with the interest of the landholders (Madison 2001:48).

The strong economic positions of the elite led to control of all aspects of political life. When private property (and free markets) secures the liberty of the wealthy class, with the help of the government, it is generally secured at the expense of a marginalized class that becomes increasingly alienated. The interests of the common person (specifically those who are poor and of color) become subordinated to the interests of this ruling class. Questioning the ruling class becomes paramount to revolution or treason. Even though there is a guise of universal participation in government, the wealthy class is instrumental in deciding by its political contributions who become governmental officers. This holds true whether the property owners are individuals or corporations. In return, the governmental officers protect the power and privilege of the wealthy class.

When John Locke first commodified land, he reduced its importance to nothing more than a unit of capital. He overlooked the rights of the land itself. In other words, he failed to see land as a gift of nature; instead it was viewed as passive and worthless until the active principle of human labor was applied to it (ibid. 26). By and large, economists have ignored the importance of land. It is merely one commodity among many rather than a precondition of economic life or as as the giver and sustainer of life. All living creatures share a common heritage in the land. While labor and capital remain reproducible, the land and its resources (such as fossil fuels and minerals) are exhaustible, as is seen in many parts of the world today.

Wealth-building through the use of land falls short of biblical standards.[2] Biblical texts clearly emphasize that all land is the sole possession of God.[3] As ultimate Creator and Sustainer, God alone is given absolute property rights. The biblical regulations concerning the sabbatical year, gleaning, Jubilee, and interest were attempts to keep the land available to all and to avoid great extremes of wealth and poverty. The biblical concepts of gleaning and Jubilee were not utopian dreams nor abstract principles from which to derive systems of ethics; rather, they provided a valid economic structure designed to ensure an equitable distribution of resources. When these concepts were flagrantly ignored, they awakened the prophets to call upon the people to repent.

STEP 3. PRAYING

Both the evolutionist and the biblical literalist agree that land preceded the advent of human beings. Land was not produced or

---

[2] For some time, papal encyclicals have wrestled with issues of property rights. Unfortunately, their historic allegiance to "landed" interests has caused a credibility gap in their attempt to define land for the common good. Pope John XXIII, while affirming the right of private ownership in *Mater et Magistra* (1961), extends this right to all classes through equitable distribution. Property is to be shared among all since it has a social destiny. Pope Paul VI's *Populorum Progressio* (1967) questioned the exclusive claim to property by some individuals while others lack necessities, and Pope John Paul II's *Laborem Exercens* (1981) balanced the rights of private property with the Christian responsibility for other members of society. Likewise, ecumenical movements among predominately Protestant churches have provided insight into ways of reestablishing an inclusive use of land.

[3] God's ownership of land can be noted in Ex. 9:29, 19:5; Dt. 10:14, 26:10; Ps.:24:1, 50:12; Jb. 41:11; and 1 Cor. 10:26.

created by humans, rather, it pre-existed as a gift of the Creator. But, the land also has rights over its inhabitants. The book of Leviticus dictates that, "When you come into the land which I [God] am giving you, the land shall keep a Sabbath to Yahweh" (25:2). According to Old Testament scholar Walter Brueggemann, "Sabbath in Israel is the affirmation that people, like land, cannot be finally owned or managed" (1977:64). The "right" to use the land is limited by humane, ecological, and economic concerns.

God's sole ownership of land makes personal possession impossible: "The land shall not be sold in perpetuity, for the land is [God's] and you are but aliens and tenants" (Lv. 25:23). To live on the land requires obedience to the Lord, who is in fact the landlord. Improper land stewardship defiles the land. Safeguards provided by the biblical texts established justice and prevented land ownership from unjustly stratifying the population.

The idea of the rights of the land itself ensures a just distribution of its fruits. By biblical law, one was not allowed to reap to the very edges of the field or pass through a second time to glean missed produce. The overlooked grain remained for the poor and the aliens (Lv. 19:9–10). In addition, the law of Moses forbade the selling of land for profit. Land was to be the inheritance of the family (Lv. 25:23–24). When property was purchased, absolute ownership was never transferred to the new owner. Instead, the land was returned to the original owner in the year of Jubilee (Lv. 25:13); if land had been sold due to financial difficulties, the property could be reclaimed (Lv. 25:25–28).

Nevertheless, the story of King Ahab, Queen Jezebel, and Naboth tells how the land was misused by the rich and powerful to the detriment of the marginalized. According to 1 Kings 21,

> "[Naboth] had a vineyard in Jezreel, near the palace of Ahab the king of Samaria. And Ahab spoke to Naboth saying, "Give me your vineyard so it can be a garden of green herbs for me." . . . But Naboth said to Ahab, "Far be it from me, by Yahweh, that I should give the inheritance of my fathers to you." . . . [Ahab told Jezebel his wife these things, and she said to Ahab], "Do you now rule over Israel? . . . I will give you the vineyard of Naboth." . . . [Jezebel then had Naboth stoned by bearing false witness against him], and when Ahab

heard that Naboth was dead, Ahab rose to go down to the vineyard . . . to take possession of it.

This view of land as a commodity to be acquired by whatever means necessary to increase personal wealth at the expense of the dispossessed produces injustices. The prophets frequently condemned their own communities for their avarice for land. During times of economic crisis, the biblical distribution of land rights was sometimes ignored as some people purchased the "inheritance" of their weaker neighbors and in the process created an urban elite profiting from the conversion of subsistence farming to exportable cash crops. The prophet Isaiah denounced this practice: "Woe to those touching house to house, bringing near field to field until no end of space, and you are made to dwell alone in the middle of the land" (5:8). Likewise, the prophet Micah proclaimed, "Woe to those plotting wickedness . . . they covet fields and seize them and houses, and carry them off. And they oppress people along with their inheritance" (2:1–2).[4]

As we have already seen, two types of claims can be made on property. Biblical texts champion inclusiveness, the belief that the land should be openly available. This pattern of land usage liberates both the individual and society from the perpetual grip of capitalism and neoliberalism. The land is held in stewardship for God so that the owner and her or his neighbors can obtain the basic necessities of life. Property serves the livelihood of all in the community, rather than becoming the form of their subjugation. Such is the paradigm established by Leviticus. This paradigm of land

---

[4] Another biblical example of the oppressive effects of ownership of land appears in the account of Pharaoh's appropriation of all the land at the expense of the Egyptians' economic welfare.

And Joseph bought all the land of Egypt for Pharaoh, because each one of the Egyptians sold their fields, because the famine was severe upon them. The land became Pharaoh's. As for the people, he reduced them to servitude from one end of Egypt to the other (Gn. 47:20–21).

In short, the biblical text declared that the right to land is subordinate to the rights of the disenfranchised to earn a just living and the rights of the land itself. Human beings are given biblical rights to be stewards of the land for the purposes of providing basic needs for sustaining life.

ownership was also employed in the early Christian church, where all believers shared their possessions (including their real property) according to each person's needs (Acts 2:44–45). This biblical concept has its roots in the wilderness experience of Israel when the bread (manna) provided by God was sufficient to meet each person's daily needs (Ex. 16:18). When accumulated in excess, it spoiled. The inclusive use of land can be used to atone for injustice and to restore broken relationships.

The concept of Trinity, one of the most important teachings of the Christian church, is a doctrine of a God whose life is an inclusive life of sharing. Tertullian's classic formula "one substance and three persons" introduced the Greek word *oikonomia* into theological discourse. This one God exists according to an inner order, the sharing of *substantia* (substance). *Substantia*, the legal terminology used by Tertullian, also meant "property." Hence, Trinity can be understood as three persons, equal in power, sharing one *substantia*, one property (González 1990b:111–15). This "economic" doctrine of the Trinity models a social order that avoids the socioeconomic consequences of exclusiveness.

Diametrically opposed to this inclusive claim on property is our modern Western form of land ownership, whose roots lie in Roman law. One of Rome's enduring contributions to Western civilization is its construction of land. Ownership constituted the right to use, to enjoy, and even to abuse the land. It was the function of the state and the backbone of Roman law to protect private property rights (idem 1990a:14–19). The title to property was exclusive. Nowhere in nature does this concept exist. It is a social construction designed to protect the appropriation of land by a single person. When this happens, the world's marginalized are generally left to barter for a small piece of land, often no longer fertile, in order to raise the bare necessities of life. This arrangement contributes to the fragmentation of our covenant with our God, our neighbor, and our land.

Many of the early church leaders condemned private property. Among the church's greatest exponent for common property was Ambrose, who wrote:

> The land was made to be common to all, the poor and the rich. Why do you, of the rich, claim for yourselves alone

the right to the land? . . . When you give to the poor, you give not of your own, but simply return what is his, for you have usurped that which is common and has been given for the common use of all. The land belongs to all, not to the rich; and yet those who are deprived of its use are many more than those who enjoy it. . . . God our Lord willed that this land be the common possession of all and give its fruit to all. But greed distributed the right of possessions. Therefore, if you claim as your private property part of what was granted in common to all human beings and to all animals, it is only fair that you share some of this with the poor, so that you will not deny nourishment to those who are also partakers of your right (by which you hold this land). (Ibid. 191)

Adolfo Perez Esquivel, the 1980 Nobel laureate, calls for neither the exclusive use of land nor the abolition of land ownership. Rather, he maintains that the land should be distributed according to need. Speaking against the backdrop of South American economies, where cash crops grown for export contribute to a deficiency in food crops, he challenges the notion that land title obtained through purchases is more legitimate than property earned through need and toil. The people who work the land for their sustenance hold a nobler title than the *patrón* who "never sowed a solitary seed" (1983:99). Enrique Dussel agrees by stating that all people have a natural right to whatever is required to live, be it calories, clothing, or housing. The excess of the unjust accumulation of real property is responsible for subjugating those who have none (1974:50).[5] This is consistent with the biblical messianic dream found in Isaiah, "They shall build houses and live in them; and they shall plant vineyards and eat their fruit. They shall not build and another live in them, or plant and another eat" (65:21–22).

---

[5] Dussel views private property as an offshoot of original sin, which, for him, is colonial domination. I maintain the opposite: that it was avarice for land and its resources that led to colonial domination, thus making land accumulation the original sin and colonialism its offshoot.

STEP 4. CASE STUDIES

- 1. Richard Robinson, Jr., a member of the Ojibwe people, remembers how his grandfather, a hospital janitor, looked forward to retiring and returning to his land. But Robinson's grandfather quickly learned that "his" land was no longer his. The Bureau of Indian Affairs told him he had signed the land over to the United States in exchange for a few thousand dollars. "He swore until he died that he never received a check and never signed any papers," said Mr. Robinson. "He was dead certain."[6] Robinson's grandfather's story is a common one concerning what once was Amerindian land, before the relentless westward push of white settlers and railroads. Like most Native Americans, Robinson rejects the argument that their dispossession from their tribal lands was some past event. Although several Christian denominations have apologized to Native Americans for the conquest of their land, there is a lack of recognition that the taking of Native lands constitutes an ongoing theft. Native Americans do not believe the apology is sufficient. Referring to apartheid, Archbishop Desmond Tutu said, "If you take my pen, what good does an apology do, if you still keep my pen?" (Kidwell et al. 2001:170).

    — Does the sin of theft constitute a sin that continues to be passed down to each succeeding generation?
    — How are the social and economic hardships of Native nations today linked, if at all, with how Native Americans have been historically treated?
    — Once Euroamerican Christians apologize, should Native Americans simply "get over it" because it happened in the past? If not, then what specifically should Christians do?
    — What responsibility, if any, do Euroamerican Christians who continue to profit from the lands stolen from the Native Americans have toward them?

---

[6] Stephanie Strom, "Indians Fight to Regain Lands Lost to Railroad," *The New York Times*, December 25, 2002.

— If the U.S. government is unable to produced an authentic bill of sale from Robinson's grandfather, what is due Mr. Robinson? Does it matter if a bill of sales does exist? Why or why not?

- 2. Thirty-one-year-old Matwa, a South African woman, is infected with HIV.[7] She is among one in every twelve African adults who has the AIDS virus. Two-thirds of AIDS fatalities and new HIV infections around the world will occur in Africa in 2004. About 2.3 million Africans died from AIDS during 2003, and at least three million more Africans became infected. Compare this with an estimated death toll around the world of three million, and five million new infections.[8] Anti-AIDS drugs offer hope now as powerful medicines have changed AIDS from a death sentence to a chronic disease in wealthier countries. But, according to health-care activists, thousands of deaths will occur in East Africa because of a lack of access to low-cost anti-AIDS drugs, and the United States has played a role in limiting access. U.S. demands for tougher review standards for generic copies of patented AIDS drugs will prevent use of cheaper versions of the drugs in the anti-AIDS program in Africa. U.S. officials say they are concerned about the safety and effectiveness of the generic drugs. However, critics charge that present generic copies have been successful.

  The Bush administration is accused of seeking to protect the profits of large U.S. drug companies, some of whose executives have contributed to the president's re-election campaign. "The Bush project is to ensure the dominance of big pharmaceuticals in poor countries," says Sharonann Lynch, leader of Washington-based NGO Healthgap. According to activists, up to four times as many Africans could be treated with life-extending drugs if the U.S. would permit purchase of the generic equivalents.[9]

---

[7] Ravi Nessman, "Government Delay Blamed for Hundreds of Thousands of AIDS Deaths in South Africa," *Associated Press Worldstream*, September 24, 2003.

[8] Richard Ingham, "World AIDS Crisis: Africa Enters the Death Phase," *Agence France Presse*, November 23, 2003.

[9] "U.S. Trying to Block Generics in Africa, Say Aids Activists," *Africa News*, March 29, 2004.

Dominance over the African drug industry is maintained through the intellectual-property rights held by the pharmaceutical companies. Intellectual-property laws and regulations insure that royalties are paid to creators of intellectual property. According to the World Bank, it is estimated that global intellectual-property rules result in the yearly transfer of $40 billion from poor countries to corporations in industrial nations. The World Trade Organization (WTO) is saddled with such regulations as special interest groups attempt to protect their interests. Jagdish Bhagwati, an economics professor at Columbia University, claims, "This is not a trade issue. It's a royalty-collection issue. It's pharmaceuticals and software throwing their weight around."[10]

— Do corporations have a right to protect their royalties from countries with the capability to reproduce their products?
— Should such corporations pursue copyright violators through the WTO?
— The major obstacle to poor nations developing and providing cheap generic AIDS drugs for their inhabitants is intellectual-property rules that insure that the pharmaceutical creator of the medicine continues to be compensated. Is this system just?
— Is the ultimate purpose of medicine to provide healing to Matwa or to increase the pharmaceutical's corporate bottom line?

• 3. President James H. Polk ran for president on the promise that if elected he would annex Texas and start a war with Mexico. In July 1845, four months after being inaugurated as the eleventh president of the United States, he sent General Zachary Taylor to encroach on Mexican territory by deploying his troops to bait the Mexicans. When Mexico met the invading army in the field, Polk seized the opportunity to request a declaration of war from Congress. A military invasion by U.S. forces led to their victory, formally recognized in the 1848 Treaty of Guadalupe-Hidalgo. The treaty ceded half of Mexico's territory to the United States.

---

[10] Tina Rosenberg, "The Free-Trade Fix," *The New York Times Magazine*, August 18, 2002.

This land included gold deposits that would be discovered in California in 1849, silver deposits in Nevada, oil in Texas, and the natural harbors needed for commerce. This is why many people of Mexican descent insist that they did not cross the border, but rather that the border crossed them. Mexico's loss of natural resources, plus the military cost of defending Mexico from the United States' invading armies led to a collapse of the Mexican economy, whose ramifications continue to be felt today. As early as 1836, John Quincy Adams was denouncing before Congress any war with Mexico as a naked act of aggression (1838:119). Ulysses S. Grant, who served in the conflict, viewed the war as an injustice forced upon Mexico for the sake of acquiring land (1885:54–56).

— Is it just for one nation to invade another nation to acquire the natural resources of that nation?
— Does the invading nation have any responsibility to the invaded nation? To its people?
— Is the flow of people across the artificially created border between the U.S. and Mexico just?
— Do Mexicans have any right to the land that was theirs until the U.S. military forces said differently?
— What should be done today about the issue of undocumented persons of Mexican descent living in the U.S.?

• 4. In Victor Hugo's classic, *Les Miserables*, Jean Valjean smashed the window of Maubert Isabeau, the baker on Church Square in Faverolles, to steal a loaf of bread to feed his widowed sister's seven hungry children. Even though he and his sister worked several jobs, it was not sufficient to place food on the table. The story of Jean Valjean is the story of many today who live in the margins of society.

— Is it moral to steal property (bread) to meet a basic human need and avert the greater evil of malnutrition?
— Is stealing food any greater a sin then the stealing of Jean Valjean's labor by refusing to pay him a living wage?
— What about the rights of Maubert Isabeau, the baker? Does stealing property, even if it is food, destroy community because it destroys trust?

— Are property laws designed to protect the property of those who can afford property while ignoring the intangible property of the poor in the form of their labor?

— Do property rights supercede the rights of humans to consume the daily requirement of calories needed to sustain life?

- 5. Former CEO L. Dennis Kozlowski went on trial in 2003 for alleged executive looting at Tyco International. Apparently, Tyco paid for an $18 million New York apartment and the $11 million supposedly spent on antiques, art, and other furnishings, including a $6,000 shower curtain. Additionally, Kozlowski, who made $293 million from 1998 to 2001 in salary, bonuses and stock proceeds, threw a lavish week-long birthday party for his wife, complete with scantily clad models in Roman-theme attire, a stage resembling a Roman temple, an anatomically correct ice sculpture of Michelangelo's David dispensing vodka, and a performance by Jimmy Buffett — all at a cost of $2 million.

  From General Electric to Adelphia, corporate coffers have paid for over-the-top perks including private jets, luxury vacations, private golf courses and multimillion-dollar corporate homes in resort towns and big cities.[11] The value of personal property often does not exist within the commodity itself, for such value is secondary. Rather, the conspicuous consumption of a commodity mainly seeks recognition by others of the consumer's higher social standing. Hence, conspicuous consumption fails to satisfy any particular need of the consumer; instead, it is the display of commodities, in and of itself, that enhances the reputation of the consumer (Veblen 1953:21–80).

  — Is conspicuous consumption moral?

  — Does a person have a right to spend his or her money on any commodity he or she chooses to own, even when the sole purpose of owning that commodity is to flaunt a higher social standing?

  — Should people be allowed to accumulate luxury items while their neighbors go hungry? If so, is this a governmental

---

[11] Rachel Beck, "Corporate Excesses Live on Tyco Birthday Video," *The Associated Press*, October 30, 2003.

responsibility? If not, are there any ways to create a more balanced society?
— What responsibility does Dennis Kozlowski have to his corporation, his stockholders, the community at large, and the poor?

Epilogue

As mentioned in this book's preface, the thoughts, ideas, and methodologies appearing within this text were forged within the "privileged" classroom at the college where I teach. At the end of the semester, as students discussed and "recapped" what they un(cover)ed during the course, one particular student said, "Every issue we discuss, no matter how clear-cut it may have appeared to be, seems always to boil down to issues of race, class, and gender. Are there any issues void of these three perspectives?"

Although I said nothing, I really wanted to respond, "Welcome to my world!" For those from the margins of society, race, class, and gender matter each and every day. The privilege of whiteness and maleness lies in not having to deal with these characteristics in order to survive within society. These factors represent the norm. White men, and white women to a lesser degree, can be good Christians without ever needing to consider how this culture privileges their very existence.

Ethics for the Christian must become the means to dismantle structures that privilege one group at the expense of another. Christian ethics also is the path by which God is known, by which justice is created, by which liberation for the oppressed is chosen. Nevertheless, Christian ethical discipline continues to be formed and shaped by those who benefit from the present structures of power. The ethical perspectives discussed throughout this book have avoided discussion of the moral deliberation of the powerful, the privileged, the intellectuals in favor of the ethics that resonates among the oppressed, the disenfranchised, and the marginalized.

For a system of ethics to be Christian, it must be forged contextually within the margins of society, specifically within the faith community. Such an ethics, by its very nature, serves as a critique of the reasoning employed by ethicists from the dominant culture whose so-called objectivity, in the final analysis, remains situated in a culture of privilege, a context that is either consciously or unconsciously justified.

This book has attempted to hold the dominant culture accountable for not addressing how race, class, and gender are embedded in Christianity. Christian ethics has ignored and continues to ignore its complicity with oppressive structures, refusing to take responsibility for creating a morality that does not adequately address the concerns of the marginalized. The benefactors of the status quo, in order to maintain their privilege, create certain principles that attempt reform without changing the very way in which power is constructed. For this reason, doing ethics from the margins is not simply an interesting ethical perspective, nor is it an extension of eurocentric ethics. Rather, to do ethics from the margins is to participate in a Christian social ethics that fully considers 1) the privilege of power, 2) the causes of supposed superiority, and 3) the rules by which power is maintained. Only then can Christians expose and debunk the obstacles preventing all of God's creatures from living the abundant life.

Bibliography

Abell, John D. "Defence Spending and Unemployment Rates: An Empirical Analysis Disaggregated by Race." *Cambridge Journal of Economics*, Vol. 14 (1990): 405–19.

———. "Military Spending and Income Inequality." *Journal of Peace Research*, Vol. 31, No. 1 (1994): 35–43.

Adams, John Quincy. *Speech of John Quincy Adams, May 25, 1836*. Washington, DC: Gale and Seaton, 1838.

Amnesty International. *United States of America: Death by Discrimination — The Continuing Role of Race in Capital Cases*. London: Amnesty International, 2003.

Anderson, Sarah, John Cavanagh, Chris Hartman, and Betsy Leondar-Wright. *Executive Excess 2001: Layoffs — Tax Rebates — The Gender Gap*. Washington, DC: Institute for Policy Studies and United for a Fair Economy, 2001.

Aquino, María Pilar. "Theological Method in U.S. Latino/a Theology: Toward an Intercultural Theology for the Third Millennium." In *From the Heart of Our People: Latino/a Explorations in Catholic Systematic Theology*. Ed. Orlando O. Espín and Miguel H. Díaz. Maryknoll, NY: Orbis Books, 1999.

Arendt, Hannah. *The Human Condition*. Chicago: University of Chicago Press, 1958.

Augustine. *The City of God Against the Pagans*, Vol. 6. Ed. T. E. Page et al. Trans. William Chase Greene. Cambridge: Harvard University Press, 1960.

Baker-Fletcher, Karen. *Sisters of Dust, Sisters of Spirit: Womanist Wordings on God and Creation*. Minneapolis: Fortress Press, 1998.

———. "Spirituality." In *Handbook of U.S. Theologies of Liberation*. Ed. Miguel A. De La Torre. St. Louis: Chalice Press, 2004.

Barlett, Donald L. and James B. Steele. *America: What Went Wrong?* Kansas City: Andrews and McMeel, 1992.

Barth, Karl. *This Christian Cause: A Letter to Great Britain from Switzerland*. New York: Macmillan Company, 1941.

——. *The Word of God and the Word of Man*. Trans. Douglas Horton. Philadelphia: Pilgrim Press, 1928.

Becker, Patricia C., ed. *A Statistical Portrait of the United States: Social Conditions and Trends*, 2nd ed. Lanham, MD.: Bernan Press, 2002.

Bell, Daniel M. *Liberation Theology After the End of History: The Refusal to Cease Suffering*. New York: Routledge, 2001.

Bhabha, Homi K. *The Location of Culture*. New York: Routledge, 1994.

Blount, Brian K. *Then the Whisper Put on Flesh: New Testament Ethics in an African American Context*. Nashville: Abingdon Press, 2001.

Boff, Clodovis. *Theology and Praxis: Epistemological Foundations*. Trans. Robert R. Barr. Maryknoll, NY: Orbis Books, 1987.

Boff, Clodovis and George V. Pixley. *The Bible, the Church, and the Poor*. Trans. Paul Burns. Maryknoll, NY: Orbis Books, 1989.

Boff, Leonardo. *Cry of the Earth, Cry of the Poor*. Trans. Phillip Berryman. Maryknoll, NY: Orbis Books, 1997.

Boff, Leonardo and Clodovis Boff. *Salvation and Liberation: In Search of a Balance between Faith and Politics*. Trans. Robert R. Barr. Maryknoll, NY: Orbis Books, 1988.

Bonino, José Míguez. *Doing Theology in a Revolutionary Situation*. Philadelphia: Fortress Press, 1975.

——. *Toward a Christian Political Ethics*. Philadelphia: Fortress Press, 1983.

Bouma-Prediger, Steven. "Environmental Racism." In *Handbook of U.S. Theologies of Liberation*. Ed. Miguel A. De La Torre. St. Louis: Chalice Press, 2004.

Bourdieu, Pierre. *Outline of a Theory of Practice*. Trans. Richard Nice. Cambridge, England: Cambridge University Press, 1977.

Bowen, William G. and Sarah A. Levin. *Reclaiming the Game: College Sports and Educational Values*. Princeton: Princeton University Press, 2003.

Brubaker, Rogers. "Rethinking Classical Theory: The Sociological Vision of Pierre Bourdieu." *Theory and Society*, Vol. 14 (1985): 745–75.

Brueggemann, Walter. *The Land*. Philadelphia: Fortress Press, 1977.

Brunner, Emil. *The Divine Imperative*. Trans. Olive Wyon. Philadelphia: Westminister, 1947.

Buber, Martin. *I and Thou*. Trans. Walter Kaufmann. New York: Scribner, 1970.

Bullard Robert D. "Anatomy of Environmental Racism." In *Toxic Struggles: The Theory and Practice of Environmental Justice*. Ed. Richard Hofrichter. Philadelphia: New Society Publishers, 1993.

——. *Dumping in Dixie: Race, Class, and Environmental Quality*. Boulder, CO: Westview Press, 1994.

Calvin, John. *The Institutes of the Christian Religion*, Vol. I & II. Trans. Henry Beveridge. Grand Rapids: Eerdmans Publishing Company, 1983.

Cannon, Katie. *Black Womanist Ethics*. Atlanta: Scholars Press, 1988.

———. *Katie's Canon: Womanism and the Soul of the Black Community*. New York: Continuum, 1995.

CELAM. *La iglesia en la actual transformacion de america latina a la luz del concilio, II Conclusiones*, 3rd ed. Bogotá: Secretariado General del CELAM, 1968.

Chávez, César. "Farm Workers at Risk." In *Toxic Struggles: The Theory and Practice of Environmental Justice*. Ed. Richard Hofrichter. Philadelphia: New Society Publishers, 1993.

Cobb Jr., John B. "Liberation Theology and the Global Economy." In *Liberating the Future: God, Mammon and Theology*. Ed. Joerg Rieger. Minneapolis: Fortress Press, 1998.

Cone, James H. *Black Theology and Black Power*. New York: Seabury Press, 1969.

———. *A Black Theology of Liberation*, 20th Anniversary Ed. Maryknoll, NY: Orbis Books, 1999a.

———. *God of the Oppressed*. New York: Seabury Press, 1975.

———. *Speaking the Truth: Ecumenism, Liberation, and Black Theology*. Maryknoll, NY: Orbis Books, 1999b.

Cooper, Mary H. "Campaign Finance Reform." *Congressional Quarterly Researcher*, Vol. 10, No. 12 (March 31, 2000): 257–80.

———. "Income Inequality." *Congressional Quarterly Researcher*, Vol. 8, No. 15 (April 17, 1998): 339–59.

Correll, Joshua, Bernadette Park, Charles M. Judd, and Bernd Wittenbrink. "The Police Officer's Dilemma: Using Ethnicity to Disambiguate Potentially Threatening Individuals." *Journal of Personality and Social Psychology*. Vol. 83, No. 6 (December 2002): 1314–29.

Costanzo, Mark. "The Death Penalty Is Discriminatory: Part I." In *The Death Penalty: Opposing Viewpoints*. Ed. Mary E. Williams. San Diego: Greenhaven Press, 2002.

Dalton, Frederick John. *The Moral Vision of César Chávez*. Maryknoll, NY: Orbis Books, 2003.

Daly, Lois K. "Ecofeminism, Reverence for Life, and Feminist Theological Ethics." In *Feminist Theological Ethics: A Reader*. Louisville: Westminister John Knox Press, 1994.

de Coulanges, Numa Denis Fustel. *The Ancient City: A Study on the Religion, Laws, and Institutions of Greece and Rome*. Baltimore: Johns Hopkins University Press, 1980.

de la Cruz, Juan. "Ascent of Mount Carmel." In *John of the Cross: Selected Writings*. Ed. Kieran Kavanaugh. New York: Paulist Press, 1987.

De La Torre, Miguel. "The Challenge of Lazarus." *Celebration: An Ecumenical Worship Resource*. Vol. 31, No. 3 (March 2003a): 99–100.

———. *La Lucha for Cuba: Religion and Politics on the Streets of Miami*. Berkeley: University of California Press, 2003b.

———. *Reading the Bible from the Margins*. Maryknoll, NY: Orbis Books, 2002.

———. *Santería: The Beliefs and Rituals of a Growing Religion in America*. Grand Rapids: Eerdmans Publishing Co., 2004.

De La Torre, Miguel A. and Edwin Aponte. *Introducing Latino/a Theologies*. Maryknoll, NY: Orbis Books, 2001.

Durkheim, Emile. *Division of Labor in Society*. Trans. George Simpson. New York: MacMillan, 1933.

Dussel, Enrique. *Ethics and Community*. Trans. Robert R. Barr. Maryknoll: Orbis Books, 1988.

———. *Ethics and the Theology of Liberation*. Trans. Bernard F. McWilliams. Maryknoll, NY: Orbis Books, 1978.

———. *The Invention of the Americas : Eclipse of "The Other" and the Myth of Modernity*. Trans. Michael D. Barber. New York: Continuum, 1995.

Ehrenreich, Barbara. *Nickel and Dimed: On (Not) Getting By in America*. New York: Henry Holt, 2001.

Ehrenreich, Barbara and John Ehrenreich. "The Professional–Managerial Class." In *Between Labor and Capital*. Ed. Pat Walker. Boston: South End Press 1972.

Fanon, Frantz. *The Wretched of the Earth*. Trans. Constance Farrington. New York: Grove Press, 1963.

Feinberg, Joel. *Rights, Justice, and the Bounds of Liberty: Essays in Social Philosophy*. Princeton: Princeton University Press, 1980.

Foucault, Michel. *The Foucault Reader*. Ed. Paul Rabinow. New York: Pantheon Books, 1984.

———. *Madness and Civilization: A History of Insanity in the Age of Reason*. Trans. Richard Howard. New York: Pantheon Books, 1965.

———. *Technologies of the Self: A Seminar with Michel Foucault*. Ed. Luther H. Martin, Huck Gitman, Patrick H. Hutton. Amherst, MA: University of Massachusetts Press, 1988.

Frankenberg, Erica and Chungmei Lee. *Race in American Public Schools: Rapidly Resegregating School Districts*. Cambridge, MA: The Civil Rights Project at Harvard University, 2002.

Freire, Paulo. *Pedagogy of the Oppressed*. 20th Anniversary Ed. Trans. Myra Bergman Ramos. New York: Continuum, 1994.

Friedman, Milton. *Capitalism and Freedom*. Chicago: University of Chicago Press, 1962.

Fukuda-Parr, Sakiko, ed. *United Nations Development Programme's Human Development Report 2003.* New York: Oxford University Press, 2003.

George, Henry. *Progress and Poverty: An Inquiry into the Cause of Industrial Depressions and of Increase of Want with Increase of Wealth,* 50th Anniversary Edition. New York: Robert Schalkenbach Foundation, 1951.

George, Susan. "Food Strategies for Tomorrow." In *The Hunger Project Papers.* Ed. Beverly Tangri. No. 6 (December 1987):1–21.

———. "A Short History of Neoliberalism." Paper presented at *The Conference on Economic Sovereignty in a Globalising World.* Bangkok, Thailand, March 24–26, 1999.

George, Susan and Fabrizio Sabelli. *Faith and Credit: The World Bank's Secular Empire.* Boulder, CO: Westview Press, 1994.

Gilligan, Carol. *In a Different Voice: Psychological Theory and Woman's Development.* Cambridge, MA: Harvard University Press, 1982.

Gnanadason, Aruna. "Toward a Feminist Eco-Theology for India." In *Women Healing Earth: Third World Women on Ecology, Feminism, and Religion.* Ed. Rosemary Radford Ruether. Maryknoll, NY: Orbis Books, 1996.

González, Justo. *Faith and Wealth: A History of Early Christian Ideas on the Origin, Significance, and Use of Money.* San Francisco: Harper & Row, 1990a.

———. *Mañana: Christian Theology from a Hispanic Perspective.* Nashville: Abingdon Press, 1990b.

Grant, Ulysses S. *Personal Memoirs,* Vol. I. New York: Charles L. Webster & Company, 1885.

Griffiths, Brian. "The Challenge of Global Capitalism: A Christian Perspective." In *Making Globalization Good: Moral Challenges of Global Capitalism.* Ed. John H. Dunning. Oxford: Oxford University Press, 2003.

Grimmett, Richard F. *Conventional Arms Transfers to Developing Nations, 1994–2001.* Washington, DC: Congressional Research Service, 2002.

Gustafson, James M. *Can Ethics Be Christian?* Chicago: University of Chicago Press, 1975.

———. *Christ and the Moral Life.* New York: Harper & Row, Publishers, 1968.

———. *Theology and Christian Ethics.* Philadelphia: Pilgrim Press Book, 1974.

Gustafson, James M. and James Laney, eds. *On Being Responsible: Issues in Personal Ethics.* New York: Harper & Row, Publishers, 1968.

Gutiérrez, Gustavo. "Liberation Theology and the Future of the Poor." In *Liberating the Future: God, Mammon and Theology.* Ed. Joerg Rieger. Minneapolis: Fortress Press, 1998.

———. *The Power of the Poor in History*. Trans. Robert R. Barr. Maryknoll, NY: Orbis Books, 1984.

———. *A Theology of Liberation*, 15th Anniversary Edition. Trans. and ed. Sister Caridad Inda and John Eagleson. Maryknoll, NY: Orbis Books, 1988.

Hamilton, Cynthia. "Environmental Consequences of Urban Growth and Blight." In *Toxic Struggles: The Theory and Practice of Environmental Justice*. Ed. Richard Hofrichter. Philadelphia: New Society Publishers, 1993.

Hartung, William D. *And Weapons for All*. New York: HarperCollins Publishers, 1994.

Henderson, Errol Anthony. "Military Spending and Poverty." *Journal of Politics*, Vol. 60, No. 2 (May 1998): 503–20.

Hegel, G. W. F. *The Phenomenology of Mind*. Trans. J. B. Baillie. New York: Harper & Row, 1967.

Heyward, Carter. "Jesus Christ." In *Handbook of U.S. Theologies of Liberation*. Ed. Miguel A. De La Torre. St. Louis: Chalice Press, 2004.

Hinkelammert, Franz J. *Cultura de la Esperanza y Sociedad sin Exclusión*. San José, Costa Rica: Departamento Ecuménico de Investigaciones, 1995.

———. "Globalization as Cover-Up." In *Globalization and Its Victims*. London: SCM Press, 2001.

———. "Liberation Theology in the Economic and Social Context of Latin America." In *Liberation Theologies, Postmodernity, and the Americas*. Ed. David Batstone, Eduardo Mendieta, Lois Ann Lorentzen, and Dwight N. Hopkins. London: Routledge, 1997.

Hobbes, Thomas. *Leviathan*. Oxford: Clarendon Press, 1909.

Hopkins, Dwight N. *Shoes That Fit Our Feet: Sources for a Constructive Black Theology*. Maryknoll, NY: Orbis Books, 2000.

Institute of Medicine, Committee on the Consequences of Uninsurance — Board on Health Care Services. *Coverage Matters: Insurance and Health Care*. Washington, DC: National Academy Press, 2001.

Iyasu, S., K. Tomaskek, and W. Barfield. "Infant Mortality and Low Birth Weight among Black and White Infants — United States, 1980–2000." *The Journal of the American Medical Association*, Vol. 288, No. 7 (April 21, 2002): 825–26.

Jackson, Jesse. *Legal Lynching: Racism, Injustice, and the Death Penalty*. New York: Marlowe and Company, 1996.

Jones, Major J. *Christian Ethics for Black Theology*. Nashville: Abingdon Press, 1974.

Jost, Kenneth. "Campaign Finance Showdown." *Congressional Quarterly Researcher*, Vol. 12, No. 41 (November 22, 2002): 971–91.

Kahn, Katherine L. "Health Care for Black and Poor Hospitalized Medicare Patients." *The Journal of the American Medical Association*, Vol. 271, No. 15 (April 20, 1994): 1169–74.

Kammer III, Charles L. *Ethics and Liberation: An Introduction.* Maryknoll, NY: Orbis Books, 1988.

Kennedy, Paul. *The Rise and Fall of the Great Powers: Economic Change and Military Conflict from 1500 to 2000.* New York: Random House, 1987.

Kidwell, Clara Sue, Homer Noley, and George E. "Tink" Tinker. *A Native American Theology.* Maryknoll, NY: Orbis Books, 2001.

King, Jr., Martin Luther. "Pilgrimage to Nonviolence." In *A Testament of Hope: The Essential Writings of Martin Luther King, Jr.* Ed. James M. Washington. New York: HarperCollins, 1986.

———. *Strength to Love.* Philadelphia: Fortress Press, 1963.

———. *Stride Toward Freedom: The Montgomery Story.* New York: Harper, 1958.

———. "The Trumpet of Conscience." In *A Testament of Hope: The Essential Writings of Martin Luther King, Jr.* Ed. James M. Washington. New York: HarperCollins, 1986.

———. *Why We Can't Wait?* New York: Mentor Book, 1964.

Kozol, Jonathan. *Savage Inequalities: Children in America's Schools.* New York: Crown Publishers, 1991.

Kwok Pui-lan. *Introducing Asian Feminist Theology.* Cleveland: Pilgrim Press, 2000.

Lacan, Jacques. *Écrits: A Selection.* Trans. Alan Sheridan. New York: W. W. Norton, 1977.

LaDuke, Winona. "A Society Based on Conquest Cannot Be Sustained: Native Peoples and the Environmental Crises." In *Toxic Struggles: The Theory and Practice of Environmental Justice.* Ed. Richard Hofrichter. Philadelphia: New Society Publishers, 1993.

Locke, John. *The Second Treatise of Government.* Ed. Thomas P. Peardon. Indianapolis: Bobbs-Merrill Educational Publishing, 1952.

Luther, Martin. *Luther's Works: The Christian in Society III*, Vol. 46. Ed. Robert C. Schultz. Philadelphia: Fortress Press, 1967.

Madison, James. "Federalist Paper #10." In *The Federalist by Alexander Hamilton, John Jay, and James Madison.* Ed. George W. Carey and James McClellan. Indianapolis: Liberty Fund, 2001.

Maher, Timothy. "Environmental Oppression: Who Is Targeted for Toxic Exposure?" *Journal of Black Studies*, Vol. 28, No. 3 (January 1998): 357–67.

Malcolm X. "The Leverett House Forum of March 18, 1964." In *The Speeches of Malcolm X at Harvard.* Ed. Archie Epps. New York: William Morrow & Company, 1968.

Masci, David, "The Consumer Culture." *Congressional Quarterly Researcher*, Vol. 9, No. 44 (November 19, 1999): 1001–16.

McCann, Dennis P. and Charles R. Strain. *Polity and Praxis: A Program for American Practical Theology.* Minneapolis: Winston Press, 1985.

McConnell, D. R. *A Different Gospel: Biblical and Historical Insights into the Word of Faith Movement.* Peabody, MA.: Hendrickson Publishers, Inc., 1995.

Meeks, M. Douglas. "Economy and the Future of Liberation Theology." In *Liberating the Future: God, Mammon, and Theology.* Ed. Joerg Rieger. Minneapolis: Fortress Press, 1998.

———. *God the Economist.* Minneapolis: Fortress Press, 1989.

Michalos, Alex C. *A Pragmatic Approach to Business Ethics.* Thousand Oaks, CA: Sage Publications, 1995.

Mitchem, Stephanie Y. *Introducing Womanist Theology.* Maryknoll, NY: Orbis Books, 2002.

Moltmann, Jürgen. "Political Theology and Theology of Liberation." In *Liberating the Future: God, Mammon and Theology.* Ed. Joerg Rieger. Minneapolis: Fortress Press, 1998.

Morgan, Edmund S. *American Slavery, American Freedom: The Ordeal of Colonial Virginia.* New York: W. W. Norton, 1975.

Morrison, R. Sean et al. "'We Don't Carry That'—Failure of Pharmacies in Predominantly Nonwhite Neighborhoods to Stock Opioid Analgesics." *The New England Journal of Medicine*, Vol. 342, No. 14 (April 6, 2000): 1023–26.

Nelson-Pallmeyer, Jack. *School of Assassins: Guns, Greed, and Globalization.* Maryknoll, NY: Orbis Books, 2001.

Niebuhr, H. Richard. *The Responsible Self: An Essay in Christian Moral Philosophy.* New York: Harper & Row, 1963.

Niebuhr, Reinhold. *Moral Man and Immoral Society: A Study in Ethics and Politics.* New York: Charles Scribner, 1960.

———. *The Nature and Destiny of Man: Human Destiny*, Vol. II. New York: Charles Scribner, 1943.

Ortega, Bob. *In Sam We Trust: The Untold Story of Sam Walton and How Wal-Mart Is Devouring America.* New York: Random House, 1998.

Parenti, Christian. *Lockdown America: Police and Prisons in the Age of Crisis.* New York: Verso, 1999.

Pedraja, Luis G. "Trinity." In *Handbook of U.S. Theologies of Liberation.* Ed. Miguel A. De La Torre. St. Louis: Chalice Press, 2004.

Pérez Esquivel, Adolfo. *Christ in a Poncho: Witnesses to the Nonviolent Struggles in Latin America.* Ed. Charles Antoine. Trans. Robert R. Barr. Maryknoll, NY: Orbis Books, 1983.

Phillips, Kevin. *The Politics of Rich and Poor: Wealth and the American Electorate in the Reagan Aftermath.* New York: Random House, 1990.

Pixley, George V. *On Exodus: A Liberation Perspective.* Trans. Robert R. Barr. Maryknoll, NY: Orbis Books, 1987.

Raboteau, Albert J. *Slave Religion: The "Invisible Institution" in the Antebellum South.* New York: Oxford University Press, 1978.

Ramsey, Paul. *Christian Ethics and the Sit-In.* New York: Association Press, 1961.

Rawls, John. *A Theory of Justice.* Cambridge, MA: Belknap Press of Harvard University Press, 1971.

Rejón, Francisco Moreno. "Fundamental Moral Theory in the Theology of Liberation." In *Mysterium Liberationis: Fundamental Concepts of Liberation Theology.* Ed. Ignacio Ellacuría and Jon Sobrino. Maryknoll, NY: Orbis Books, 1993.

Rousseau, Jean-Jacques. *The First and Second Discourses.* Ed. Roger D. Masters. Trans. Roger D. Masters and Judith R. Masters. New York: St. Martin's Press, 1964.

Ruether, Rosemary Radford, ed. *Women Healing Earth: Third World Women on Ecology, Feminism, and Religion.* Maryknoll, NY: Orbis Books, 1996.

Sanders, Cheryl. *Empowerment Ethics for a Liberated People: A Path to African American Social Transformation.* Minneapolis: Fortress Press, 1995.

Sanders, Rickie and Mark T. Mattson. *Growing Up in America: An Atlas of Youth in the USA.* New York: Prentice Hall International, 1998.

Schubeck, Thomas L. *Liberating Ethics: Sources, Models, and Norms.* Minneapolis: Fortress Press, 1993.

Schulman, Kevin A. et al. "The Effect of Race and Sex on Physician's Recommendations for Cardiac Catheterization." *The New England Journal of Medicine,* Vol. 340, No. 8 (February 25, 1999): 618–25.

Seager, Joni. "Creating a Culture of Destruction: Gender, Militarism, and the Enviroment." In *Toxic Struggles: The Theory and Practice of Environmental Justice.* Ed. Richard Hofrichter. Philadelphia: New Society Publishers, 1993.

Segundo, Juan Luis. "Conversion and Reconciliation in the Perspective of Modern Liberation Theology." In *Signs of the Times: Theological Reflections.* Trans. Robert R. Barr. Maryknoll, NY: Orbis Books, 1993.

Shiva, Vandana. "Let Us Survive: Women, Ecology and Development." In *Women Healing Earth: Third World Women on Ecology, Feminism, and Religion.* Ed. Rosemary Radford Ruether. Maryknoll, NY: Orbis Books, 1996.

Sider, Ronald J. *Rich Christians in an Age of Hunger: Moving from Afflu-ence to Generosity.* Revised ed. Nashville: Word Publishing, 1997.

Smith, Adam. *An Inquiry into the Nature and Causes of the Wealth of Nations,* Vol. I. Ed. R. H. Campbell, A. S. Skinner, and W. B. Todd. Oxford, England: Clarendon Press, 1976.

Snell, Tracy L., and Laura M. Maruschak. *Capital Punishment 2001.* Washington, DC: Bureau of Justice Statistics, 2002.

Sobrino, Jon. *Christology at the Crossroads: A Latin American Approach.* Trans. John Drury. Maryknoll, NY: Orbis Books, 1978.

———. *Jesus the Liberator: A Historical-Theological Reading of Jesus of Nazareth.* Trans. P. Burns and F. McDonagh. Maryknoll, NY: Orbis Books, 1993.

Taylor, Mark Lewis. *The Executed God: The Way of the Cross in Lockdown America.* Minneapolis: Fortress Press, 2001.

Teninty, Ellen. "The S&L Crises: Time to Strike Back." In *Ethics in the Present Tense: Readings from Christianity and Crisis 1966–1991.* Ed. Leon Howell and Vivian Lindermayer. New York: Friendship Press, 1991.

Thandeka. *Learning to Be White: Money, Race, and God in America.* New York: Continuum, 1999.

Tinker, George. "Spirituality, Native American Personhood, Sovereignty and Solidarity." In *Spirituality of the Third World: A Cry for Life.* Ed. K. C. Abraham and B. Mbuy-Beya. Maryknoll, NY: Orbis Books, 1994.

Townes, Emilie. *In a Blaze of Glory: Womanist Spirituality as Social Witness.* Nashville: Abingdon Press, 1995.

Trimiew, Darryl M. "Ethics." In *Handbook of U.S. Theologies of Liberation.* Ed. Miguel A. De La Torre. St. Louis: Chalice Press, 2004.

———. *Voices of the Silenced: The Responsible Self in a Marginalized Community.* Cleveland: Pilgrim Press, 1993.

Tutu, Desmond. "South Africa's Blacks: Aliens in Their Own Land." In *Ethics in the Present Tense: Readings from Christianity and Crisis 1966–1991.* Ed. Leon Howell and Vivian Lindermayer. New York: Friendship Press, 1991.

Veblen, Thorstein. *The Theory of the Leisure Class.* New York: New American Library, 1953.

Velasquez, Manuel G. *Business Ethics: Concepts and Cases,* 4th Ed. Upper Saddle River, N.J.: Prentice Hall, 1998.

Von Rad, Gerhard. *Old Testament Theology: A Theology of Israel's Historical Traditions,* Vol. I. Trans. D. M. G. Stalker. New York: Harper & Row, 1962.

Warren, Karen. "Feminism and Ecology: Making Connections." *Environmental Ethics,* 9 (Spring 1987): 3–20.

Welch, Sharon D. *A Feminist Ethic of Risk*. Minneapolis: Fortress Press, 1990.

West, Cornel. *Prophesy Deliverance: An Afro-American Revolutionary Christianity*. Philadelphia: Westminster Press, 1982.

Williams, Delores S. "Black Women's Surrogacy Experience and the Christian Notion of Redemption." In *After Patriarchy: Feminist Transformation of World Religions*. Ed. Paula M. Cooey et al. Maryknoll, NY: Orbis Press, 1991.

———. *Sisters in the Wilderness: The Challenge of Womanist God-Talk*. Maryknoll, NY: Orbis Books, 1993.

Williams, Preston N. "An Analysis of the Conception of Love and Its Influence on Justice in the Thought of Martin Luther King, Jr." *Journal of Religious Ethics*, Vol. 18, No. 2 (Fall 1990):15–31.

Wilson, William Julius. *The Bridge over the Racial Divide: Rising Inequality and Coalition Politics*. Berkeley: University of California Press, 1999.

Wright, Beverly Hendrix and Robert D. Bullard. "The Effects of Occupational Injury, Illness, and Disease on the Health Status of Black Americans." In *Toxic Struggles: The Theory and Practice of Environmental Justice*. Ed. Richard Hofrichter. Philadelphia: New Society Publishers, 1993.

Wright, Erik Olin. *Classes*. London: Verso, 1985.

Yang, Seung A. "Asian-American." In *Handbook on U.S. Theologies of Liberation*. Ed. Miguel A. De La Torre. St. Louis: Chalice Press, 2004.

Index